CONTENTS

PREFACE

This book is a thoroughly revised version of my 1988 dissertation, "Royal Ideology and the Technology of Faith: A Comparative Midrash Study of 1 Kgs 3:2-15." In revising that study for publication I have fundamentally reoriented the argument and attempted to eliminate many of the stylistic characteristics specific to the dissertation genre. Still, I have included in this book the complete bibliography from the original dissertation and some references to deleted discussions for readers with an interest in them. Because of the scale of the revision and limits of time, I have only occasionally been able to incorporate references to articles and books which have appeared or become available to me since the dissertation was completed.

A number of individuals have contributed to the genesis of this monograph, some of whom have already been acknowledged at the beginning of the dissertation on which it is based. In addition to those mentioned there I wish to acknowledge the help provided by Sterling Bjorndall and John Daniels, both of whom were staff members of the Q project of the Institute for Antiquity and Christianity (Claremont, CA) at the time when the dissertation was being completed. They generously provided access to the library and data-base of the Q project, including an invaluable working paper by M. G. Steinhauser, which outlined the Q variants discussed in the appendix to the book.

It has been my pleasure to work with the editors and staff of Scholars press in the process of producing what has turned out to be an unusually difficult manuscript. In particular, I would like to acknowledge the gracious help provided by the Editor of the Monograph series, Edward F. Campbell, and the Associate manager for Publications, Darwin Melnyk.

Finally, I dedicate this book to my father, John Lynn Carr, still one of my most admired role models.

David Carr
Delaware, Ohio
June, 1991

Chapter One

INTRODUCTION

This book is a study of the earliest Jewish interpretations of the story of God's appearance to Solomon at Gibeon (hereafter termed "the Gibeon story"). This chapter discusses the context and purposes of the overall study. The chapters which follow give a detailed history of early Jewish interpretation of the Gibeon story. The book concludes with a summary of this interpretation history and discussion of its potential implications for contemporary Biblical interpretation.

Stated briefly, this book is written in the conviction that these early Jewish interpretations exemplify an interpretive flexibility which corresponds in exciting ways with the contemporary methodological pluralism in Biblical scholarship.[1] In previous years Biblical critics might have

---

[1] Such use of ancient interpretation to illuminate modern interpretation originates in James Sanders and others' work in "canonical criticism." I do not build primarily on Brevard Childs and others' work on an approach to the Bible as Scripture (with a particular focus on its final, canonical shape). Indeed, Childs would not take his work to be the creation of a separate discipline, "canonical criticism," but rather a reconstrual of the proper role and focus of present methods in Christian interpretation.

This study continues some aspects of the canonical critical program. In particular, like the canonical critics, I will examine the dialectic of stability and adaptability in each interpretation of the Gibeon story. Unlike the canonical critics, however, I will not focus on theological characterization of inner-Biblical interpretation over against extra-Biblical interpretation, nor will I search for a "canonical hermeneutic" (characterized as "prophetic," "theocentric," or "monotheistic") over against which contemporary interpretation can be judged. For a survey of canonical criticism see James Sanders, *Canon and Community: A Guide to Canonical Criticism*, Guides to Biblical Scholarship (Philadelphia: Fortress, 1984) and the "Select Bibliography in Canonical Criticism," in *From Sacred Story to Sacred Text: Canon as Paradigm*

dismissed such interpretations as pre-critical violations of the original intentions of their texts. But in the current context we are better prepared to appreciate the interpretive achievements of early Jewish interpreters. Just as early interpreters took the text beyond and even against its original intention, so contemporary interpreters—including "new" literary critics, structuralists, reader response, deconstructionist and other literary critics—have persuasively attacked earlier Biblical scholarship's preoccupation with original intention.

In particular, contemporary movements such as feminism have demonstrated the inadequacy of the historical-critical paradigm to allow the Bible to interact productively with our contemporary sense of truth. Biblical texts are not focused on overcoming patriarchy in the same way many of us today are. The best an honest feminist historical-critical investigation of the Bible's *own* thought world can often achieve is a three by three foot plot in an acre of that world.[2] In this context, movements like feminism have begun to seek new, more creative ways of interacting with the Biblical text. And they have begun to find interpretive modes which draw on the Bible's potential to both transform and be transformed by a situation of struggle for life, often in ways unrelated to—or even contradictory to—the original intention of the Biblical texts.[3]

To be sure, not all of Biblical scholarship is comfortable with these methodological developments. The field is still dominated by the old historical-critical paradigm to the extent that some interpreters either advocate historical-critical exegesis as the only legitimate approach to the

---

(Philadelphia: Fortress, 1987), 195-200. For antecedents to this study see particularly James A. Sanders, "Adaptable for Life: The Nature and Function of Canon," in *Magnalia Dei, The Mighty Acts of God: Essays on the Bible and Archeology in Memory of G. Ernest Wright*, eds. Frank Moore Cross, Werner E. Lemke and Patrick D. Miller (Garden City, NY: Doubleday & Co., 1976), 531-560.

[2] For a superb survey of Biblical traditions regarding women see Phyllis A. Bird, "Images of Women in the Old Testament," in *The Bible and Liberation: Political and Social Hermeneutics*, ed. Norman K. Gottwald (Orbis: Maryknoll, NY, 1983), pp. 252-279.

[3] Jewish feminists have been particularly creative in rewriting tradition. See in particular: Judith Plaskow, "The Coming of Lilith: Toward a Feminist Theology," in *Womanspirit Rising: A Feminist Reader in Religion*, ed. Carol P. Christ and Judith Plaskow (San Francisco: Harper & Row, 1979), 198-209; idem. "Jewish Memory from a Feminist Perspective," *Tikkun* 1 (1987): 28-34 and reprinted in *Weaving the Visions: New Patterns in Feminist Spirituality*, Judith Plaskow and Carol Christ, eds (San Francisco: Harper & Row, 1989), 39-50; and Jane Sprague Zones, ed. *Taking the Fruit: Modern Women's Tales of the Bible*, 2nd ed. (San Diego: Woman's Institute for Continuing Education, 1989).

Biblical text or deny the usefulness and viability of such exegesis altogether.[4] Treatments which accept the usefulness of both historical-critical exegesis and other approaches often either juxtapose the methods or collapse the literary approach into the historical-critical one—seeing attention to literary form as yet another type of evidence for original intention.[5]

However much methodological pluralism increasingly dominates the academic discussion of the Bible and secular college courses, the historical-critical paradigm is still dominant in much seminary Bible teaching. Many of us who teach the Bible in religious contexts still teach as if historical-critical exegesis is required for any legitimate reading of the Bible. Our introductory Bible courses focus almost exclusively on introducing students to the ancient contexts and theology of the Scriptures and motivating them to investigate these contexts and theology in their use of the Bible. We then often require students preparing for the pastoral ministry to take "exegesis" courses which focus more specifically on the context and original intention of individual books of the Bible.[6] Similarly, homiletics courses often build on lectionary commentaries which briefly summarize Biblical scholars' views of the original context and message of the lectionary passages. This entire program teaches the student to "understand a Biblical text on its own terms" before extending all or part of it to their contemporary situation. Conversely many of them feel the need to qualify creative approaches to Scripture (say in a sermon or church class) with comments like "I realize that this probably does not correspond to the text's original intention, but..." The tone of such comments often suggests that the interpreter thinks that the interpretation

---

[4] Take for example David Robertson, *The Old Testament and the Literary Critic*, Guides to Biblical Scholarship (Philadelphia: Fortress, 1977).

[5] Cf. Norman Gottwald's discussion in *The Hebrew Bible: A Socio-Literary Introduction* (Philadelphia: Fortress, 1985), 20-34.

[6] Cf. Edgar Krentz, *The Historical-Critical Method*, Guides to Biblical Scholarship (Philadelphia: Fortress, 1975), 65; Otto Kaiser, "Old Testament Exegesis" in *Exegetical Method: A Student's Handbook*, Otto Kaiser and Werner G. Kümmel, trans. E. V. N. Goetschius and M. J. O'Connell (New York: Seabury, 1980), p. 2; Douglas Stuart, Old Testament Exegesis: A Primer for Students and Pastors (Philadelphia: Westminster, 1980), 142 (See also pp. 47 and 72-73); John Hayes and Carl Holladay, *Biblical Exegesis: A Beginner's Handbook*, rev. ed. (Atlanta: John Knox, 1987), 133; see also pp. 5-32 and 152; Raymond Brown, *The Critical Meaning of the Bible* (New York: Paulist Press, 1981), particularly his chapter on "What the Biblical Word Meant and What It Means," pp. 23-44. These scholars are well aware of the interpreter's role in historical-critical exegesis. Nevertheless, they continue to maintain the primacy of a search for original intention, still seen as the proper locus of canonical authority.

being offered is less legitimate for not agreeing with the text's original intention.[7]

Such an emphasis on historical criticism is an outgrowth of the crucial role historical criticism has played, is playing, and will continue to play in maintaining the vital connection between the Bible and modern religious communities. To be sure, the historical-critical method has appeared to threaten the Bible's authority by exposing its pre-modern context and worldview. But (at its best) historical criticism has allowed modern readers to see how the Bible's truth is not identical with its pre-modern worldview, nor is its meaning confined to its original context. Moreover, historical criticism has illuminated many aspects of the Biblical text which would otherwise have remained obscure. It has made possible a culturally cued reading of new dimensions of the Biblical text, opening up a glorious new and alien theological world to its Enlightenment and Post-Enlightenment readers. Indeed, historical-critical method has enabled modern readers to engage in a bi-directional interaction with the Biblical tradition: they relativize some aspects of the Biblical text as mere artifacts of its ancient origins, while allowing other aspects of the Bible's quite different perspective to call their modern presuppositions into question. Though the modern interpreter remains in ultimate control of this process, through it the Bible can (at least initially) speak a new word over against the reader as never before.

This latter phenomenon, where historical-critical exegesis allows the Bible to speak over against the presuppositions of the interpreter, is the basis for the dominance of this approach in contemporary *religious* interpretation of the Bible. To be sure, most contemporary Biblical scholars recognize the necessary and positive role the interpreter's presuppositions play in interpretation of ancient texts. Nevertheless, the major basis for any present exclusive emphasis on historical criticism has been its claim to prevent *eis*egesis, where the interpreter merely subjectively reads his or her beliefs *into* the text. Through reconstruction of the text's original intention, historical criticism makes *ex*egesis possible, where (at least to some extent) the interpreter reads beliefs and understandings different from his or her own *out* of the text.

This study is an exercise in historical-critical exegesis subverting its own supremacy. Out of the kind of questions feminists and others are

---

[7] The disclaimer ("I realize that this probably . . .") can also mean that students presume that an authority present (for example, the Bible specialist) considers their interpretation less legitimate for not corresponding to the original intention of the text.

raising about the predominance of the historical-critical paradigm, I focus in this study on some examples of what might be termed "*sunegesis*," where early Jewish interpreters both "combined" and "did battle" with traditions held dear by their communities.[8] Whereas many historical critics focus on how Biblical texts (or aspects of them) can be legitimately *extended* to their contemporary situation, many of these early Jewish interpreters only invoked their traditions in order to *subvert* them. Whereas historical critics are preoccupied with proper *understanding of the text*, these early Jews were focused on proper *textual understanding of their situations*. In this task, they were passionately engaged with a living tradition. Whether for or against it, they continually imaged their hopes and visions through the medium of this tradition. In what follows, after establishing the early redaction history of 1 Kgs 3:2-15, we will look at how they did this.

---

[8] The word "sunegesis" is an artificial construct. Just as "eisegesis" is understood in English as "reading into" rather than its ancient Greek meaning "proposing, advising" (see Henry George Liddell and Robert Scott, A *Greek-English Lexicon* [Oxford: Clarendon, 1940], 495), so the word "sunegesis" partakes of inter-English rather than ancient Greek language development. In particular, in search of a term to serve as an English alternative to the exegesis/eisegesis contrast, I built on the ancient Greek meaning of the word συνάγω (Liddell-Scott, A *Greek-English Lexicon*, 1691-1692).

Chapter Two

THE REDACTION HISTORY
OF 1 KGS 3:2-15

A long history of dialogue and re-interpretation lies behind the Deuteronomistic account of Solomon's dream at Gibeon (1 Kgs 3:2-15). In this chapter—after a brief literature review—I will attempt to disentangle the various strands of redaction in this text. This then will serve as the basis for investigation of the earliest interpretation of the Gibeon story, the interpretation implicit in the story's redaction.

PREVIOUS STUDY OF 1 KGS 3:2-15

Tradition-Critical Studies of 1 Kgs 3:2-15

The redactional character of 1 Kgs 3:2 and 3 is so clear that commentators as early as Thenius (1849) and Schrader (1869) recognized them as secondary to the story as a whole.[9] These verses focus on the problem raised by Solomon sacrificing at Gibeon. This sacrifice is a problem because it conflicts with the Deuteronomic laws on centralization of the cult. This clear conflict between the apparent Deuteronomic ethics of the author(s) of 1 Kgs 3:2-3 and the events narrated in 1 Kgs 3:4 is the best evidence for at least two layers in the Gibeon story: a pre-Deuteronomistic Vorlage and Deuteronomistic redaction(s).

---

[9] Otto Thenius, *Die Bücher der Könige*, KEHAT 9 (Leipzig: Weidmann, 1849), v-vi; Wilhelm Martin Leberecht De Wette, *Lehrbuch der historisch-kritischen Einleitung in die kanonischen und apokryphischen Bücher des Alten Testaments*, revised by Eberhard Schrader (Berlin: G. Reimer, 1869), 349-352.

Ever since this initial recognition of Deuteronomistic redaction in the Gibeon story, scholars have identified ever increasing amounts of the text as Deuteronomistic. Kuenen (1887) and Benzinger (1899) recognized the Deuteronomistic characteristics of 3:14.[10] Kittel (1900) and Wellhausen (1900) saw Deuteronomistic elements in 3:15 as well.[11] In his pathbreaking 1903 study, Burney discerned Deuteronomistic influence in 3:6aβb, 8a, and 12b,[12] but most commentaries which appeared soon after his book still did not see Deuteronomistic influence in the middle of the story.[13] Šanda's 1911 commentary was the major exception. He anticipated later scholarship by observing the secondary character of 3:8b and the incomparability formulae in 12bβγ and 13b.[14]

This gradual trend toward increasing recognition of the Deuteronomist's work in the Gibeon story was briefly interrupted by scholars attempting to extend the Pentateuchal sources beyond the Pentateuch. In the nineteen-twenties, Smend, Sellin, Benzinger, and Hölscher assigned the middle of the Gibeon story to the Elohist on the basis of two main factors: the story's overall focus on a dream and the occurrence of אלהים in 3:5b and 11.[15] With the 1943 appearance of Noth's *Überlieferungs-*

---

[10] Abraham Kuenen, *Historisch-critisch onderzoek naar het ontstaan en de verzameling van de boeken des Ouden Verbonds*, vol. 1 (2nd ed.; Amsterdam: S.L. van Looy, 1887), 402-404; Immanuel Benzinger, *Die Bücher der Könige*, KHAT 9 (Freiburg: J.C.B. Mohr, 1899), 14-15. Cf. Schrader, *Lehrbuch*, 351-352.

[11] Rudolph Kittel, *Die Bücher der Könige*, HAT 1:5 (Göttingen: Vandenhoeck & Ruprecht, 1900), 28; Julius Wellhausen, *Die Komposition des Hexateuchs und der historischen Bücher des Alten Testaments*, 4th ed. (Berlin: de Gruyter, 1900), 271.

[12] Charles Fox Burney, *Notes on the Hebrew Text of the Books of Kings* (Oxford: at the Clarendon Press, 1903), 30-32. In his diagram on pp. 29-30 Burney indicates possible Deuteronomistic origins for parts of 5a and 6aα along with 10 and 15.

[13] Bernard Stade with Friedrich Schwally, *The Books of Kings: Critical Edition of the Hebrew Text Printed in Colors Exhibiting the Composite Structure of the Books with Notes*, trans. R. E. Brünnow and Paul Haupt, The Sacred Books of the Old Testament 9 (Leipzig: J. C. Hinrichs'sche Buchhandlung, 1904), 72-73; John Skinner, *Kings*, The Century Bible (Edinburgh: T. C. & E. C. Jack, 1904), 84-88.

[14] A. Šanda, *Die Bücher der Könige*, EHAT 9 (Münster: Aschendorffsche Verlagsbuchhandlung, 1911), 63.

[15] Rudolph Smend, "J E in den geschichtlichen Büchern," ZAW 39 (1921): 205; Ernst Sellin, *Introduction to the Old Testament*, trans. W. Montgomery (London: Hodder and Stoughton Ltd., 1923), 122-123 (translation of 3rd ed. [1920] of Sellin's *Einleitung in das Alte Testament*); Immanuel Benzinger, *Jahwist und Elohist in den Königsbüchern*, Beiträge zur Wissenschaft vom Alten Testaments, new series, no. 2 (Berlin, Stuttgart, Leipzig: W. Kohlhammer, 1921), 19; Gustav Hölscher, "Das Buch der Königen, Seine Quellen und seine Redaktion," in ΕΥΧΑΡΙΣΤΗΡΙΟΝ: *Studien zur Religion und Literatur des Alten und Neuen Testaments*, ed. Hans Schmidt, vol. 1: *Zur*

geschictliche Studien, however, attempts to find the J, E, or P sources in the Deuteronomistic history became much less frequent.[16]

In subsequent studies, scholars such as Montgomery, Carlson, and Noth (in his later commentary on 1 Kings) returned to Burney's analysis and began seeing the Deuteronomistic characteristics of the middle of the Gibeon story, particularly in 3:6-8 and 13b.[17] Though some recent studies have found a pre-Deuteronomistic redaction in the story (usually centered on verses 5a, 10 and 15),[18] most have continued the trend toward increasing recognition of the Deuteronomist's work here. For example, though he still recognizes the framework of the story as pre-Deuteronomistic, Weinfeld assigns the entire contents of the Gibeon dream (3:6-14) to the Deuteronomist.[19]

Kenik's dissertation represents the final extension of the tendency to see Deuteronomistic redaction in 1 Kgs 3:2-15. She attempts to establish Deuteronomistic redaction in every verse of the story. Whereas most tradition historians presuppose a pre-Deuteronomistic *Vorlage* for the Gibeon story, Kenik explicitly rejects that approach. Instead, she

---

Religion und Literatur des Alten Testament. FRLANT 36/1 (Göttingen: Vandenhoeck & Ruprecht, 1923), 159.

[16] In this early work Noth assigned only 3:2-3 and 14-15 to the Deuteronomist. Martin Noth, *Überlieferungsgeschichtliche Studien: Die sammelnden und bearbeitenden Geschichtswerke im Alten Testament* (Tübingen: M. Niemeyer, 1943), 67-68.

[17] James A. Montgomery, *A Critical and Exegetical Commentary on the Books of Kings.* ICC 10. New York: Scribner's, 1951), 107-108; Rolf A. Carlson, *David the Chosen King—A Traditio-Historical Approach to the Second Book of Samuel,* trans. Eric J. Sharpe and Stan Rudman (Uppsala: Almqvist & Wiksell, 1964), 206; Martin Noth, *Könige,* vol. 1, 1, 1-16, BKAT 9, part 1 (Neukirchen: Neukirchener Verlag, 1968), 44-45.

[18] Manfred Görg, *Gott-König-Reden in Israel und Ägypten,* BWANT, 6th series, no. 5 (Stuttgart: W. Kohlhammer, 1975), 33-36 (he includes 13b in his non-Deuteronomistic redaction); Gwilym H. Jones, *1 & 2 Kings,* vol. 1: *1 Kgs 1-16:34,* New Century Bible Commentary (Grand Rapids: Eerdmans, 1984), 121-128. Ernst Würthwein's discrimination of a younger layer of Deuteronomistic redaction in the additions to 3:8 and 9 is similar to Görg's and Jones' efforts to provide a more nuanced tradition history (*Die Bücher Könige,* vol. 1: *Könige 1-16,* ATD 11.1 [Göttingen: Vandenhoeck & Ruprecht, 1977], 35).

[19] Moshe Weinfeld, *Deuteronomy and the Deuteronomic School* (Oxford: Clarendon Press, 1972), 246-257. Here he provides detailed argumentation for a position earlier adopted by R. B. Y. Scott, "Solomon and the Beginning of Wisdom in Israel," in *Wisdom in Israel and in the Ancient Near East: Festschrift H. H. Rowley,* eds. Martin Noth and D. Winston Thomas, VTSup 3 (Leiden: Brill, 1955), 271-272.

attempts to show that the Deuteronomist produced all of the Gibeon story *ex nihilo.*[20]

Though Kenik's study is quite thorough and includes many helpful individual insights, her overall argument is not convincing. First, she is not able to explain adequately why the Deuteronomist chose *Gibeon* as the particular sanctuary for this narrative.[21] Second, many of her tradition-critical arguments are atomistic, often focusing on individual vocabulary items. Obviously she has done her concordance work thoroughly, but it is still not clear that the Deuteronomist presupposed such knowledge in his readers.[22] In sum, Kenik's thorough study indicates that some middle ground must be found between assigning none of the story to the Deuteronomist and assigning all of it.

Ancient Near Eastern Parallels to 1 Kgs 3:2-15

The Deuteronomistic account of Solomon's dream at Gibeon has been a battleground for those interested in comparing the Bible with Ancient Near Eastern materials. Scholars have found Sumerian, Egyptian, Assyrian, Neo-Babylonian, and Northwest Semitic parallels to parts or all of the Gibeon story.[23] Furthermore many of them have used these parallels to support particular theories regarding the tradition history of 1 Kgs 3:2-15.

The priorities of such studies can be described using a continuum with tradition historical method prior on one end and comparative method prior on the other. On the former end of the continuum, studies such as those by Görg and Weinfeld attempt a sustained traditio-historical analysis of the Gibeon story prior to their attempts to compare it with

---

[20] Helen A. Kenik, *Design for Kingship: The Deuteronomistic Narrative Technique in 1 Kings 3:4-15,* SBLDS 69 (Chico, CA: Scholars Press, 1983), 33 and passim.

[21] Kenik, *Design for Kingship,* 185-188, argues on the basis of 1 Kgs 3:2 that the choice of Gibeon is motivated by the Deuteronomist's intent to contrast pre-temple with post-temple sacrificial practices. As I argue below, 3:2 is not part of the first Deuteronomist's redaction of the story.

[22] Here Kenik seems to partake of the old Biblical Theology movement's tendency to see individual words as bearers of special theological meaning. On this see James Barr's classic work, *The Semantics of Biblical Language* (New York: Oxford University Press, 1961).

[23] For detailed summary, see David Carr, "Royal Ideology and the Technology of Faith: A Comparative Midrash Study of 1 Kgs 3:2-15," (Ph.D. Diss., Claremont Graduate School, 1988), 30-41.

ancient Near Eastern materials.[24] Zalevsky's study of the Gibeon story stands at the other end of the continuum: priority of comparative method. He is aware of traditio-historical treatments of the Gibeon story. Nevertheless, on the basis of his comparison of the story with extra-Biblical Northwest Semitic materials, Zalevsky claims that only two words in the Gibeon story (חקי ומצותי: "my statutes and command-ments" in 3:14) are Deuteronomistic.[25] Similarly, Gray takes all of 3:4-15 except 3:14 and part of 15 as "genuinely Solomonic."[26]

Most traditio-historical and comparative studies are less explicit in relating traditio-historical and comparative concerns. On the one hand, most treatments of tradition history do not offer new and compelling comparative proposals. On the other hand, many comparative studies—such as those by Oppenheim, Kapelrud, and Seow—do not discuss tra-ditio-historical questions.[27] Other comparative studies—such as Ehrlich's and Herrmann's—only deal with a few traditio-historical questions in footnotes.[28] In almost all cases, the comparative studies seem to exclude Deuteronomistic influence for any parts of the Gibeon story other than 3:2-3 and 3:14-15. Thus, except for Görg's and Weinfeld's work, most comparative studies assume a picture of the tradition history of the Gibeon story identical to that of Kittel and Wellhausen at the turn of the century.

Conclusions: Methodology

This study will follow the example of Görg and Weinfeld in putting prior emphasis on the redaction analysis of 1 Kgs 3:2-15. First, most of

---

[24] Görg, *Gott-König-Reden*, 25-36; Weinfeld, *Deuteronomy and the Deuteronomic School*, 246-257. Both apparently assume that comparison to extra-Biblical materials will only illuminate the pre-Deuteronomistic version of the Gibeon story. The present author does not share this assumption.

[25] Saul Zalevsky, "התגלות ה' לשלמה בגעון," *Tarbiz* 42 (1973): 233.

[26] John Gray, *I & II Kings: A Commentary*, 2nd ed. (Philadelphia: Westminster, 1963), 121.

[27] A. Leo Oppenheim, *The Interpretation of Dreams in the Ancient Near East*, Transactions of the American Philosophical Society, New Series, no. 46, part 3 (Philadelphia: The American Philosophical Society, 1956), 188; Arvid S. Kapelrud, "Temple Building, a Task for Gods and Kings," *Or* 32 (1963): 56-62; C. L. Seow, "The Syro-Palestinian Context of Solomon's Dream," *HTR* 77 (1984): 141-152.

[28] Ernst Ludwig Ehrlich, *Der Traum im Alten Testament*, BZAW 7 (Leipzig: J. C. Hinrichs'sche Buchhandlung, 1914), 13-27; Siegfried Herrmann, "Die Königsnovelle in Ägypten und Israel," *Wissenschaftliche Zeitschrift der Karl Marx Universität, Leipzig* 3 (1953/54), Gesellschaft und sprachwissenschaftliche Reihe, Heft 1 [Festschrift Albrecht Alt]: 33-39.

the Ancient Near Eastern parallels to 1 Kgs 3:2-15 are vague by comparison with Biblical (particularly Deuteronomistic) counterparts. Second,
tradition history proceeds on firmer ground in identifying late redaction
than when it posits early tradition. The tradition historian already has at
his or her disposal a knowledge of the vocabulary, narrative framework,
and theology which characterize a given redactional stratum. This is
particularly true of analyses of Deuteronomistic redaction. From
Deuteronomy to 2 Kings a number of passages are easily isolated from
their contexts, passages which exhibit consistent Deuteronomistic
phraseology and theology.

Noth's 1943 monograph has played a particular role in leading to the
recognition that Deuteronomy through 2 Kings form a coherent work
known as "the Deuteronomistic history." Furthermore, studies since
Noth's monograph have shown that the history has undergone multiple
redactions. The overall shape of the work is probably best explained by
taking it as originally being a rationale for Josiah's cultic centralization
and national re-unification reforms. Indeed, most ancient Near Eastern
histories outside Israel seem to have supported just such concrete political projects. In this case, the Josianic editors of the history composed a
history stretching from Moses' reprise of Israel's formative traditions
(Deuteronomy) to Josiah's climactic re-unification of the Davidic kingdom around a centralized cult purified of post-Mosaic influences (2 Kgs
22:1-23:25). Once this work was produced, however, it required significant retouching throughout later periods, in light of further events such
as Josiah's death at Megiddo, the Judean exile, and the struggles of the
post-exilic community.[29]

The findings of this study correspond to the above background on the
redaction(s) of the Deuteronomistic history. In the following I isolate not
one, but several different strands of Deuteronomistic redaction in the
text. The discussion begins with treatment of those passages which I

---

[29] For a more detailed argument for this position and survey of literature, see Carr
"Royal Ideology and the Technology of Faith," pp. 128-139. In advocating a Josianic
redaction, I am closest to advocates of the "Double Redaction" hypothesis. See particularly Frank Moore Cross, "The Themes of the Book of Kings and the Structure of
the Deuteronomistic History," in *Canaanite Myth and Hebrew Epic: Essays in the History
of the Religion of Israel* (Cambridge: Harvard University Press, 1973), 274-289; and
James Nelson, *The Double Redaction of the Deuteronomistic History*, JSOTSup 18
(Sheffield: Dept. of Biblical Studies, University of Sheffield, 1981). Note that I do not
follow Cross, Nelson and others in focusing on a single exilic redaction of the original
seventh century history.

assign to the Josianic editors of the overall history. Then I proceed to the verses which belong to later redactions of the history.

REDACTION OF THE GIBEON STORY

The Deuteronomistic Redaction:

1 Kgs 3:3: Regnal Evaluation: Solomon's Patronage of במה in Context

1 Kgs 3:3 - Solomon loved Yahweh, living according to the norms of David, his father, but he sacrificed and made smoke offerings in the [non-Jerusalemite] sanctuaries.

The Deuteronomistic editors typically introduce each king's reign with an evaluation like this one. These evaluations often include a comparison of the king to a standard of virtue (usually David) or vice (usually Ahab). The praise for Solomon in 1 Kgs 3:3a includes such a comparison (to David in this case), along with Deuteronomistic terminology ("loved Yahweh").[30] In addition, Deuteronomistic regnal formulae almost always include a statement about how the king did or did not comply with the Deuteronomistic requirement of cultic centralization. 1 Kgs 3:3b ("but he sacrificed...") is just such a statement, qualifying the praise for Solomon in 3a with a description of his patronage of sanctuaries outside Jerusalem.[31] In sum, 1 Kgs 3:3 is a typical Deuteronomistic regnal evaluation.

1 Kgs 3:6aβ: Conditions for God's Loyalty to David

[Context - Pre-deuteronomistic description of God's loyalty, 6aα: Solomon said, "You have acted with great faithfulness towards your servant, David, my father,]
[Deuteronomistic addition: 6aβ] when he walked before you in total loyalty and in integrity of heart with you

Though some scholars associate the description of God's loyalty in 6aα with the qualification of it in 6aβ, there are important differences in intention between these two units. 6aα has no specifically Deuteronomistic characteristics. Moreover, it can stand alone as a pre-Deuteron-

---

[30] Cf. Deut 6:5; 10:12; 11:1, 13, 22; 13:4; 19:9; 30:6, 16, 20; Josh 22:5; 23:11. Also in Exod 20:6//Deut 5:10; Judg 5:31; Isa 56:6; Pss 5:12; 31:24; 69:37; 97:10; 119:132; 145:20; Dan 9:4//Deut 7:9; Neh 1:5//Deut 7:9. Citations from Weinfeld, *Deuteronomy and the Deuteronomic School,* 33, item 4.

[31] The negative use of the term במות ("local sanctuaries") in 3:3b is typical of such Deuteronomistic pronouncements.

omistic reference to God's loyalty to David and the possibility of transferal of that loyalty to Solomon upon his succession. This emphasis on succession and God's *unconditional* promise to David is quite distinct from that in 6aβ.

In 6aβ the emphasis is on God's loyalty to David *because of his faithfulness*. Like several other Deuteronomistic verses, 6aβ characterizes David as an ideal king, and describes that ideal in terms of "walking before [Yahweh]" and the trueness of the king's "heart."[32] Scholars such as Herrmann, Gray, and Zalevsky have attempted to use extra-Biblical Ancient Near Eastern texts to establish the pre-Deuteronomistic character of 6aβ. Their parallels, however, pale in comparison with its Deuteronomistic characteristics.[33]

1 Kgs 3:6b: Evidence of God's Loyalty to David

(6bα) And you observed this great loyalty toward him:

(6bβ) You gave to him a son sitting on his throne as on this very day.

The description of evidence for God's loyalty in 6b is closely related to the pre-Deuteronomistic description of God's loyalty in 6aα. In 6aα Solomon asserts that God has "acted with great faithfulness toward your servant, David." Through almost repeating 6aα, the beginning of 6b resumes its themes. Moreover, it refers back to 6aα through adding a near demonstrative to indicate that the loyalty will be specified: "You observed *this* great loyalty toward him." This resumption of themes and back reference would not have been necessary prior to the Deuteronomistic insertion in 6aβ. Moreover, the slight terminological differences between 6bα and its pre-Deutero-nomistic parallel (6aα) confirm the former's Deuteronomistic character. In 6b the expression עשה חסד ("act loyally") of the pre-Deuteronomistic layer (6aα) is replaced with the primarily Deuteronomistic expression - שמר חסד ("observe loyalty").[34]

---

[32] 1 Kgs 9:4 (also refers to Solomon); 14:8; 15:3 . Cf. also 1 Kgs 11:4; 2 Kgs 22:2. These citations are from Weinfeld, *Deuteronomy and the Deuteronomic School*, 77; Carlson, *David, the Chosen King*, 23; and Zalevsky, "התנלות ה' לשלמה בנעון," p. 228, note 50.

[33] Herrmann, "Die Königsnovelle in Ägypten und Israel," 36-37; Gray, *I & II Kings*, 125; Zalevsky, "התנלות ה' לשלמה בנעון," 228-230.

[34] שמר חסד (observe loyalty") is particularly characteristic of materials related to or dependent on the Deuteronomist. The phrase first occurs in Hosea 12:7 as a concluding exhortation: שמור חסד ומשפט ("observe loyalty and justice"). Though this occurrence is probably pre-Deuteronomistic, the links between Hosea and the Deuteronomist are well established. Another possibly ancient occurrence of the

Together, these indicators show that 6bα is Deuteronomistic, introducing a Deuteronomistic specification of evidence for the pre-Deuteronomistic description of loyalty in 6aα.

The next unit, 6bβ, is the Deuteronomistic specification of evidence for God's loyalty. It includes two elements, a reference to God's giving David a successor (6bβ1-4) and a fulfillment formula (6bβ5-6). The Deuteronomistic character of the fulfillment formula has long been recognized,[35] but the status of the preceding description of God's gift of a successor has not been as clear. Rather than having close Deuteronomistic parallels, this 3:6b description of God's gift of a successor is most nearly parallel to succession narrative references to God's promise to David.[36] Nevertheless, even this portion of verse six is probably Deuteronomistic, quoting from the succession narrative in order to make a point about God's fidelity to promises. The immediately preceding succession narrative (2 Sam 7 - 1 Kgs 2*)[37] revolves around God's fulfillment of the promise to David of a successor (2 Sam 7:1-17*) through having Solomon succeed him. Then in our text (3:6bβ1-4) Solomon quotes from succession narrative descriptions of the Davidic promise in order to assert that God has fulfilled it.[38] Such emphasis on God's fidelity

---

phrase is Ps 89:29. The next occurrence of this formula is a confessional formula in Deuteronomy 7:9, a Deuteronomic adaptation of the pronouncement in Deut 5:10. עשה חסד ("act loyally") occurs in Deut 5:10 rather than שמר חסד ("observe loyalty"). Note that the parallel in Exod 20:6 has the first person throughout whereas the Deut 5:10 version switches from first to third person. All the rest of the examples of שמר חסד ("observe loyalty") occur in variants of this confessional formula. Some stick close to the formula (Neh 1:5; Dan 9:4), while others deviate somewhat (Neh 9:32; 2 Chr 6:14), but all are post-exilic.

[35] Although this fulfillment formula occurs occasionally in possibly pre-Deuteronomistic contexts (Gen 50:20; 1 Sam 22:8, 13), it is particularly typical of Deuteronomistic literature: Deut 4:38; 8:18; 10:15; 29:27; 1 Kgs 8:24, 61; Jer 11:5; 25:18; 32:20; 44:6, 23. Cf. Zalevsky, "התגלות ה' לשלמה בגבעון," p. 232, and note 68; Weinfeld, *Deuteronomy and the Deuteronomic School,* 174, 252-253.

[36] 1 Kgs 1:13, 17, 20, 24, 27, 30, 35, 46, 48. 1 Kgs 1:48 is the closest to 1 Kgs 3:6bβ. It is a blessing spoken by David which not only includes the succession formula concerning Solomon, but also the verb נתן with יהוה as subject, and the expression היום functioning adverbially.

[37] Here and throughout the rest of this study, an asterisk indicates that the indicated text block includes some later redaction.

[38] Though Zalevsky points out that the language used in this section (בן ישב על-כסאו) is typically used to refer to successors in Northwest Semitic materials, this parallel only extends as far as 6bβ1-4, the phrase also occurring in the succession narrative. Zalevsky, "התגלות ה' לשלמה בגבעון," 230-232. His references are Kilamu *KAI* 24:9, 14; Karatepe *KAI* 26A (I) 11; and Sefire *KAI* (III) 224:17.

to promises, particularly the Davidic promise, is characteristic of the Deuteronomistic theology of history.[39] Therefore, 6b as a whole appears to be Deuteronomistic creation, a verse building on this theology of promise in order to specify God's loyalty to David.

1 Kgs 3:8 and 9b: The Consequences of Solomon's Placement Over God's Great Chosen People

1 Kgs 3:8a: Your servant is in the midst of your people whom you have chosen,

1 Kgs 3:8b: a great people who cannot be counted or numbered because of their multitude...

1 Kgs 3:9b: For who is able to judge this, your great people?

The election theme and use of the verb בחר ("choose") to refer to that theme clearly mark 8a as Deuteronomistic.[40] Furthermore, the description of the chosen people in 8b is in apposition to an element in 8a: (8a) "Your servant is in the midst of your people . . . (8b) a great people who cannot be counted or numbered because of their multitude." If the insertion in 8a were excised, 8b would not make sense. This is preliminary evidence that both 8a and 8b are Deuteronomistic.

The Deuteronomistic description of Moses' request for divine aid in judging Israel (Deut 1:9-18) provides additional evidence for the Deuteronomistic origins of 8b, along with 9b. Deuteronomy 1:9-18 is one of three stories which describe Moses as overwhelmed with the task of judging Israel (Exod 18:13-27; Num 11:14-17). In all three accounts Moses responds to the dilemma by asking for relief, eventually delegating his legal responsibilities to officials among the Israelites. The Deuteronomy text, however, is unique in describing Moses' predicament as a result of God's fidelity to God's promises to the patriarchs (Deut 1:10-11). Moses requires help because the God of the fathers has fulfilled the promise to bless and multiply Israel, making them too numerous to judge. As men-

---

[39] Gerhard von Rad, "Die deuteronomistiche Geschichtstheologie in den Königsbüchern," in *Gesammelte Studien zum Alten Testament*, vol. 1 (Munich: Chr. Kaiser, 1958), 189-204.

[40] Burney, *Notes on the Hebrew Text of the Books of Kings*, 31, compares 1 Kgs 3:8aβ 2-4 to Deut 4:37; 7:6; 14:2. Kenik, *Design for Kingship*, 89-92, summarizes the literature and cites the central texts. See in particular her note 79 on p. 90. For survey of the verb בחר referring to election, see Weinfeld, *Deuteronomy and the Deuteronomic School*, 226-228 and 327, item 5. He cites Deut 4:37; 7:6, 7; 10:15; 14:2; and Jer 33:24 (along with our text, 1 Kgs 3:8). Cf. Pss 33:12; 78:68; Isa 14:1; 41:8, 9; 43:10; 44:1, 2; 49:7; Ezek 20:5.

tioned above, this emphasis on God's fulfillment of promises is characteristically Deuteronomistic.

1 Kgs 3:8b shares these themes with Deut 1:9b-11. Solomon, like Moses, is unable to judge God's great chosen people. Just as Deut 1:10 recalls the patriarchal promises through use of the phrase "like the stars of the heavens in multitude," so 1 Kgs 3:8b recalls the promises through describing God's chosen people as a people "who cannot be counted or numbered because of their multitude."[41] In emphasizing the problems caused by God's fulfillment of promises to David (succession) and then the "fathers" (multiplication), the arguments of both 3:6b and 3:8 are Deuteronomistic. 1 Kgs 3:9b then summarizes Solomon's arguments, focusing on his final argument (1 Kgs 3:8) that judging Israel is difficult.[42]

1 Kgs 3:11aα4-b: The Reasoning Behind the Divine Promises

1 Kgs 3:11aα4-12βb: Because you asked this thing, and did not ask for yourself many days, nor did you ask for yourself riches, or ask for the life of your enemies, but you asked for yourself discrimination to hear cases, . . .

Language and ideology indicate the Deuteronomistic origins of this prologue to the divine response to Solomon. The conjunction which introduces it, יַעַן אֲשֶׁר ("because"), is favored by the Deuteronomist for explanatory insertions.[43] Moreover, the ideology of the prologue is thoroughly Deuteronomistic. Here Solomon is praised for fulfilling two aspects of the Deuteronomistic kingship ideal:

1)   The positive requirement to pursue legal wisdom and enable the people to live by the law:

Solomon requests "discrimination in order to hear cases."

---

[41] The text of this section is highly uncertain. Nevertheless, whether one follows the Old Greek, Proto-"Lucianic," or Massoretic and majority of proto-Massoretic witnesses, all formulations of 3:8b somehow parallel the patriarchal promises. For more detailed discussion, see Carr, "Royal Ideology and the Technology of Faith," 71-76.

[42] To be sure, the term, כבד ("heavy, difficult, great") occurs in 3:9b, a term also central to the non-Deuteronomistic parallels to Deut 1:9-18. Exodus 18:18 uses the word to describe the *difficulty* of Moses' *job* while Num 11:14 clearly refers to the *difficulty* (stubbornness) of *Israel*. 3:9b diverges from those parallels in using the word כבד to refer to the *greatness* of *Israel*.

[43] Walter Dietrich, *Prophetie und Geschichte: Eine redaktionsgeschichtliche Untersuchung zum deuteronomistischen Geschichtswerk*, FRLANT 108 (Göttingen: Vandenhoeck & Ruprecht, 1972), 64-70.

2)   The negative requirement to avoid a "kingship like the nations."

Solomon *does not* request a list of things which the Deuteronomist saw other
nations as typically valuing: long life, riches, and military victory.

The positive requirement is clearly indicated in the Deuteronomistic
king's law (Deut 17:18-19), regnal evaluations, and description of Josiah's
reign.[44] The negative requirement, however, merits further discussion.
The list of things which Solomon did not request (long life, riches, military victory) diverges from the list of unconditionally granted items
(wisdom, riches, and honor).[45] Whereas the latter list anticipates
widespread and often ancient traditions about Solomon's reign ("riches
and honor) which appear later in 1 Kgs and throughout the Bible,[46] the
list of non-requested things in 3:11 does not match his reign. Solomon
did not have either extraordinarily long life or military victories. Thus,
the list of unconditionally granted items (wisdom, riches and honor) is
the part of the divine speech which anticipates and explains Solomon's
subsequent reign, while the list of things which he did not request (long
life, riches and military victory) remains unexplained.

Though both Biblical and extra-Biblical Ancient Near Eastern materials are full of references to royal valuing of individual items in the 1 Kgs
3:11 list,[47] this catalogue of royal needs particularly resembles a stereo-

---

[44] For a more comprehensive argument see Gerald Eddie Gerbrandt, *Kingship
According to the Deuteronomistic History*, SBLDS 87 (Atlanta: Scholars, 1986), passim.

[45] The conditional promise in 13:14 is discussed below.

[46] Cf. in particular: 1 Kgs 5:9-14 and 10:23.

[47] Biblical: Pss 21:4-7 (long life, riches, honor); 61:7 (long life/reign); 72:5, 8-11, 15-
17 (long life, prosperity in the land, military victory, honor); 110 (military victory);
Prov 9:11 (long life). References are from my own survey along with C. H. W.
Brekelmans, "Solomon at Gibeon," in *Von Kanaan bis Kerala, Festschrift für Prof. Mag.
Dr. Dr. J. P. M. van der Ploeg O. P. zur Vollendung des siebzigsten Lebensjahres am 4. Juli
1979*, ed. W. Delsman, et. al. (Neukirschen-Vluyn: Neukirchener Verlag, 1982), 55;
Burke Long, *1 Kings with an Introduction to the Historical Literature*, FOTL 9 (Grand
Rapids: Eerdmans, 1984), 66; Würthwein, *Die Bücher Könige*, 32; and Zalevsky, "בנעון
התגלות ה' לשלמה," 234-235. I do not include some of Zalevsky's references because
they are not directly parallel to 1 Kgs 3:11.

Other Northwest Semitic: *KTU* 1.17 VI:20-25, 34-40 (Ugarit (Aqhat): riches and
long life); *KTU* 1.14 [I:51-II:3] (Ugarit (Keret): wealth and military power); *KAI* 4:3-7
(Byblos, long life); 6:2-3 (Byblos, long life); 7:4-5 (Byblos, long life); 10:9 (Byblos, long
life); 25:4-7 (Zinjirli, long life); *KAI* 26 A III:16-IV:12 (Karatepe: long life, peace, military strength, prosperity). Note the almost exclusive emphasis on long life.

Egyptian: Herrmann, "Die Königsnovelle," p. 38 notes 7 and 8; Görg, *Gott-
König-Reden*, 105-111; N. Shupak, "Some Idioms Connected with the Concept of
"Heart in Egypt and the Bible," in *Pharaonic Egypt: The Bible and Christianity*, ed. S.

typed list of things sought by kings in the blessing and dedicatory sections of Mesopotamian royal inscriptions.[48] These Mesopotamian dedications and blessings followed a fairly standard catalogue of royal needs: long life, abundance in agriculture, stability of reign, unity, progeny, military victory, and other items.[49] Furthermore, Northwest Semitic cultures with special contact with Mesopotamia seem to have known this Mesopotamian royal need catalogue tradition. Similar catalogues of royal needs occur in two bi-lingual Northwest Semitic royal inscriptions: the

---

Israelit-Groll (Jerusalem: Magnes Press, 1985), 205. Akkadian: Brekelmans "Solomon at Gibeon," pp. 56-57.

[48] Previously observed by Brekelmans, "Solomon at Gibeon," 56-57, especially notes 2 and 3; A. Malamat, "Longevity: Biblical Concepts and Some Ancient Near Eastern Parallels," in *Recontre Assyriologique Internationale in Wien. 6-10. Juli 1981*, AfO Beiheft 19 (Horn, Austria: Ferdinand Berger & Söhne Gesellschaft, 1982), 220 and note 28.

[49] Early Sumerian and Babylonian Expanded Blessing and Dedicatory Formulae: E. Sollberger and J.-R. Kupper, *Inscriptions royales Sumériennes et Akkadiennes*, Littératures anciennes du Proche-orient, no. 3 (Paris: Les Éditions du Cerf, 1971) 94-95. (IH2b); Ilmari Kärki, *Die Sumerischen und Akkadischen Königsinschriften Der Altbabyloniaschen Zeit*, vol. 1, *Isin, Larsa, Uruk*, StudOr 49 (Helsinki: Finnish Oriental Society, 1980), 51-52 (Nūr-Adad 3); Sîniddinam 5:19-25 (Kärki, 60); 88-89 (Waradsîn 6:24-29), 89-91 (Waradsîn 7:32-41), 91-93 (Waradsîn 8:44-50), 94-96 (Waradsîn 10:45-50), 97-98 (Waradsîn 11:40-50), 98-99 (Waradsîn 12:33-39), 100-101 (Waradsîn 13:35-39), 126-132 (Waradsîn 29:108-116), 136-137. (Waradsîn 36:2,29'-34'), 142-143, (Rîmsîn 2:24-30), 145-146 (Rîmsîn 4:20-28), 146-147 (Rîmsîn 5:20-28), 157-158 (Rîmsîn 12:20-28), 44-46 (Abī-sarē 4, 5:4-20).

Old Babylonian Expanded Dedicatory and Blessing Formulae: I. J. Gelb, "A New Clay-Nail of Ḫamurabi," *JNES* 7 (1948): 269 (A:ii:8-10; B:ii:26-iii:1; note the expanded emphasis on military victory); E. Sollberger, "Šamšu-ilūna's Bilingual Inscriptions C and D," *RA* 63 (1969): 37, 40; G. Dossin, "L'inscription de foundation de Iaḫdun-Lim, roi de Mari," *Syria* 32 (1955): 16 (lines 14-23; again, note emphasis on military victory).

Early Assyrian exemplars: Albert Kirk Grayson, *Assyrian Royal Inscriptions*, vol. 1: *From the Beginning to Ashur-resha-ishi I*, RANE 1 (Wiesbaden: Otto Harrassowitz, 1972), 1:42-43, (no. 2, § 278); 1:84 (no. 1, § 536); 1:90 (no. 8, § 578); 1:97 (no. 23, § 646).

Later Assyrian Expanded Dedicatory formulae: A. K. Grayson, *Assyrian Royal Inscriptions*, vol. 2, *From Tiglath-pileser I to Ashur-nasir-apli II*, RANE 2 (Wiesbaden: Otto Harrassowitz, 1976) 2:79 (no. 3, § 381; note that he uses Aššur-nasir-apli's dedicatory formulae to restore this section because the fragments which are preserved show a resemblance); 2:196-197 (no. 40, § 779; no. 41, § 783; and 42, § 787).

Later Assyrian Blessings: Grayson, *Assyrian Royal Inscriptions*, 2:18-19 (no. 1, § 58), 2:177 (no. 18, § 686); 2:178-179 (no. 19, § 690), 2:182 (no. 24, § 708).

For more detailed discussion, translations, and a tradition history, see Carr, "Royal Ideology and the Technology of Faith," 109-114 (Egyptian materials are briefly discussed on pp. 115-116).

Tell Fekhariya dedication (Part A:7-10; Akkadian/Aramaic) and the Karatepe blessing (III:2-11; Neo-Hittite/Phoenician).

1 Kgs 3:11 describes God as rewarding Solomon for *rejecting* exactly those things which this Mesopotamian royal need catalogue tradition describes other kings as *wanting*.[50] Such a reward for avoiding pagan royal values is typical of the Deuteronomist's overall nationalistic orientation.[51] In particular, the Deuteronomistic redaction of Deut 17:14-20 and 1 Sam 8:4-22 negatively portrays the people's request for "a king like the nations." Moreover, in both passages, the Deuteronomist makes a special effort to avoid portraying Solomon as a king like the nations. Both include early anti-Solomonic traditions (Deut 17:16a, 17; 1 Sam 8:11b-17*) which originally condemned his search for wealth and military security.[52] In their Deuteronomistic contexts, however, these condemnations no longer refer to Solomon, but to the kingship "like the nations" which Israel should avoid, and Solomon (in 1 Kgs 3:9; cf. 3:11) does avoid.

In conclusion, the prologue to the divine speech in 11aα4-12βb is Deuteronomistic.[53] The total point is the following: Solomon's fabled

---

[50] Note that 3:11 does not necessarily accurately represent the priorities of non-Israelite royalty. It is polemical and represents Israelite perceptions of non-Israelites.

[51] Seow, "The Syro-Palestinian Context of Solomon's Dream," 148 points out that there are a couple of examples from Ugaritic literature of human refusal of divine offers of certain goods. Two stories in Ugaritic literature describe human refusal of divine offers, the Keret dream epiphany (*KTU* 1.14 [I:51-II:3]) and Aqhat's encounter with Anat (*KTU* 1.17 VI:20-25, 34-40). 1 Kgs 3:11, however, is distinctive in using the human refusal of potential divine gifts *to explain further divine favor*.

[52] Frank Crüsemann's study of 1 Sam 8 (*Der Widerstand gegen das Königtum: Die antiköniglichen Texte des Alten Testamentes und der Kampf um den frühen israelitischen Staat*, WMANT 49 [Neukirchen: Neukirchener Verlag, 1978], 66-73) has established the existence of a pre-Deuteronomistic layer in it which is close to, but not identical with, the Deuteronomistic position on kingship. This hypothesis better accounts for the genre and intention of this passage than previous theories, including the "late source" approach, assignment of this passage wholly to the Deuteronomist, and the "prophetic redaction" approach. Note that one of the recent "prophetic redaction" studies leaves 1 Sam 8 out of that redaction: Anthony F. Campbell, *Of Prophets and Kings: A Late Ninth-Century Document (1 Sam 1 - 2 Kings 10)*, CBQMS 17 (Washington D. C.: Catholic Biblical Association of America, 1986).

For inclusion of Deut 17:16a and 17 in this stratum see note 325 of Carr, "Royal Ideology and the Technology of Faith," 117-118.

[53] This assignment of 11aα4-12βb to the Deuteronomist agrees with Würthwein, *Die Bücher Könige*, 1:35; and Simon J. De Vries, *1 Kings*, WBC 12 (Waco, TX: Word Books, 1985), 47. Jones, *1 & 2 Kings*, 128, argues that the prologue is an addition by court redactors emphasizing Solomon's wisdom as his charisma (but cf. 1:121 on 1 Kgs 3:11b!).

wealth and power were produced not by his desire to emulate foreign ways, but by his rejection of those ways and his choice of judicial wisdom, a quality of the true king. This positive picture of Solomon is part of the Deuteronomistic presentation of him. In this presentation, the Deuteronomist decontextualizes anti-Solomonic texts and describes him, for now, as the wise temple builder with the right priorities. Only after Solomon builds the temple will the Deuteronomist return to the subject of Solomon's apostasy.[54]

1 Kgs 3:12bβγ and 13ba: The Incomparability Formulae

1 Kgs 3:12bβγ: so that none like you will have existed before you, nor after you will one arise like you.

1 Kgs 3:13ba: so that no one among the kings will be like you [13bβ all your days].[55]

Many passages roughly similar to 1 Kgs 3:12bβγ, 13ba occur in Biblical materials. Formulae describing humans as unique in degree occur in the Deuteronomistic history, Pentateuch (J and E), Job, and Nehemiah. The formulae in 1 Kgs 3:12bβγ and 13ba, however, particularly resemble the following Deuteronomistic descriptions of the incomparability of great kings.

2 Kgs 18:5b: ואחריו לא־היה כמהו בכל מלכי יהודה ואשר היו לפניו

And after him [Hezekiah] there was none like him among the kings of Judah or those who were before him.

---

[54] Such a picture better explains the prologue than the often cited parallel from the prologue to Proverbs (Prov 3:13-18). Cf. Long, *1 Kings,* 66 and Weinfeld, *Deuteronomy and the Deuteronomic School,* 257. Similar passages occur elsewhere in the prologue (Prov 2:4-8; 4:7; 8:10-21; 9:11), but they assert that a personified Wisdom brings riches, honor, long life, etc. They do not argue that a *preference* for wisdom would lead God to provide riches, honor, long life, etc, nor do they include any positive evaluation of the rejection of those valued items along with military victory. For discussion of an actual parallel between Prov 3:13-18 and the pre-Deuteronomistic form of the Gibeon story see the next chapter.

[55] The phrase, כל־ימך ("all your days"), at the end of verse 13 is difficult to interpret. With the preceding incomparability formula the phrase seems to specify the range of incomparability, that is Solomon's contemporaries. Generally such specifications in incomparability formulae are prepositional phrases introduced by the preposition ב ("in"). This led Noth (citing Ehrlich) to postulate the secondary character of 13ba on the basis of its separation of כל־ימך from 13a (*Könige,* 44).

2 Kgs 23:25: וכמהו לא־היה לפניו מלך אשר...ואחריו לא־קם כמהו

And none like him [Josiah] were before him . . . nor after him did one arise like him.

The formulae in 1 Kgs 3:12-13 share all the Deuteronomistic formal characteristics, but focus on Solomon's wisdom, wealth and honor rather than his piety.[56] The common form indicates the probable Deuteronomistic origins of 1 Kgs 3:12bβγ and 13bα, while the divergence in focus is explained by the Deuteronomist's interest in reworking pre-Deuteronomistic references to Solomon's incomparable wisdom, wealth, and fame (1 Kgs 5:9-14; 10:23; cf. 10:10b, 12b, 20b for similar formulae).[57]

Kgs 3:14a: The Condition for the Promise of Long Life

1 Kgs 3:14a: And if you walk in my ways, observing my norms and commandments like David, your father,

The comparison to David and terminology (חקי ומצותי, "my statutes and commandments")[58] and הלך בדרכי, "walk in my ways")[59] identify

---

[56] Aside from the above cited clearly Deuteronomistic texts such incomparability formulae occur only twice: 1 Kgs 3:12-13 and Neh 13:26, a description of Solomon probably dependent on 1 Kgs 3:12-13. For more detailed comparison see Gottfried Johannes, *Unvergleichlichkeitsformulierungen im Alten Testament* (Mainz: Un. Mainz, 1968), 81-87.

[57] The lack of description in 1 Kgs 3:12-13 of Solomon's incomparable virtue is also consistent with the Deuteronomist's mild qualification of praise for Solomon in 1 Kgs 3:3b and later description of his apostasy in 1 Kgs 11:1-8.

On the pre-Deuteronomistic character of 1 Kgs 5:9-14 and the above cited texts from chapter 10 see Noth, *Könige*, 80-81, 208-209, contra Scott, "Solomon and the Beginning of Wisdom in Israel," 262-279.

Zalevsky, "התגלות ה' לשלמה בגעון," 235, attempts through adducing extra-Biblical Ancient Near Eastern Incomparability formulae to establish that the Deuteronomist borrowed from a pre-Deuteronomistic source in 1 Kgs 3:12-13 for the form of his other comparisons. His parallels, however, show few patterns amongst themselves, focus on different subjects from the formulae in 12bβγ and 13b, and share few formal characteristics with them. Johannes (*Unvergleichlichkeitsformulierungen*, 49-50) and Görg (*Gott-König-Reden*, 101-111) propose Egyptian parallels. These parallels, however, are shaped by the Egyptian ideology about divine kingship and thus diverge significantly from the incomparability formulae in 1 Kgs 3:12bβγ, 13b.

[58] The combination occurs in Deuteronomistic literature in Deut 4:40; 1 Kgs 8:58; Jer 32:11. Other occurrences include 2 Chr 19:10; Ezra 7:11.

[59] See Nelson, *The Double Redaction of the Deuteronomistic History*, p. 136, note 28, and Weinfeld, *Deuteronomy and the Deuteronomic School*, 333-334 (nos. 6, 6a, 7) for this and related expressions.

the condition in 14a as Deuteronomistic.[60] This has often been enough to establish the Deuteronomistic origins of the verse as a whole, but other indicators suggest that the promise of long life in 3:14b was originally unconnected to the condition in 3:14a. To be sure, many purpose clauses in the Deuteronomistic law portray long life as a reward for obedience.[61] Nevertheless, the actual promise of long life in 14b diverges from the Deuteronomistic purpose clauses in two ways: having God as the subject of the verb (God, not Solomon, is to lengthen his life) and lacking any reference to long life *in the land* or *long rule* (as in Deut 17:20).[62] Instead, the promise of long life in 1 Kgs 3:14b is closer to the first part of the blessing in several 10th century Phoenician dedicatory inscriptions. These inscriptions read: "may (god[s] X) lengthen the days of (king X) and his years over Byblos." For example, the restored text of Elibaal reads "may the lady of Byblos lengthen the days of Elibaal and his years over Byblos" (*KAI* 6:2-3). Both 1 Kgs 3:14b and the first part of these Byblos blessings share vocabulary (ארך causative, יום with following suffix or construct) and subject (God) over against the Deuteronomistic purpose clauses. These similarities between 3:14b and the Byblos inscriptions along with a lack of uniquely Deuteronomistic phraseology in 14b indicate that the latter half of verse fourteen is probably not Deuteronomistic.

In conclusion, while 14a is clearly Deuteronomistic, the similarities between 3:14b and the Byblos promises along with lack of Deuteronomistic characteristics indicate that 3:14b was probably part of the pre-Deuteronomistic version of 1 Kgs 3:2-15. The promise in 14b is dependent on either the Byblos blessing tradition or an Israelite tradition

---

[60] Moreover, 14a makes verse 14 as a whole a religious conditional promise. Such religious conditional promises occur almost exclusively in materials redacted by the Deuteronomistic school (Deuteronomistic history and Jeremiah) or influenced by its style (Chronicles). See Harry Wesley Gilmer, *The If-You Form in Israelite Law*, SBLDS 15 (Missoula: Scholars Press, 1975), 32-37 and 78-80.

[61] The term "Deuteronomistic" is used rather than "Deuteronomic" because the present form of the Deuteronomic law is Deuteronomistic. For example, the Deuteronomistic character of Deut 17:18-19 is indicated most of all by the reference in verse 18 to the writing of the Torah in a book. Similar references to the law book occur in the (covenant) curses in Deut 29:19, 20 and 28 and then the description of the law (ספר התורה) found and read during the time of Josiah in 2 Kgs 22:8, 10.

[62] For other Deuteronomistic purpose clauses cf. Deut 4:1, 40; 5:16; 6:2, 24; 8:1; 11:9; 22:7; 25:15; 30:6, 15-20; and 32:47. Occurrences outside unquestionably Deuteronomistic literature include Exod 20:12; Isa 53:10; Prov 28:16; Eccl 8:13. In all cases, the persons are said to prolong their own days.

resembling that tradition.[63] In either case, the fixed character of the early formula was enough to force a shift to using a causative form of אָרךְ ("lengthen") from using a form of the verb נתן ("give"), the one used in God's initial query (1 Kgs 3:5bβ) and God's promises of wisdom, wealth, and honor (1 Kgs 3:12-13).

The Adonai Redaction

1 Kgs 3:10 and 15ba1-6 ("he went to Jerusalem and stood before the ark of the covenant of Adonai") are distinguished from their context by their use of the term "Adonai" (אֲדֹנָי) to refer to God, rather than the "Yahweh" of the Deuteronomistic additions, and the "Elohim" of most of the pre-Deuteronomistic story.[64] "Adonai" is used as a divine designation in late materials.[65] Its appearance as a divine designation in parts of the Gibeon story is evidence for their being secondary and later than the first Deuteronomistic redaction of the Gibeon story.[66] For this reason in

---

[63] The regularity of the long life blessing in the Byblos inscriptions suggests that it was not the creation of an individual writer but a formula, shared within the Byblos tradition and possibly elsewhere. Solomon's relations with Phoenicia are well documented and the tradition may have originated there. The geographical and chronological proximity of the Byblos inscriptions to Solomon and his period provide further support for this hypothesis (see Seow, "The Syro-Palestinian Context of Solomon's Dream," 142), but it is also possible that the promise of long life in 14b is dependent on an Israelite tradition resembling the one which appears in the Byblos inscriptions.

[64] "Yahweh" is used twice in the pre-Deuteronomistic version, once when God first appears and once in Solomon's vocative address to God.

[65] אֲדֹנָי and אֲדֹנָי are widely attested in Biblical and extra-Biblical Northwest Semitic literature as popular forms for vocatives at the beginnings of addresses to superiors. אֲדֹנָי, however, only became prevalent as a divine designation in the exilic period. It is common in the Psalms and framework portions (introductions and concluding formulae) of the prophetic books (especially Ezekiel). It probably only occurred five times in the earliest texts of Genesis-Kings (excluding 1 Kgs 3:10 and 15ba): Exod 15:17 (possibly secondary - see Samaritan Targum, Cairo Geniza fragments, and several Hebrew manuscripts); 34:9; 1 Kgs 2:26 (possibly secondary - see Syriac and Old Greek); 22:6; 2 Kgs 7:6; 19:23. This does not include the 28 occurrences of אֲדֹנָי in addresses to God which were probably originally אֲדֹנָי or אֲדֹנָי: Gen 15:2, 8; 18:3, 27, 30, 31; 20:4; Exod 4:10, 13; 5:22; 34:9 (second occurrence in the Massoretic text); Num 14:17; Deut 3:24; 9:26; Josh 7:7, 8; Judg 6:22; 13:8; 16:28; 2 Sam 7:18, 19 (2), 20, 22, [25b in some MSS], 28, 29; 1 Kgs 8:53. Cf. Otto Eissfeldt, "אֲדֹון, אֲדֹנָי," in *Theologisches Wörterbuch zum Alten Testament*, vol. 1, אב-גלה (Stuttgart: W. Kohlhammer, 1970), 66; Abraham Even-Shoshan, A New Concordance to the Torah, Prophets, and Writings (Jerusalem: Kiryat Sepher, 1982), 107-108.

[66] For a brief discussion of criteria for use of divine names in redaction analysis see below, pp. 27-28 and note 73. In this case אֲדֹנָי is allowed to serve as a prima facie

the following material these verses are referred to as "the Adonai redaction." Additional evidence of the secondary and post-Deuteronomistic character of this redaction follows.

The Description of God's Affective Reaction to Solomon's Response

1 Kgs 3:10: The thing pleased Adonai, that Solomon had asked this thing.

This addition supplements the first Deuteronomist's explanation of God's favorable reaction in 1 Kgs 3:11. 3:11 emphasized the value of both Solomon's request for wisdom and rejection of other items commonly valued by pagan kings. In contrast, 3:10 exclusively emphasizes the value of Solomon's request for wisdom. It does not mention his rejection of other items. Moreover, this description of God's response prematurely and repetitively anticipates the prologue in 11, even repeating one of its phrases: את־הדבר הזה ("this thing").

1 Kgs 3:15ba1-6: Solomon's trip to before the ark in Jerusalem

1 Kgs 3:15ba1-6: He went to Jerusalem and stood before the ark of the covenant of Adonai.

The main indication of the secondary nature of this phrase is the fact that it produces a significant deviation from the epiphany form otherwise followed in 1 Kgs 3:2-15. Epiphany reports such as the Gibeon story almost always promote the reputation of sanctuaries by describing the receiver of the epiphany as building an altar and/or offering sacrifices *at the sanctuary site where the epiphany took place.*[67] With the removal of Solomon from Gibeon, the Gibeon story now lacks any such description.

Whereas the pre-Deuteronomistic epiphany story probably described Solomon as offering burnt offerings and holding a banquet in Gibeon, the addition in 15ba1-6 removes Solomon from Gibeon, so that his thanksgiving sacrifice takes place in Jerusalem, the only legitimate sanctuary according to the Deuteronomistic perspective. But removal of Solomon's thanksgiving offering to the ark in Jerusalem is not necessary

---

cause for literary distinctions for several reasons. First, the form אֲדֹנָי is a special form which develops specifically to refer to יהוה and, as such, is very close to a proper name. Second, the widespread use of אֲדֹנָי as a semi-proper name is demonstrably exilic and later. Third, unlike אלהים, when not used as a proper name אֲדֹנָי occurs in a specific, easily identifiable context, introduction to direct address, and even there was probably originally not אֲדֹנָי but אֲדֹנָי/אֲדֹנִי.

[67] Argumentation for this point will be given in the next chapter.

within the first Deuteronomist's perspective. The first Deuteronomistic editor, who authored 3:3b, is clearly aware of Solomon's patronage of sanctuaries outside Jerusalem. Indeed he explicitly mentions this patronage in the regnal evaluation rather than disguising it.

Nevertheless, the Adonai editor's addition is Deuteronomistic in tone. This is signaled by both the inclination to portray Solomon as sacrificing in Jerusalem and by the expression, "ark of the covenant of the Lord," an expression closest to Deuteronomistic references to the ark.[68]

A Deuteronomistic Gloss: 1 Kgs 3:2

1 Kgs 3:2   The people, however, were sacrificing at the [non-Jeru-salemite] sanctuaries because the temple had not yet been built to the name of the LORD in those days.

The Deuteronomistic terminology and focus on centralized worship and terminology[69] indicate that 3:2 is a Deuteronomistic secondary addition. Like the second half of Deuteronomistic mixed evaluations of kings (2 Kgs 12:3-4; 14:3-4; 15:3-4, 34-35), 1 Kgs 3:2 begins with רק ("only, however") and mentions the people's continued sacrifices at sanctuaries. There are also, however, some crucial differences between 1 Kgs 3:2 and the Deuteronomistic mixed regnal evaluations. Most importantly, the negative half of the mixed evaluations has been modified in 3:2 in order to excuse Solomon's sacrifice at Gibeon. Unlike the mixed regnal evaluations, 3:2 does not mention that Solomon failed to remove the non-Jerusalemite sanctuaries. Moreover, 3:2 explains Solomon's sacrifice through explicitly stating that everyone had to sacrifice at the non-Jerusalemite sanctuaries before the temple was built.[70]

Verse 3:2 is also different in important ways from the Deuteronomistic regnal evaluation in 3:3. Rather than criticizing Solomon (as does 3:3b), 3:2 justifies his worship outside Jerusalem in terms of pre-temple practices. Through placing Solomon's worship outside Jerusalem *in the context of* the people's necessary pre-temple practices, this verse justifies

---

[68] Cf. particularly Josh 3:11, 13; 1 Kgs 2:26. These verses are probably late. They are distinguished from 1 Kgs 3:15 by the word ארון without a suffix in construct with כל-הארץ. This and a like epithet, ארון חולי ארץ, occur four other times in the Bible, each time in a post-exilic context (Zech 4:14; 6:5; Pss 97:5; 114:7).

[69] במה: "sanctuary" used in a negative sense and לשם יהוה ("to the name of Yahweh").

[70] Also, the mixed regnal evaluations usually describe sacrifice at non-Jerusalemite sanctuaries using the terms מזבחים ומקטירים ("sacrificing and offering incense"). In 3:2 this has been shortened to מזבחים ("sacrificing") alone.

Solomon's practices as in accord with general pre-temple conditions. In other words, 1 Kgs 3:2 implies that the qualification of praise in 1 Kgs 3:3b is anachronistic.

In sum, differences between 3:2 and the framework Deuteronomist regnal evaluations (1 Kgs 3:3 and 2 Kgs 12:3-4; 14:3-4; 15:3-4, 34-35) indicate the 3:2 was probably not authored by the editor(s) of the overall Deuteronomistic history. Instead, 3:2 was probably written as a marginal comment next to verse 3:3 in order to correct the negative description of Solomon's sacrifice in 3:3b. Since the qualification of praise in 3:3b begins with the particle רק ("only"), the author of 3:2 connected it to 3:3b by likewise beginning it with רק ("only"). Only later did a scribe insert the verse in its present context. Once this happened, however, the particle became problematic, since 3:2 could not qualify the preceding verse about Solomon's marriage to Pharaoh's daughter.[71] This then explains the origins of the awkward רק ("only") at the beginning of 3:2.

Other Verses Previously Isolated as Deuteronomistic[72]

1 Kgs 3:5a and 7

Other redaction analyses have singled out 1 Kgs 3:5a and 7 as Deuteronomistic, but these verses are not identified as such here. To be sure, both verses share with the Deuteronomistic material the use of יהוה ("Yahweh") as a divine name, rather than אלהים ("God") characteristic of other parts of the pre-Deuteronomistic version. Nevertheless, divine designations cannot serve as an *a priori* argument for the separation of

---

[71] This difficulty has led some scholars to propose that verse 2 originally stood after 3:3 or 2:46. For examples of this see Šanda, *Könige*, 56 (with emendations); and Carl Steurnagel, *Lehrbuch der Einleitung in das Alte Testament* (Tübingen: J.C.B. Mohr, 1912), 356. 3:2, however, cannot qualify either verse. If it followed 2:46, we would have the anomaly of Solomon's successful consolidation of power being juxtaposed to the continued practice of sacrifice outside Jerusalem. If 3:2 followed 3:3, the somewhat parallel statements in 3:3b and 3:2 would be juxtaposed by the particle רק.

For other's arguments for a "marginal gloss" hypothesis for 3:2 see Immanuel Benzinger, *Die Bücher der Könige*, 15; Burney, *Notes on the Hebrew Text of the Books of Kings*, 28; and Skinner, *Kings*, 84.

[72] Through use of the word "isolated" I mean to exclude discussion of the Kenik, Scott, and Weinfeld analyses which attempt to establish Deuteronomistic redaction of the entire Gibeon story (Kenik) or its contents (Scott, Weinfeld). Scott's and Weinfeld's arguments only pertain to select parts of the Gibeon story, and—though quite helpful for those parts—do not establish Deuteronomistic redaction of the whole. For discussion of Kenik, see above, pp. 9-10.

layers.[73] Rather, the proper name יהוה ("Yahweh") serves specific functions in both 3:5a and 7. In 1 Kgs 3:5a, יהוה serves to introduce Yahweh on the epiphany scene. Once introduced, God is referred to in the pre-Deuteronomistic Gibeon story by the general divine designation, אלהים ("God"). The one exception, יהוה אלהי ("Yahweh, my God" in 3:7), is Solomon's vocative address to God. In this context a distinction appears between address to God by God's proper name, יהוה ("Yahweh") and the use of אלהים ("God") as a divine designation combined with the possessive suffix.[74]

1 Kgs 3:9a

The multivalence of Solomon's request in 9a make it the most problematic part of the Gibeon story for redaction analysis. Outside of 9a there seems to be a tension between an original request for general wisdom and the Deuteronomist's interpretation of that as a request for

---

[73] Here I depend most on the penetrating methodological discussions by Erhard Blum (*Die Komposition der Vätergeschichte*, WMANT 57 [Neukirchen: Neukirchener Verlag, 1984], 471-475) and Wolfgang Richter (*Exegese als Literaturwissenschaft: Entwurf einer alttestamentlichen Literaturtheorie und Methodologie* [Göttingen: Vandenhoeck & Ruprecht, 1971], 56-57). Contrary to Blum, I would maintain that divine designation usages in the Bible do not easily fit into clear cut categories of proper name versus concept terms. Rather they fit into a continuum of usage, with יהוה on one end as the divine name proper, and אֲדֹנָי and אלהים as terms which increasingly begin to serve as substitutes for יהוה, especially as Israelite religion restricted usage of the latter. Moreover, אֲדֹנָי and אלהים seem to have retained distinctiveness over against the proper name יהוה, though the particular lines of the distinctiveness of אלהים have not yet been clarified. For discussions of this problem cf. (in addition to the sources cited above): W. R. Rudolph, *Der Elohist als Erzähler: Ein Irrweg der Pentateuchkritik?*, BZAW 63 (Giessen: A. Töpelmann, 1933), 14-16; Umberto Cassuto, *The Documentary Hypothesis and the Composition of the Pentateuch: Eight Lectures*, trans. I. Abrahams (Jerusalem: Magnes, 1963), 20-41; Moses Hirsch Segal, *The Pentateuch: Its Composition and its Authorship and Other Biblical Studies* (Jerusalem: Magnes, 1967), 103-123.

[74] Other arguments for the secondary character of 3:5a and 7 are no more persuasive. Herrmann ("Die Königsnovelle in Ägypten und in Israel," p. 36, note 1) proposes that the mention of the dream in 5a seems to conflict with the surprise registered in 15a, והנה חלום ("and behold, it was a dream"), but the surprise element in 15a is from Solomon's point of view, while the notice in 5a is for the reader's benefit (cf. the similar movement in the often cited Keret parallel to 1 Kgs 3:15: [*KTU* 1.14 I: 35-37 to III:50-51]). Noth (*Könige*, 45) adds the observation that 5a resembles 1 Kgs 9:2, a clearly Deuteronomistic verse, but 1 Kgs 9:2 resembles 3:5a only enough to refer back to it. There are important differences between 3:5a and 9:2 (such as 9:2 not being a dream epiphany) which indicate that the two verses were not written by the same author.

specifically legal wisdom. (Non-Deuteronomistic) 1 Kgs 3:12 describes Solomon as requesting general wisdom ("a wise and intelligent heart"), while (Deuteronomistic) 3:11b describes Solomon as requesting legal wisdom ("discrimination in order to hear cases"). If 9a or part of it could be unambiguously interpreted as referring to either legal wisdom or general wisdom, the redaction-critical problem could be solved.

Unfortunately (from a redaction-critical perspective) all parts of the verse can be plausibly interpreted in both ways. The verse can be translated "Give your servant a hearing heart to govern your people and to distinguish good from evil" (general wisdom) or "Give your servant a hearing heart to judge your people and to distinguish right from wrong" (legal interpretation).[75] The former translation parallels the pre-Deuteronomistic 3:12, while the latter translation parallels the Deuteronomistic 3:11b.

In other parts of the story, the Deuteronomist carefully preserves, yet supplements, pre-Deuteronomistic elements (1 Kgs 3:4-5, 6aα, 7, 12bα, 13a, and 14b). The same is probably true of 1 Kgs 3:9a. Whereas Deuteronomistic additions elsewhere in the story show clear Deuteronomistic characteristics, none of 9a is distinctively Deuteronomistic.[76] Therefore, following the norms established with 3:5a and 3:7, the verse should be presumed to be pre-Deuteronomistic. At its earliest stage it was understood as a request for general wisdom (fulfilled in 3:12). Later the Deuteronomist understood the multivalent terms of this request as

---

75 The infinitive phrase, להבין בין טוב לרע, can refer to specifically legal capacities, but also can refer to comprehensive knowledge. Cf. W. Malcolm Clark, "A Legal Background to the Yahwist's Use of "Good and Evil" in Genesis 2-3," *JBL* 88 (1969): 266-278; and Weinfeld's brief critique of Clark in *Deuteronomy and the Deuteronomic School*, 247, including note 1.

The verb שפט usually means "judge," but it can also mean "govern." Similarly, the verb שמע ("hear") can refer to legal capacities (cf. Deut 1:16), but it can also refer to wisdom receptivity. On the latter expression see Kenik, *Design for Kingship*, 136; Helmut Brunner, "Das hörende Herz," *TLZ* 79 (1954):697-700; Görg, *Gott-König-Reden*, 82-88 and Shupak, "Some Idioms Connected with the Concept of 'Heart,'" 202-206.

76 The election theology implicit in עמך ("your people"), could be seen as an indicator of Deuteronomistic origins of the phrase (לשפט את־עמך: "to judge your people," but election theology is not limited to the Deuteronomist. Note the contrast between the descriptions of God's people as great in 8a and 9b versus the lack of such description in 9a. Moreover, we might expect עמך ישראל ("your people Israel"). See Weinfeld, *Deuteronomy and the Deuteronomic School*, p. 328, item 11, for the Deuteronomistic character of this phrase (items 9-12 are relevant).

referring to legal wisdom and explicitly described the request as such in additions elsewhere in the story (3:11).

Concluding Summary

In sum, I have argued here that there is indeed substantial evidence for multiple layers of Deuteronomistic redaction in the Gibeon story. In the first stage of this redaction, the Josianic editors appropriated a pre-Deuteronomistic Gibeon story and placed it in their history, pairing it with the story of Solomon's wise judgment (1 Kgs 3:16-28) and placing it right after the succession narrative as an introduction to Solomon's reign. In the process, these editors added the following material: 3:3, 6aβb, 8, 9b, 11aα4-12βb (the prologue to the divine speech), 12b$\beta\gamma$,13bα, and 14a. The next two phases in the growth of the story were part of a later Deuteronomistic "retouching" of the history. First, the Adonai editor added two transitions: 3:10 and 15bα1-6 (Solomon's journey to the ark). Second, a Deuteronomistically inclined glossator added the present 1 Kgs 3:2 as a marginal comment on 3b. During the subsequent written transmission of 1 Kings, someone inserted this marginal comment into the text.

Chapter Three

THE PRE-DEUTERONOMISTIC VORLAGE
TO THE GIBEON STORY

Having isolated the stages of redaction of the Gibeon story, I now interpret its pre-Deuteronomistic Vorlage. Through such interpretation I aim for a baseline against which to measure the transformations of the story through redaction. I presuppose that the Vorlage is an individual speech act structured by some larger generic forms, *but* tailored to speak a particular message. Form-critical investigation inevitably involves a dialectic between analysis of the individual text and observation of generically typical elements in it (its genres).[77] In order to preserve this sense of the individuality of the text, I begin with a close reading of it. Such a reading can often uncover gaps in the story and other loci of multivalence which play a major role in later interpretations of it.

I begin with the Vorlage in order to compare it with subsequent redaction, but such a beginning point brings certain methodological problems. After all, literary and form-critical analyses proceed on firmer ground with the final form of the text, 1 Kgs 3:2-15, than with a reconstructed version of the text dependent on potentially faulty redaction-critical judgments. With regard to literary analysis, this problem is unavoidable, but necessary if one wants to carefully examine the interpretation implicit in redaction. In the following I present the close reading of the Vorlage first even though I began with the final form of the text in my own literary analysis of the Gibeon story. The close reading of the

---

77 Rolf Knierim, "Old Testament Form Criticism Reconsidered," *Int* 27 (1973):435-468.

Vorlage then provides data for subsequent analysis of the forms utilized in the Vorlage.

THE TEXT OF THE VORLAGE

Through process of elimination, the following verses belong to the pre-Deuteronomistic Gibeon story: 1 Kgs 3:4-5, 6aα, 7, 9a, 11aα1-3, 12abα, 13a, 13bβ, 14b, 15a, and 15bα7-10β (Solomon's offerings and banquet). The verses in this pre-Deuteronomistic layer all lack Deuteronomistic traits and fit together into a coherent whole. The following is an English translation of the text which these verses constitute:

4)	The king went to Gibeon to sacrifice there because it was the greatest of the sanctuaries. Solomon used to offer a thousand burnt offerings on that altar.
5)	At Gibeon Yahweh appeared to Solomon in a dream of the night and said, "Ask what I should give you."
6aα)	Solomon said, "You have acted with great faithfulness towards your servant, my father David.
7)	And now, oh LORD my God, you have made your servant king after my father David, but I am a little youth. I do not know how to go out or come in.
9a)	Give your servant a hearing heart in order to govern your people and to distinguish between good and evil.
11aα1-3)	And God said to him,
12abα)	"Behold, I act according to your words. Behold I give you a wise and intelligent heart
13a)	Also that which you did not request I give you, both riches and honor
13bβ)	all your days,
14b)	and I will lengthen your days.
15a)	Solomon awoke, and behold, it was a dream,
15bα7-10β)	and he offered burnt offerings, performed communion sacrifices, and held a banquet for all his servants.

A CLOSE READING OF THE VORLAGE

The Introductions: 1 Kgs 3:4 and 5

4)   The king went to Gibeon to sacrifice there because it was the greatest of the sanctuaries. Solomon used to offer a thousand burnt offerings on that altar.

5)   At Gibeon Yahweh appeared to Solomon in a dream of the night and said, "Ask what I should give you."

These two verses work on several different levels to initiate the overall narrative. Verse four locates "the king" at Gibeon and explains his presence there. In so doing, it sets the stage for the following epiphany proper (5-15a) and response to it (15b*). The description of God's appearance in 5a is more strictly related to the epiphany which it introduces, 5b-14. Moreover, it corresponds to the description of Solomon's waking in 15a. Finally, the open ended divine offer in 5b initiates the petition scene which is the framework for the subsequent interaction (6-14). In summary, all of 4-5 introduce the Gibeon story, but the focus progressively narrows from introducing the story as a whole to setting the stage for Solomon's petition and God's reply to it.

4aα)   The king went to Gibeon to sacrifice there

The text of 4aα is trim in its referents: the king, Gibeon, and sacrifice.[78] These are the three major elements of the story at its outset. The next two clauses build on each other to account for the connection between these three elements. They answer the question: "Why did Solomon make this trip to sacrifice at Gibeon?"

4aβ)   because it was the greatest of the sanctuaries.

At the outset, 4aβ is explicitly subordinated to 4aα through the conjunction כי ("for, because"). This subordinate clause describes Gibeon as הבמה הגדולה ("the great sanctuary"). Clearly at this point, the word במה ("sanctuary") had not acquired the negative connotations that it had in

---

[78] As it stands, the first clause begins enigmatically. The definite article on הַמֶּלֶךְ ("the king") implies that this king has been discussed in a previous text, and the vav-consecutive form, וַיֵּלֶךְ ("and he went") likewise suggests that text precedes this version of the Gibeon story. These elements may have been added by the redactors responsible for placing the Gibeon story in its present context. In any case, for the present purposes, focus on the Gibeon story precludes further discussion of the possible explanations for the ways 3:4 in its present form seems to presume material which preceded it.

the Deuteronomistic and later periods. Instead, describing Gibeon as "the great sanctuary" could explain a great king's visit.

4b)   Solomon used to offer a thousand burnt offerings on that altar.

The parenthetical remark in 4b builds on and explicates the claims in 4aβ that Gibeon was *the* great sanctuary. The parenthetical, explicative character of 4b is signaled not only through its subject matter, but also through its asyndetic coordination with the preceding.[79] Moreover, central elements of 4b relate to both the 4aα description of the purpose of Solomon's trip to Gibeon ("to sacrifice there") and the 4aβ description of the greatness of the sanctuary there ("because it was the greatest of sanctuaries"). Through referring with a demonstrative pronoun (ההוא: "that") to an element in 4aβ (the Gibeon sanctuary), the prepositional phrase at the end of 4b, על־המזבח ההוא ("on that altar") connects 4b to 4aβ. But rather than simply referring back to the sanctuary at Gibeon discussed in 4aβ (במה), the word מזבח ("altar") is used. This word's root, זבח ("sacrifice"), then links the end of 4b with a verb form in 4aα (לזבח:"to sacrifice").

The main emphasis in this sentence is on the extravagance of Solomon's sacrifice. The direct object, אלף עלות ("a thousand burnt offerings"), occurs in "front extra" position at the beginning of the sentence, diverging from Hebrew's usual verb-subject-object word order. Such position is termed "front extra" because it emphasizes the item which is out of place. In this case, the placement of the direct object at the beginning of the sentence emphasizes the incredible number of sacrifices which Solomon customarily offered at Gibeon.

The rest of the sentence emphasizes the idea that it was Solomon, the great king, who habitually offered such extravagant sacrifices. The verb, יַעֲלֶה (3ms, H-stem by context) is in the imperfect conjugation, referring to habitual action.[80] Moreover, this is the point where the text goes beyond its reference to "the king" and specifies that this king was none

---

[79] P. Joüon, *Grammaire de l'Hébreu Biblique* (Rome: Pontifical Institute, 1923), § 177a. Cf. verse 7b for another example of such a construction. Such asyndetic coordination can also signal the beginning of a new unit, such as in 3:5.

[80] Since 4b clearly refers to some kind of past action (thus explaining Solomon's past trip to Gibeon), other options for the imperfect (non-past, modal) are ruled out. Though one might suppose that the prefix form here is an ancient preterite, the converted imperfect form at the beginning of verse four makes this thesis unlikely. With the disappearance of most of the differentiating criteria between the preterite and the imperfect, the converted imperfect, a more differentiated narrative form, came to occupy the morphological slot previously held by the preterite.

other than Solomon. Through explicit mention of Solomon at this point the text implies that Solomon is the kind of king whose patronage makes a sanctuary "great."

The placement of 4b after both 4aα and 4aβ suggests that 4b describes *both* how great a sanctuary Gibeon was *and* why Solomon made this particular trip there. The text could have read: "Solomon went to Gibeon to sacrifice there; he used to offer a thousand burnt offerings on that altar because Gibeon was the great sanctuary." Instead, placed after 4aβ, the clause in 4b establishes how great a sanctuary Gibeon was through reference to Solomon's sacrifice there, *and through such argument* further explains Solomon's particular trip to Gibeon on this occasion. The implication of these explicative clauses is that Solomon went to Gibeon to sacrifice there because Gibeon was the kind of great sanctuary where a great king like Solomon customarily offered a thousand burnt offerings.

5a)   At Gibeon Yahweh appeared to Solomon in a dream of the night,

With the location and circumstances of the epiphany firmly established by verse four, the description of God's appearance in 5a introduces the other major character in the Gibeon story: Yahweh. The semantic focus of the text shifts from Solomon's behavior to God's, from Solomon's arrival at Gibeon to God's appearance, from introduction of the human actor to introduction of the divine one.[81]

The placement of בגבעון ("at Gibeon") at the beginning of the clause resumes the narrative thread broken by the explicative comments in 4aβ and 4b. Moreover, through placement of בגבעון ("at Gibeon") in front extra position, the text emphasizes once again the centrality of Gibeon in the overall narrative. Gibeon figures prominently not only in the notes about Solomon's arrival, but also in the description of God's appearance.

The verb which follows בגבעון ("at Gibeon"), נראה ("appear"), indicates the new element introduced by 5a, a divine appearance. The subject of the verb is Yahweh, while Solomon is merely the passive recipient of God's epiphany, the object of a prepositional phrase (אל־שלמה, "to Solomon").

5a concludes with another prepositional phrase: בחלום הלילה ("in a night dream"). This phrase specifies the medium of the divine appearance: a night dream. Night was (and continues to be) seen as a border

---

[81] This semantic shift indicates that the asyndetic coordination at the beginning of 5a corresponds to a major break in the narrative, in contrast to asyndetically coordinated clauses in 4b and 7b.

time of encounter with the extraordinary. Dreams are the preeminent form of such encounters. The expression, "night dream" draws doubly on these associations in depicting this particular divine-human encounter.[82] As a result of 5a, the number of major elements in the Gibeon story has grown from three (in 4aα and its explicative clauses) to four: Solomon, Gibeon, sacrifice and (now) God.

> 5b)   and God said, "Ask what I should give you."

God continues to occupy center stage in the speech report which follows (5b).[83] This text clearly portrays God as having the initiative, both in appearing and initiating the petition scene. Solomon does not simply exercise his royal prerogatives with God; rather God is in control. God directly addresses Solomon, beginning with an imperative: שְׁאַל ("ask").

The following indeterminate pronoun establishes the open-endedness of the divine offer. God does not just offer particular things that God knows Solomon will want. Rather God allows Solomon to ask whatever he wants.

Solomon's Petition: 1 Kgs 3:6aα,7,9a

The reader must wait to find out what Solomon wants. Solomon begins his petition with a lengthy rationale for it. Such a prologue is typical of Biblical petitions, but in this case it serves at least two functions. First, it delays Solomon's particular request, retarding the narrative pace and focusing the reader's curiosity on what the request will be.[84] Second, the strenuous argument in the prologue re-opens the question of divine favor through implying that Solomon had to persuade God to fulfill his request. Though the divine offer seemed straightforward in 5b, now other possibilities of interpretation emerge. The prefix form in 5b, אֶתֵּן, could be interpreted in two ways: as referring to the future and implying commitment to fulfill the request ("[ask what] I will give [to you]") *or* as subjunctive, implying God's withheld judgment until Solomon makes his request ("[ask what] I might give [to you]"). At this early stage in the

---

[82] For argumentation for this claim see the discussion of dream epiphanies later in this chapter.

[83] As mentioned above, with Yahweh having been mentioned by name in 5a, the divine designation, אלהים ("God") is used in the speech report introduction.

[84] On this phenomenon see Meir Sternberg, *The Poetics of Biblical Narrative: Ideological Literature and the Drama of Reading* (Indiana Studies in Biblical Literature; Bloomington, IN: Indiana University Press, 1985), 186-320, particularly 237-240.

story, the divine disposition toward Solomon is almost as unknown as what Solomon will request.[85]

> 6aα)   Solomon said, "You have acted with great faithfulness towards your servant, my father David.

Solomon's petition begins with a description of past circumstances leading up to the present petition. This description is brief: "You acted with great faithfulness toward my father, David." A morpho-syntactically unnecessary independent pronoun אתה ("you" masculine singular) occurs in front extra position at the beginning of this sentence. Just as in 3:4b, this placement of a noun at the head of the sentence focuses attention on that noun. In this case, the existence and placement of the pronoun signals that Solomon is focusing on God's (and no one else's) behavior. Specifically, Solomon is justifying his petition through reference to God's great faithfulness toward his father, David.

> 7a)   And now, oh Yahweh my God, you have made your servant king after my father David,

At verse seven Solomon shifts from description of past to present. This shift is indicated by the placement of עתה ("now") at the beginning of the verse. The following extended vocative address to God and use (again) of a morpho-syntactically unnecessary pronoun (אתה: "you") further underscores the fact that Solomon is focusing on God's behavior. God and no one else is responsible for making Solomon succeed David. The resulting connection between 6aα and 7a may be paraphrased as follows: "In the past, you showed great faithfulness to David, my father, and now Yahweh, my God, you and you alone put me in his place." The implied argument is that God should show the same kind of loyalty to Solomon as God showed to the king whom God had him succeed.

> 7b)   but I am a little youth. I do not know how to go out or come in.

With 7b, Solomon finally turns from God's behavior to its consequences for him. The shift is dramatically signaled by the placement of the first common singular pronoun אנכי ("I") at the beginning of the verbless clause in 7ba. The result can be paraphrased as follows: "In the past, *you* showed great faithfulness to David, my father, and now *Yahweh, my God, you and you* alone put me in his place, but *I* am a little youth, I do not know how to go out or come in."

---

85 The latter narrative move is an example of retrospective gapping, opening a gap in the narrative which did not previously exist.

The first part of 7b emphasizes Solomon's youth in two ways. First, the redundant expression נער קטן ("little youth") doubly describes his youth. Second, this redundant expression may model Solomon's youth for the reader. Otherwise unknown, this expression may be an example of ancient Hebrew children's speech, resembling the semantic redundancy of some expressions used by English speaking children like "more bigger."

In sum, the pronouns, movement and focus of Solomon's prologue almost make it sound like an accusation speech. While the "you" at the beginning of 6aα might be taken as a vocative "you" of praise, the clearly vocative "you" at the beginning of 7a is an address of a wrongfully neglected party to the one who has neglected him. The accusatory tone, however, is softened by the use of the submissive vassal term עבדך ("your servant") in 7a. Through use of this term, Solomon portrays himself as loyal to God, connecting this description of himself with his description of David in 6aα. Through such a connection, Solomon is calling for a restoration of right relationship. He invokes his privileges as God's appointed successor to David; he calls on God to be loyal to him as God would be to David.

> 9a)   Give your servant a hearing heart in order to govern your
>   people and to distinguish between good and evil.

The petition in 9a refers in multiple ways to the prologue which precedes and promotes it. At the beginning Solomon repeats the verb used in God's initial speech, נתן ("give"), and the vassal language used in the prologue to connect his relationship with God to David's (עבדך, "your servant"). In its present context, the second masculine singular possessive pronoun on people, עמך (*your* people") refers back to the repeated second masculine singular independent pronouns ("You," "Yahweh, my God, You...") of his semi-accusation speech in 6aα7a.

9a ends the waiting for Solomon's actual petition, but introduces a new line of tension. The head term of Solomon's request is the enigmatic expression, "hearing heart" (לב שמע). As seen in the redaction analysis, this expression has few exact parallels, and can be interpreted in more than one direction. This metaphorical expression brings together "heart" and "hear," leaving the reader to wonder, "Exactly how can a heart 'hear.'"

The two following infinitive phrases provide the first clue to this puzzle: "to govern your people" (לשפט את־עמך) and "to discriminate between good and evil." (להבין בין־טוב לרע). These two explicating infinitive phrases link the *purpose* of Solomon's request to the problem described in his arguments for it. Solomon is requesting that God remedy his lack of general knowledge so that he may fulfill the job in which God has set him. The general nature of the knowledge intended is indicated by the military connotations of Solomon's description of his inability to do the job: "I do not know how to go out or come in." In sum, the setting of Solomon's petition and the infinitive phrases attached to it indicate that he is asking for receptivity to divine instruction, instruction which will help him govern God's people.[86]

In sum, in the Vorlage, Solomon may not know how to go out or come in, but he can construct an artful case for what he wants. His speech shows how God's past actions have resulted in a present need which can only be met through God's favorable response to the petition. The petition, then, is thoroughly integrated with the prologue which prepares for it. The whole argues for Solomon's rights before God as the divinely appointed successor to David, specifically his right to be equipped to be an able successor by being given a "hearing heart."

God's Response to Solomon's Petition: 1 Kgs 3:11aα1-3; 12aα, 13a, 13bβ, 14b

12abα)   Behold, I act according to your words.
            Behold I give you a wise and intelligent heart.

This first part of God's response resolves two of the problems which have emerged in the narrative so far: How God is disposed toward Solomon and what constitutes a "hearing heart." With regard to the first, the divine response to Solomon's speech is overwhelmingly positive. God begins by saying that הנה ("behold") God is acting in accordance with Solomon's "words" (דבריך). This reference to Solomon's intricate case for his petition seems to recognize his reasoning as compelling.

---

[86] Legal wisdom is not excluded here. In both the Bible and extra-Biblical pre-Deuteronomistic Northwest Semitic materials the king is viewed as having particular legal responsibilities. Yassib (Keret's oldest son) and Absalom based their attempted takeovers on their fathers' failure to fulfill that responsibility (*KTU* 1.16 VI:41-54; 2 Sam 15:1-6). Moreover, there are several Biblical references to kings serving a judicial role (2 Sam 12:1-6; 14:1-17; 1 Kgs 3:16-28; 2 Kgs 8:1-6). The judicial role of the king is reflected in the petition found in the pre-exilic Ps 72:5 (royal psalm) and messianic prophecies such as Isa 11:3-4; 16:5. Solomon himself made a hall of judgment in which he could perform these duties (1 Kgs 7:7).

For fuller discussion see particularly Keith W. Whitelam, *The Just King: Monarchical Judicial Authority in Ancient Israel*, JSOTSup 12 (Sheffield: JSOT, 1979).

Furthermore, God will act in accordance with his words by providing him with a "wise and intelligent heart" (לב חכם ונבון). Thus, though ostensibly in accordance with Solomon's words, God's actual promise diverges from those words. The item which God promises in accordance with God's words is a "heart," but now a "wise and intelligent" heart, that is general wisdom. This divergence within partial repetition is highly significant. Now seen in the light of the divine reference to general wisdom, the original reference to "hearing heart" appears to be a description of intellectual receptivity: "a sensitive mind." The implication of this divine clarification is that the originally requested "hearing heart" is the same as a "wise and intelligent heart." From the privileged divine perspective intellectual receptivity (לב שמע: "a hearing heart") is true wisdom.[87]

This message, in turn, corresponds to its setting. The overall narrative revolves around the theme of receptivity, specifically royal receptivity to divine gifts. God appears and commands Solomon to receive. When Solomon requests intellectual receptivity, God responds by saying Solomon had requested wisdom. The Gibeon story Vorlage clearly presupposes that God is the source of wisdom, and that wisdom consists in receptivity to divine instruction.

13aα)   Also that which you did not request I give you,

This next part of the divine speech, like the first part, is introduced by a comment about its relation to Solomon's petition. Whereas God begins the promise of wisdom by saying it is in accordance with Solomon's words, God begins the promise of additional items by mentioning that they were not implicit in Solomon's words: "and also that which you did not request I give to you, . . ." God acts in accordance with Solomon's petition in verse 12abα, only to inexplicably go beyond it (13a).

Thus, just when the "hearing heart" puzzle is resolved, the narrative goes on to explicitly pose a problem which is never explicitly addressed within the Vorlage itself: Why does God promise Solomon additional things which he did not request? The fact that this is a "gap" and not a "blank" is indicated by the explicit thematization of the contrast between

---

[87] On the play of perspectives (particularly divine versus human) see Sternberg, *The Poetics of Biblical Narrative*, 129-185 and on repetition 365-440. God's redescription of Solomon's request would be an example of deliberate variation by God in repetition of a verbal object (Solomon's request). As Sternberg (402, 406-409) points out, such variation is particularly significant since verbatim repetition is expected with verbal objects.

promising Solomon what he requested ("Behold, I act in accordance with your words.") and promising things he did not request ("and also that which you did not request I give to you.").

13a)   Also that which you did not request I give you,
         both riches and honor

13bβ)   all your days,

14b)   and I will lengthen your days.

So, after having acted in accordance with his words in providing Solomon wisdom, God goes on to promise riches and honor all his days and a longer life in which to enjoy them. This plot—wisdom leads to riches, honor, and long life—matches that found in a different form in Israel and Egypt's instruction traditions. Specifically, the extra gifts which Solomon receives are exactly the ones described as in the right and left hands of Wisdom in Proverbs 3:16: אֹרֶךְ יָמִים בִּימִינָהּ בִּשְׂמֹאולָהּ עֹשֶׁר וכבד ("Long life is in her [Wisdom's] right hand; in her left are riches and honor.") This linkage of wisdom to long life, riches, and honor occurs throughout Proverbs 1-9 (2:4-8; 4:7-9; 8:10-21; 9:11), and originates in Egyptian wisdom literature concerning Maat.[88] Within its original wisdom contexts, this theme helps emphasize the rewards of the wisdom enterprise. The Vorlage to the Gibeon story, however, applies to God the predicates reserved for Maat/Wisdom in these traditions. Now God rewards Solomon for God's own reasons. In its earliest form, the text leaves the reader to wonder what those reasons are.

Finally, the Vorlage's promise of long life is an extension of the promise of riches and honor in 13bα. God not only promises Solomon riches and honor all his life, but also a longer life to enjoy them.[89] Thus the long life promise takes a subsidiary place to the promises of things for which Solomon was particularly famous: wisdom, wealth, and honor. The already existing fame of Solomon's wisdom, wealth, and honor helps validate the Vorlage's story about the divine origin of these things.

---

[88] Shupak, "The Concept of 'Heart' in Egypt and the Bible," 205; Christa Kayatz, *Studien zu Proverbien 1-9: Eine form- und motivgeschichtliche Untersuchung unter Einbeziehung Ägyptischen Vergleichsmaterials*, WMANT 22 (Neukirchen: Neukirchener Verlag, 1966), 76-134.

[89] Only with the Deuteronomistic insertions in 13bα and 14a did this connection get obscured.

The Conclusions: 1 Kgs 3 :15abα7-10β

15a)   Solomon awoke, and behold, it was a dream,

The conclusions here in 15a and next in 15b* (α7-10β) bring to a close the narrative begun in 4-5a. As mentioned above, the description of Solomon's waking in 15a corresponds to the dream epiphany formula in 5a. 5a drew on the border-time, extraordinary associations of nighttime and dreams to introduce the epiphany of God to Solomon. Likewise, 15a emphasizes the dream character of the revelation, but this time as a transition to Solomon's waking response. Only after having woken up can Solomon go on to respond to the divine gifts promised in the epiphany.

But the notice in 15a also subtly underlines a difference in perspective between the reader and Solomon. In the dream epiphany formula in 5a, the narrator informs the reader of the dream character of Solomon's revelation. The reader has no reason to believe at that point that Solomon is not also aware that he is dreaming. In this context, the second notice of the dream accompanied by the particle הנה ("behold") suddenly reveals that Solomon was not aware that he was dreaming until he woke up. All through the dream, the reader (through the notice in 5a) had been aware of something Solomon was not.[90]

15bα7-10β)   and he offered burnt offerings, performed communion
              sacrifices, and held a banquet for all his servants.

15bα7-10β brings the narrative around to the point where it began: Solomon's worship at Gibeon. One of the most prominent elements to emerge from this close reading of the story is its strong emphasis on the location of the epiphany, Gibeon. This emphasis appears from the beginning. Solomon traveled to Gibeon because it was the great sanctuary (4aβ). He used to offer a thousand sacrifices there (4b). Furthermore, the Vorlage stresses in the description of God's appearance that it was *at Gibeon* that God appeared to Solomon in a night dream, granting both his request and things he did not request (5a). Having received such bountiful gifts from God at his favored sanctuary, 15bα7-10β describes how

---

[90] The variation in repetition is produced by a combination of shift in context and form (the shift from an epiphany formula to the particle הנה ("behold"). This is a minor example of surprise retrospective gapping (see Sternberg, *The Poetics of Biblical Narrative*, 309-320). The introduction of a surprise divergence in perspectives could function in a variety of ways, including adding narrative interest and subtly impressing on the readers the advantages of their privileged perspective.

Solomon responded in thanksgiving. Here 15b echoes almost verbatim the earlier description of Solomon's customary extravagant burnt offerings (4b), but then supplements this with a description of his additional acts of thanksgiving. Not only did he offer his usual burnt offerings, but he added communion offerings and a banquet for all his servants. The verbatim repetition of a non-verbal object (burnt offerings) highlights the variation implicit in the addition of additional acts of thanksgiving.[91] Along with the shift in context, this variation in repetition highlights a shift within Solomon's own perspective: the dream epiphany has moved him beyond his usual extravagance (4b) to yet more sacrifices and celebration (15ba7-10β).

A FORM CRITICAL ANALYSIS OF THE VORLAGE

We turn from a close reading of the various parts of the Vorlage in their individuality to a consideration of the form of the story as a whole, particularly those parts of the Vorlage's form which are generically typical. While no text is the sum total of its generic typicalities, observation of such elements can enhance appreciation of a text's setting and intention. Forsaking such observation risks unconscious and uncritical subsumption of the ancient text into the interpreter's own modern repertoire of genres. For this reason I begin with a structure diagram of the form of the Gibeon story. Then I go on to discuss the generic typicalities present in the Vorlage.

In this case, working with reconstructed text does not significantly alter the form-critical results for the whole. The Vorlage isolated in the previous chapter includes all of the critical macro-structural indicators in the Gibeon story, from its pre-Deuteronomistic version through to its final form. In other words, the overall form of the Gibeon story does not change with its subsequent redaction. Instead, redactional insertions alter lower levels of the text's structure, levels which will not figure prominently in the following genre analysis.

---

[91] See Sternberg, *The Poetics of Biblical Narrative*, 402-406.

Diagram of the Structure
of the pre-Deuteronomistic Gibeon Story

Analysis of the Major Genres in the Vorlage

Overall Genre

• *Message Epiphany*

As an epiphany, the Gibeon story is closest to a set of Biblical epiphany stories which include divine messages communicated through the epiphany. These epiphanies have three parts. They usually begin with an epiphany introduction much like 1 Kgs 3:5.[92] Then comes the

---

[92] Cf. the following occurrences of the formula with a personal name (as in 1 Kgs 3:5): Gen 12:7; 17:1; 35:9 (there is a reference to this epiphany in Gen 48:3-4); 1 Kgs 9:2. Cf. also the references to the patriarchal traditions in Exod 6:3. This formula also occurs with מַלְאַךְ יהוה in Judg 13:3. The most thorough study of these formulae to date is Herbert Mölle, *Das 'Erscheinen Gottes' im Pentateuch: Ein literaturwis-senschaftlicher Beitrag zur alttestamentlichen Exegese*, Europäische Hochschulschriften, 23rd Series, no. 18 (Bern: Herbert Lang and and Frankfurt: Peter Lang, 1973).

message, usually a divine promise to the individual (1 Kgs 3:6-14).[93] And the epiphany usually concludes with a description of the individual's cultic act in response to the epiphany and promise (1 Kgs 3:15). This cultic act consists of building an altar and/or offering offerings: most often burnt offerings, but drink, oil, and communion offerings (שְׁלָם) also occur.[94] One final shared characteristic is that the epiphany promises are almost always fulfilled in the following text.[95]

One other important characteristic which the Gibeon story shares with message epiphanies is its connection with a local cultic sanctuary. As our close reading above indicates, the Gibeon story from start to finish emphasizes that it was at Gibeon that Solomon received his famed wisdom, wealth, and honor. Similarly, other message epiphanies occur in well known Israelite sanctuaries: Shechem (Gen 12:6-9), Mamre (Gen 18:1-16), Beer-lahai-roi (Gen 16:7-13), Gerar (26:2-5), Beersheba (Gen 26:24-25), Bethel (Gen 28:10-22), Horeb (Exod 3:1-4:17), Ophrah (Judg 6:11-24), Shiloh (1 Sam 3:10-14) and the Temple mount in Jerusalem (2 Sam 24:15-25; cf. 1 Chr 22:1; 2 Chr 3:1). Generally, the cultic connections of these epiphany reports seem to derive from a common presupposition that divine epiphanies take place at sanctuaries.[96]

In some cases, however, the epiphany reports actually focus to some extent on justifying the existence of the sanctuary. For example, the ancient dream epiphany report in Gen 28:11-13aα, 16-19a served to explain the name and existence of the Bethel sanctuary. Similarly, an extra-Biblical text, the Deir 'Allā night epiphany report, may be an example of an epiphany report actually displayed at a cultic sanctuary.[97]

---

[93] Cf. T. Rendtorff, "Die Offenbarungsvorstellungen im Alten Israel," in *Offenbarung als Geschichte*, ed. Wolfhart Pannenberg (Göttingen: Vandenhoeck & Ruprecht, 1961), 24-25, and "'Offenbarung' im Alten Testament," *TLZ* 85 (1960): 833-834; also Mölle, *Das 'Erscheinen' Gottes im Pentateuch*, 249-253.

Gen 32:23-33 and 2 Sam 24:16 are examples of message epiphanies which do not include promises. In addition, the Deir 'Allā text and Abimelek's dream (Gen 20:3-7) both contain threats not promises.

[94] Gen 12:6-9; 26:23-25; 28:10-22; 35:9-15; Judg 6:11-24; 2 Sam 24:15-25.

[95] Again the Deir 'Allā text and Abimelek's dream (Gen 20:3-7) are slight exceptions to the rule.

[96] The sanctified character of ground where God has appeared is most explicit in Exod 3:5, where God tells Moses to take his sandals off his feet because the ground upon which he is standing is holy. See also Rolf Knierim, "Offenbarung im Alten Testament," in *Probleme biblischer Theologie: Gerhard von Rad zum 70. Geburtstag*, ed. Hans Walter Wolff (Munich: Chr. Kaiser, 1971), 216-217

[97] The excavators of Deir 'Allā have very tentatively identified the structure in which the night epiphany text was found as a sanctuary. Note the extreme qualifica-

The focus of the Gibeon story on the prestige of the Gibeon sanctuary makes the story similar to ancient message epiphany reports with similarly strong cultic connections, such as Gen 28:11-13aα, 16-19 and the Deir ʿAllā epiphany report. In the case of the Gibeon story, the cultic connections are evident not only in its location of the epiphany at Gibeon (a problem for later redactors of the story), but also in the emphasis in the introduction on the greatness of its sanctuary (4aβ) and Solomon's habit of sacrificing great amounts there (4b), the further emphasis at the beginning of the epiphany formula (5aα1-2) on Gibeon as the site of the epiphany,[98] and the description of his sacrifices there following the epiphany (15bα7-10). Once given this context, the epiphany proper emphasizes the great things which Solomon received at Gibeon. Specifically, like many cultic dedicatory and building inscriptions, the Gibeon story includes a divine promise of long life.[99]

- *Dream Epiphany*

More specifically, the Gibeon story is a dream epiphany.[100] Like message epiphanies, dream epiphanies have a focus on God's appearance in

---

tions of this claim in the statement by the dig's archaeologist, H. L. Franken, on this subject in the editio princeps: Jacob Hoftijzer, G. van der Kooij, *Aramaic Texts from Deir Alla*, Documenta et Monumenta Orientis Antiqvi (Leiden: E. J. Brill, 1976), 12-13. Since they have not yet published the report of the phase in which this structure occurs (Phase M), their arguments for this proposal can not yet be evaluated.

On the close relationship between the Deir ʿAllā text and Biblical traditions see Carr, "Royal Ideology and the Technology of Faith," 152-154, including note 406; and Hans-Peter Müller, "Die aramäische Inschrift von Deir ʿAllā und die älteren Bileamspruche," *ZAW* 94 (1982): 214-244; idem. "Einige alttestamentliche Probleme zur aramäischen Inschrift von Der ʿAlla," *ZDPV* 94 (1978): 56-67.

[98] Indeed, 3:5a is one point in the story where the cultic emphasis of the Gibeon story is so strong that it diverges from formulae used in other message epiphanies. Through placement of a prepositional phrase at the beginning of the sentence and the consequent use of the perfect (rather than converted imperfect) form of the verb, this half-verse diverges from other message epiphany formulae.

[99] Most of the Byblos texts close to 1 Kgs 3:14b show connections to the cult. For more discussion, see Carr, "Royal Ideology and the Technology of Faith," 176.

[100] In his study of dreams in the Ancient Near East, Oppenheim argues persuasively for a distinction between "message dream reports," which serve as the framework for messages, and "reports of symbolic dreams." Oppenheim, *The Interpretation of Dreams in the Ancient Near East*, 197-217. Since Oppenheim's "message dreams" focus on divine appearances, most form critics term such dream reports "dream epiphanies."

order to give a message to an individual.[101] Moreover, both message epiphanies and dream epiphanies have a tripartite structure consisting of the introduction, message, and human response to the message.[102] Nevertheless, the introductions and conclusions of dream epiphanies are often slightly different from their counterparts in message epiphanies. The epiphany formula or conclusion of the dream epiphany, though similar to their (non-dream) epiphany counterparts, often uses some form of the root חלם (dream).[103] In addition, dream epiphanies frequently conclude with some kind of wake-up formula, like that seen in 1 Kgs 3:15a.[104]

The final characteristic which distinguishes dreams from other types of revelation is that they are the preeminent form of revelation at night. Epiphanies and visions *can* happen during the day or night. Dreams, however, *almost always* occur at night, the usual time for sleep.[105] Night revelation reports share the generative preunderstanding that night is a border time when contact with the divine is particularly easy.[106] In addi-

---

[101] Gen 20:1-18; 28:10-22 (note the symbolic element embedded in this dream, 28:12); 31:10-17, 24; Num 22:7-14, 15-21. Quite similar night revelations include: Gen 15:1-6 (night epiphany); 26:23-30 (night epiphany); 46:1-7 (night vision); 1 Sam 3:1-18 (night epiphany); and 2 Sam 7:1-17. For examples of extra-Biblical Ancient Near Eastern dream reports see, Oppenheim, *The Interpretation of Dreams in the Ancient Near East*, 245-255 (add to this Combination One of the Deir ʿAllā plaster texts). For discussion of the relationship between dreams and visions see S. Cavalletti, "Sogno e profezia nell'Antic Testamento," *RivB* 7 (1959):356-363, particularly p. 357 and note 4; André Caquot, "Les songes et leur interprétation selon Canaan et Israel," in *Songes et leur interprétation*, ed. A.-M. Esnoul and others, Sources Orientales 2 (Paris:Éditions du Seuil, 1959), 109-11; Robert K. Gnuse, *The Dream Theophany of Samuel: Its Structure in Relation to Ancient Near Eastern Dreams and Its Theological Significance* (Lanham [MD], New York, and London: University Press, 1984), 59-60.

[102] Symbolic dreams share a more complex structure because their surreal imagery usually requires interpretation.

[103] Caquot, "Les songes et leur interprétation selon Canaan et Israel," 111.

[104] Oppenheim, *The Interpretation of Dreams in the Ancient Near East*, 191. Through his wide Ancient Near Eastern survey, Oppenheim was able to see the generic character of this wake up formula. Others such as Seow ("The Syro-Palestinian Context of Solomon's Dream," 148) mistake the formula for some kind of special connection with Ugaritic literature.

[105] The Thutmose IV Sphinx stele is an exception. Thutmose IV takes a nap under the shadow of the Sphinx during the day and has his dream epiphany then.

[106] This is particularly emphasized by two studies of Egyptian dreams: S. Sauneron, "Les songes et leur interprétation dans l'Égypte ancienne," in *Songes et leur interprétation*, 19-20; and J. Parlebas, "Remarques sur la conception de reves et sur leur interprétation dans la civilization Égyptienne antique," *Ktema* 7 (1982): 20. See also Oppenheim, *The Interpretation of Dreams in the Ancient Near East*, 184.

tion, the same other worldly character of dreams (more strictly defined) makes them likely loci for encounter with the divine. Human dreams are an extraordinary phenomenon, containing plots and images not typically found in the everyday world. Working from this cross-cultural conceptual matrix, an author could add to the plausibility of a divine epiphany report by presenting it as a dream epiphany report.

- *Conclusion: The Gibeon Story as a Dream Epiphany*

In sum, the characterization of the pre-Deuteronomistic Gibeon story as a "dream epiphany" report accounts for many factors in the story. It has the three-part internal form of dream epiphanies: the dream-epiphany introduction (3:5a, using a form of the root חלם), dream focused on a divine message (3:6-14), and wake-up formula (3:15a). Since dreams were often seen as the loci for divine encounters, this dream form helps underscore the plausibility of God's appearance to Solomon at Gibeon. Furthermore, as a "dream epiphany" the Gibeon story participates in the wider genre of "message epiphanies," and comparison of the story with other message epiphanies corroborates the cultic focus found in our close reading of it: from the lengthy introduction focusing on Gibeon in 1 Kgs 3:4 and 5aa1-2, through the dream itself focusing on God's open-ended offer and generous gifts (3:6-14), to Solomon responding to God's appearance and gifts by offering even more sacrifices than he customarily did at Gibeon (3:15b; cf. 3:4).

To be sure, "dream epiphany report" is only one of an array of generic identifications proposed for the Gibeon story by Biblical and Ancient Near Eastern scholars. Nevertheless, the characterization of the Gibeon story as a "dream epiphany report" incorporates the strengths of previous proposals while avoiding their weaknesses. Though the Gibeon story is often characterized as an incubation, this hypothesis has several weaknesses; it is based on a misunderstanding of 3:4 as referring to a specific sacrifice; it misses the emphasis in the story on God's initiative; and there are no clear Semitic exemplars of the genre.[107] The widespread identifi-

---

107 Caquot, "Les songes et leur interprétation selon Canaan et Israel," 107; A. Resch, *Der Traum im Heilsplan Gottes: Deutung und Bedeutung des Traums im Alten Testament* (Freiburg/Basel/Wien: Herder, 1964), 114-115.

The Ugaritic Aqhat epiphany is often cited as an incubation, but it clearly describes God as appearing on the seventh day. J. Obermann, a proponent of the incubation hypothesis himself sees this difficulty, as is evident in such references as the following: ". . . there can be no doubt that the sprinkling and the incubation proper, no less than the *uzr* sacrifice, were repeated for six days, or as we should rather say,

cation of the Gibeon story as resembling Egyptian Königsnovellen like-wise misses this emphasis on God's initiative. Moreover, the similarities often adduced between the Gibeon story and the Thutmose IV stele are superficial, and unlike Egyptian Königsnovellen, the Gibeon story is not designed to explain actions, events and institutions as originating solely from the king's initiative.[108] Of course, there are many similarities between the Gibeon story and extra-Biblical texts such as Egyptian Königsnovellen, Mesopotamian temple building reports, Greek incuba-tion scenes, and Ugaritic epiphanies. These parallels, however, are a function of the texts' common participation in the more general epiphany or more specific dream epiphany genres.[109]

The Petition Scene Initiated by the Petitioned

The above discussion of the dream epiphany genre helped uncover the cultic origins and focus of the Gibeon story Vorlage. As we turn from the genre of the whole Vorlage to that of its main part (1 Kgs 3:5b-14*),

---

for six nights." *How Daniel was Blessed with a Son: An Incubation Scene in Ugaritic*, JAOS Supplements 6 (New Haven: Yale U. Press, 1946), 11. An additional example adduced by Oppenheim, *The Interpretation of Dreams*, 250, and Gnuse, *The Dream Theophany of Samuel*, 34 is an Akkadian psalm asking for a favorable dream. This psalm, however, merely seems a variant of familiar Mesopotamian prayers for good omens (as subsequent lines in the prayer indicate), and the prayer does not concern the initiation of a divine visit through some kind of ritual (incubation). The clear ex-emplars of the incubation genre are limited to Greece and Hatti, cultures whose dream reports are similar in other respects as well (Oppenheim, *The Interpretation of Dreams in the Ancient Near East*, 197-199). For opposing views, cf. Ehrlich, *Der Traum im Alten Testament*, 13-27; Oppenheim, *The Interpretation of Dreams in the Ancient Near East*, 188, 250; Gray, *I & II Kings*, 124; Seow, "The Syro-Palestinian Context of Solomon's Dream," 141-152; Gnuse, *The Dream Theophany of Samuel*, 34.

[108] Cf. Herrmann, "Die Königsnovelle in Ägypten und Israel," 33-34 and Görg, *Gott-König-Reden*, 54-65. Scholars who have followed Herrmann (with few additions) include Tryggve Mettinger, *Solomonic State Officials: A Study of the Civil Government Officials of the Israelite Monarchy*, ConBOTS 5 (Lund: Gleerup, 1971), 150-151; Leonidas Kalugila, *The Wise King: Studies in Royal Wisdom as Divine Revelation in the Old Testament and Its Environment*, ConBOTS 15 (Lund: Gleerup, 1980), 109-115. For more detailed discussion see Carr, "Royal Ideology and the Technology of Faith," 172-173.

[109] For the Mesopotamian temple building report hypothesis see Arvid S. Kapelrud, "Temple Building, a Task for Gods and Kings," 56-62 and Weinfeld, *Deuteronomy and the Deuteronomic School*, 247-248. For refutation of Kapelrud see Zalevsky, "התבלות ה' לשלמה בנבעון" 221-222; Stan Rummel "Narrative Structures in the Ugaritic Texts," in *Ras Shamra Parallels: The Texts from Ugarit and the Hebrew Bible*, vol. 3, ed. Stan Rummel (Rome: Pontifical Institute, 1981), 277-284; and Carr, "Royal Ideology and the Technology of Faith," 171-172.

we gain insight into how the cultic focus of the Gibeon story intersects with aspects of royal ideology. The open ended divine offer in 1 Kgs 3:5bβ works out of Northwest Semitic royal ideology. In particular this verse is based on the pre-understanding that pious kings are particularly favored by God and can ask the God(s) for whatever they want and receive it. This pre-understanding is evident in the Panammu inscription reference to the divine offer of whatever the king wanted (*KAI* 214:4, 22-23), description of similar offers to Aqhat by Anat in the Aqhat epic (*KTU* 1.17 VI:15-46), and references within Royal psalms to divine offers of whatever the king wants (Pss 2:8; 20:5-6; 21:3-5).[110]

The open ended divine offer in 5bβ in turn, serves as the cornerstone of an overall petition scene structure which dominates the description of Solomon's epiphany. In both Ugaritic and Biblical literature there are a number of similar petition scene reports, many of which closely resemble part II of the Gibeon story in structure and character. By "petition scene report" is meant an account where the occasion for, process of, and response to a petition is narrated. A minimum of two parties participates in such a process: the one who eventually offers a petition and the one who responds to it. Moreover, there is an unequal power relationship between these two parties; either a subject petitions his or her king, or the king petitions his god.

Petition scene reports can be divided into two groups. The first group consists of those texts which describe petition scenes initiated by one who offers a petition: 1 Kgs 1:11-40; 2:13-25; Jer 37:20-21; 38:14-28 (especially 26); Ruth 3:6-13; Esth 8:3-17.[111] The Gibeon story is a member of the second group, those texts where the petition scene is initiated by

---

110 Cf. Zalevsky, "התבלות ה' לשלמה בנבעון", 234-235, especially note 76; Brekelmans, "Solomon at Gibeon," 55-56; Seow, "The Syro-Palestinian Context of Solomon's Dream," 149-151. These scholars attempt to establish a relationship between the Gibeon story and coronation through combining the parallels mentioned above with parallels to elements from the prologue to Solomon's speech (primarily parallels to 6aβ: באמת ובצדקה ובישרת לבב עמך, "in truth and in righteousness and in integrity of heart with you"). For discussion of the Deuteronomistic characteristics of 6aβ, see the preceding chapter, p. 14. In addition, with the exception of Ps 2, the parallels to the open ended offer in 5bβ do not show a clear relationship to coronation. The main common theme linking the royal Psalm references (Pss 2:8; 20:5-6; 21:3-5) is not coronation, but military concerns. Moreover, the Panammu inscription and Psalms 20 and 21 show the possibility of positive divine response to the king's (or his son's) wishes outside the context of coronation.

111 Occasionally, the one who is petitioned asks what the petitioner wants (1 Kgs 1:16b), but this only follows the petitioner's prior initiation of the petitioning process (1 Kgs 1:16a).

the one who would eventually respond to a petition (hereafter termed the "one to be petitioned"): Keret *KTU* 1.14 I:35-III:51; Aqhat *KTU* 1.17 VI:15-46; 1 Kgs 3:5b-14; Isa 7:10-17; Neh 2:1-8; Esth 5:1-14; 7:1-8:2; 9:12-15. Through offering a person whatever she or he wants, the one to be petitioned (usually a king or god) constitutes that person as a potential petitioner.[112] If that person responds by offering a petition, then they become the petitioner proper, and the one to be petitioned becomes "the petitioned" proper.[113]

The petition scene proper of "petition scenes initiated by the one to be petitioned" follow a standard pattern consisting of three parts:

1) The initiation of the petition scene by the one to be petitioned (*KTU* 1.14 I:42-[51]; 1 Kgs 3:5b; Isa 7:11; Neh 2:4a; Esth 5:3, 6; 7:2; 9:12). This first part typically consists of an open offer to the potential petitioner by the one to be petitioned.

2) A response by the potential petitioner (*KTU* 1.14 I:[51]-II:5; *KTU* 1.17 VI:19-25, 33-41; 1 Kgs 3:6-9; Isa 7:12; Neh 2:5; Esth 5:4, 7-8; 7:3-4; 9:13).

3) A response by the one to be petitioned. When part of the petition scene, this consists of an evaluational (1 Kgs 3:10; Neh 2:6) and/or verbal response by the petitioned (*KTU* 1.14 II:6-III:49; *KTU* 1.17 VI:42-45; 1 Kgs 3:11-14; Isa 7:13-17).

Unlike some other genres, this fairly stereotyped form does not seem to arise out of a typical institutional matrix (Sitz im Leben). Instead, the form presupposes cross-cultural patterns of social interaction in monarchal societies, where petitions are a primary medium of interaction between people of unequal position.

Nevertheless, though they do not share a common institutional context, many of these petition scenes do share a common intention. But before investigating the typical intention of petition scenes like the one in the Gibeon story, we must make a further distinction between the forms of two types of petition scenes initiated by the petitioned. In some such petition scenes the one to be petitioned makes an offer for some other reason than favor for the potential petitioner: Isa 7:10-17 and the Aqhat epic (*KTU* 1.17 VI:17-19, 26-33 (Cf. VI:10-14)). In these cases the potential

---

[112] In the case of Aqhat and Isa 7:10-17 the person receiving the offer does not actualize this potentiality.

[113] Since some such "petition scenes" never actually result in a petition, one might term them "potential petition scenes." Such terminology, however, is unwieldy, particularly in light of the fact that in all such petition scenes a petition is under discussion, although it is not always executed.

petitioner refuses to offer a petition and the one to be petitioned (both times a god) responds with judgment. Other such petition scenes, however, presuppose the favor of the one to be petitioned for the potential petitioner: Neh 2:1-8; *KTU* 1.14 I:35-III:51 (Keret) and Esth 5:1-14; 7:1-8:2; 9:12-15.[114] In these cases, the one to be petitioned makes the open-ended offer, the potential petitioner responds with a petition[115] and the petitioned grants it.[116] For example, Neh 1:1-11 describes Nehemiah's sadness over the state of Jerusalem and mentions that he is Artexerxes' cupbearer. This is the occasion for a petition scene where Artexerxes perceives Nehemiah's sadness and makes an open offer. Nehemiah asks to go to Jerusalem, and Artexerxes grants Nehemiah's petition.

At least part of the intention of this latter group of petition scenes is to demonstrate the favor of the petitioned for the petitioner. In the Keret epic, the positive relationship between Keret and El in their petition scene (initiated by the one to be petitioned, El) directly contrasts with the negative relationship between Keret and Asherah (*KTU* 1.15 III:25-30). The Nehemiah and Esther petition scenes serve to establish the favor which Jews enjoyed with their Persian overlords. Such portrayals could serve as propaganda in their struggles with other subjects of the Persian empire.

The Gibeon story is a member of this latter group of petition scenes designed to demonstrate the god's favor for the petitioner. In the Gibeon story, this favor takes the particular form of God's initiation of the petition situation through the open-ended offer in 1 Kgs 3:5bβ. This offer then serves as the beginning of a larger petition scene initiated by the one

---

114 Esth 5:1-2 describes Esther's appearance before the king and his favorable reaction to it. The petition scenes in Esther diverge from similar petition scenes in so far as the petition process is extended over several different occasions (5:1-8; 7:1-8:2; 8:3-17; 9:12-15). The mention in 5:1-2 of the king's favor for her helps explain the later petition scenes along with the petition scene which immediately follows in 5:3-8.

115 See *KTU* 1.14 I:[51]-II:5; 1 Kgs 3:6-9; Neh 2:5; Esth 5:4, 7-8; 7:3-4; 9:13. Some such petitions include questions of clarification by the petitioned (Neh 2:6a; Esth 7:5) and the petitioner's clarification (Esth 7:6a).

116 In these cases, the one to be petitioned has already indicated a positive predisposition toward the petitioner by initiating the petition situation. The third part of these petition scenes usually contains promises that the petition will be fulfilled. In some cases the one to be petitioned's response is described in the following narrative of their fulfillment of the petition (Neh 2:8b; Esth 5:5; 7:1-10; 9:14). Such fulfillment descriptions are integrated with the petition scene more than those fulfillment descriptions which follow petition scenes containing an evaluative and or verbal response (examples of the latter include *KTU* 1.14 III:50 - 1.15 III:25 and 1 Kgs 3:16-10:29).

to be petitioned, one which results in a petition and its granting (3:5b-14). In so far as the scene revolves around the presupposition that God looks favorably on Solomon, the story shares the typical intention of such petition reports, to emphasize the favor of the petitioner with the petitioned—in this case Solomon with God.

COMBINED INSIGHTS FROM THE LITERARY
AND FORM CRITICAL ANALYSES

As seen in the literary analysis, the Vorlage has several gaps and points of multivalence. Primary among these are the nature of the "hearing heart" which Solomon requests and the reason for God's grant of gifts which Solomon did not request. The former point of ambiguity is at least partially resolved by the divine description of Solomon as requesting a "wise and intelligent heart," general wisdom. The latter point of ambiguity, however, is never explicitly resolved. The story never says why, after having acted in accordance with Solomon's words in granting him wisdom, God went beyond Solomon's words in granting him wealth and honor along with a long life to enjoy them.

In contrast with the promise of riches, wealth and long life, God's grant of wisdom is not problematic. In accordance with royal ideology God offers Solomon whatever he wants and grants him his request. Moreover, in doing so, God is granting Solomon the capacity to fulfill the vocation into which God has put him. But the story is designed to claim the divine origins of not only Solomon's wisdom, but also his wealth and fame. Riches and fame are not necessary for Solomon's job. He did not request or need them. A lot rests on this unresolved gap in the story. The plot keeps playing itself out in the reader's mind, leaving him or her to ponder its resolution.

The form-critical analysis provides a proximate resolution to this puzzle *from the perspective of original intention.* The analysis of the dream epiphany and petition scene forms in the story uncovered an intersection of cultic and royal ideological perspectives behind it. Specifically, God shows favor to Solomon at Gibeon because he is a *pious* king; he customarily offers a thousand burnt offerings at the great sanctuary at Gibeon. Thus the royal ideological element of the Gibeon story petition scene feeds back into the overall cultic focus of the overarching dream epiphany framework. As a pious king Solomon is favored, but it is specifically *at the great Gibeon sanctuary,* where he frequently makes extravagant offerings, that he receives the kind of bountiful divine favor which produced his fabled wisdom, wealth, and honor.

Thus, the Vorlage's dream epiphany form and cultic emphasis imply that Solomon's preference for Gibeon played an important role in the extra divine promises to him. Through implying that Solomon's faithful patronage of the Gibeon sanctuary led to God's generosity toward him, the Vorlage subtly claims some of Solomon's prestige for the Gibeonite sanctuary. Now Gibeon appears as the "great sanctuary" where important people go and God acts in wonderful ways toward them.[117] Solomon's famous wisdom, wealth, and honor then become evidence of God's favor shown toward him. Perhaps, this unexplicit implication is more potent when only unconsciously perceived by the reader.

As we analyze later interpretations of this story we will consider two aspects of interpretation: stability and adaptability. On the one hand, every interpretation of an early tradition preserves something of that early tradition. Otherwise, why bother with interpretation at all? This preservation of early tradition—its wording, plot, and/or spirit—is what is meant by "stability" in interpretation. On the other hand, interpretation also involves adaptation of that tradition to the present concerns of the author (authorial intent) and audience (rhetoric). Rarely, does the tradition continue to function in community without undergoing some kind of transformation.

There is no evidence for a version of the Gibeon story which was earlier than the one represented by the reconstructed pre-Deuteronomistic Vorlage discussed above.[118] Nevertheless, this Vorlage both builds on and contradicts traditions which preceded it. Thus, it betrays the royal ideological presupposition that God is responsible for taking care of the legitimate king. The Vorlage also builds on ancient traditions about Solomon's wisdom, wealth, and honor. These things are now evidence of God's favor toward Solomon, divine gifts to the legitimate

---

[117] Having concluded arguments for the literary focus on Gibeon in the Vorlage to 1 Kgs 3:2-15, it is appropriate to mention Joseph Blenkinsopp's attempt to establish that Gibeon was Saul's capital: "Did Saul Make Gibeon His Capital?," *VT* 24 (1974): 1-7, and *Gibeon and Israel: The Role of Gibeon and the Gibeonites in the Political and Religious History of Early Israel*, SOTSMS 2 (Cambridge: At the University Press, 1972), see especially pp. 53-64. Blenkinsopp refers to the relevant archaeological research at el-Jîb, but his hypothesis remains rather speculative, as he himself admits ("Did Saul Make Gibeon His Capital?," 4). In any case, such historical concerns are not the focus of this study.

[118] For brief discussion of possible evidence in 3:4 for the Vorlage once being part of another literary context see above, note 78.

and pious king. Finally, the story appropriates the ancient message dream epiphany and petition scene genres to imply that Solomon received his fabled wisdom, wealth and honor because of his piety exhibited at Gibeon.

All of the above examples of Vorlage interpretation are examples of ways the Vorlage builds on preceding traditions, preserving them essentially unchanged. In some cases, however, the Vorlage clearly alters earlier traditions while appropriating them. It uses a long life formula, much like that found at Byblos, but subordinates it to the larger message of how Solomon got his great wisdom, riches and honor. Moreover, the Vorlage theocentrically appropriates ancient traditions regarding Maat/Wisdom, arguing that God, not Maat/Wisdom, provides the riches, honor and long life which come with wisdom.[119] As mentioned above, this plot—wisdom leads to riches, honor and long life—originated in the wisdom instruction traditions of Egypt and Israel. In those contexts, it was part of an overall effort to promote the wisdom enterprise by claiming its benefits. In contrast, the Gibeon story Vorlage appropriates this wisdom theme to promote God and worship of God at the sanctuary at Gibeon. Considered in the overall context of the Vorlage, this emphasis on God's responsibility for the extra gifts implies that worship at the great Gibeon sanctuary, not study in the wisdom academy, is the way to riches and honor.

The overall result is an explanation of Solomon's wisdom, riches and honor as divine gifts. Once Solomon arrives at Gibeon, God has the initiative throughout the story. God initiates not only the petition situation, but also the extra gifts. Though this God reveals Godself as the power behind Solomon's great power, this God is nevertheless a God of the few. The pre-Deuteronomistic Gibeon story is thoroughly infused with ancient royal ideology, an ideology which sees the king as enjoying special privileges with the God of Israel. In sum, the story has not yet made its pilgrimage into the life of this people, and become a resource for them.

Such is a preliminary reading of the Vorlage to the Gibeon story. Already we have seen ways the Vorlage preserved and adapted earlier traditions to make its own point about Solomon and the divine origin of his wisdom, wealth, and honor. Moreover, we have located loci of multivalence inherent within the story, loci which will play important roles in later interpretation of it. These are in addition to aspects of the Vorlage

---

[119] Whether the author works directly from Egyptian traditions is difficult to say.

which clashed with the theological perspectives of its later redactors and interpreters. It is to these later interpretations and the perspectives behind them that we now turn.

Chapter Four

INTERPRETATION IN REDACTION

We are able to reconstruct the Vorlage thanks to the later communities who found the story meaningful and preserved it for ages to come. These communities, however, did not preserve the story unchanged, but retold it, incorporating their interpretations in the retelling. In chapter two we disentangled their contributions from the original version of the story, and in chapter three we discussed the literary features, generic shape, setting, and intention of that original version. Now we turn to an investigation of the interpretive contributions of later communities.

THE FIRST DEUTERONOMISTIC EDITION

The Introduction: 1 Kgs 3:3-5

Pre-Deuteronomistic Vorlage	*First Deuteronomistic Edition*
	1 Kgs 3:3
	Solomon loved the LORD, living according to the norms of David, his father, but he sacrificed and made smoke offerings in the local sanctuaries.

1 Kgs 3:4	1 Kgs 3:4
The king went to Gibeon to sacrifice there because it was the greatest of the sanctuaries. Solomon used to offer a thousand burnt offerings on that altar.	The king went to Gibeon to sacrifice there because it was the greatest of the sanctuaries. Solomon used to offer a thousand burnt offerings on that altar.

1 Kgs 3:5	1 Kgs 3:5
At Gibeon the LORD appeared to Solomon in a dream of the night and said, "Ask what I should give you."	At Gibeon the LORD appeared to Solomon in a dream of the night and said, "Ask what I should give you."

One way the Deuteronomist preserved the interpreted tradition, the Vorlage, was by preserving its wording, even where the Vorlage's intent is fundamentally at odds with the Deuteronomistic program. Whereas the Vorlage introduction subtly promotes the local sanctuary at Gibeon (1 Kgs 3:4), the Deuteronomist considers such sanctuaries to be so illegitimate that they must be destroyed. Nevertheless, the Deuteronomist preserves the wording of 3:4, but recontextualizes the story with a prior introduction modeled on other Deuteronomistic regnal formulae (1 Kgs 3:3).

The Deuteronomist's introduction does several things. First, 1 Kgs 3:3 evaluates Solomon, measuring him against the criteria which the Deuteronomist applies to all of Israel's kings. As such, the verse resembles the evaluative component of the Deuteronomistic regnal summaries, whether introductory overviews or concluding resumés.[120] As in the cases of six out of the nine rulers between Abijam (911-908) and Ahaz (742-726),[121] the Deuteronomist gives Solomon a mixed review. Though he did what was right as his father did, he sacrificed at sanctuaries outside Jerusalem.

---

[120] On the regnal resumé, see Long, *1 Kings,* 259. He emphasizes the summaries which conclude reigns, and for that reason his use of the term "resumé" is appropriate. His list, however, includes an example of an introductory overview. These Deuteronomistic introductory and concluding summaries share enough in common to share a general generic designation (regnal summary), which may then be split into introductory (overview) and concluding (resumé).

[121] Asa (1 Kgs 15:11-15), Jehoshaphat (1 Kgs 22:43-44), Jehoash (2 Kgs 12:3-4), Amaziah (2 Kgs 14:3-4), Uzziah (2 Kgs 15:3-4), and Jotham (2 Kgs 15:34-35). The exceptions are Jehoram (2 Kgs 8:18), Ahaziah (2 Kgs 8:27), and Athaliah, granddaughter of Omri (2 Kgs 11).

This evaluation of Solomon contradicts any implication in the Vorlage that God rewarded Solomon for sacrificing at Gibeon. To be sure, the Deuteronomist shares the author of the Vorlage's belief that Solomon was favored by God. We will soon see the Deuteronomist's explanation of God's graciousness toward him. At this point, however, the Deuteronomist uses this introduction to make it perfectly clear that whatever things Solomon may have done right, sacrificing at non-Jerusalemite sanctuaries was not among them.[122]

Thus 1 Kgs 3:3 plays a particular role in relation to the Gibeon story. This role appears yet more clearly when 1 Kgs 3:3 is compared with the mixed evaluations of six kings between Abijam and Ahaz. The Deuteronomist says that each of them did what was right, "only the [non-Jerusalemite] sanctuaries were not removed."[123] In contrast, 1 Kgs 3:3 does not criticize Solomon for failing to remove those sanctuaries, but for sacrificing at them. Specifically, the Deuteronomist expresses clear disapproval of Solomon's practice of sacrificing at the non-Jerusalemite sanctuary at Gibeon.

This disapproval, however, only occurs as a qualification to the Deuteronomist's general praise of Solomon. 1 Kgs 3:3 as a whole endorses Solomon, though not on the Vorlage's terms. In addition, the verse integrates the Gibeon story into the Deuteronomist's narration of Solomon's reign. Now, the Gibeon story introduces the good part of Solomon's reign (1 Kgs 3-10), by explaining the divine origin of Solomon's fabled wisdom, wealth and honor (1 Kgs 3:16-28; 5:1-14, 21, 26; 10:1-29). Already the ethical emphasis of the Deuteronomistic introduction suggests that the Deuteronomistic edition will explain Solomon's good fortune as a divine reward for his goodness (1 Kgs 4-10), and his bad fortune as divine punishment for apostasy (1 Kgs 11).

Finally, as with the mixed evaluations of the Judean kings, the Deuteronomist portrays Solomon's goodness as consistent with his father's behavior. Asa did what was right as David, his father did (2 Kgs

---

[122] In the redaction analysis, this characteristically Deuteronomistic emphasis on Jerusalem as the only legitimate sanctuary was used to establish the Deuteronomistic character of this verse. The redactional character of this verse having been established, the present discussion focuses on the type of interpretation involved in the addition of this Deuteronomistic perspective to the Gibeon story in particular. Similarly, in the following, the focus is no longer on establishing the redactional character of additions, but on the interpretive implications of texts previously established as redactional.

[123] רק הבמות לא סרו

15:11). Jehoshaphat walked in the way of Asa, doing right in the sight of the Lord (1 Kgs 22:43). Jehoash did what was right because Jehoiada, the priest instructed him (2 Kgs 12:3), while his son, Amaziah, did what was right as he did (2 Kgs 22:3b). Uzziah did what was right in the eyes of the Lord in accordance with all which his father Amaziah had done (2 Kgs 15:3), and Jotham, his son, likewise followed in his father's footsteps (2 Kgs 15:34). Finally, Solomon loved the Lord, walking according to the norms of his father David (1 Kgs 3:3).

A wider look at the Deuteronomistic evaluations of Judean kings shows the context and significance of the Deuteronomist's evaluation of Solomon. In cases where the good Judean king in question was raised by another good king, the Deuteronomist introduces the son's reign by mentioning that the son ruled like his father (Solomon, Jehoshaphat, Amaziah, Uzziah, Jotham). When the good king's reign followed the reign of a bad king, the Deuteronomist introduces his reign by saying that he did what was right as David, his father, did (Asa, Hezekiah (2 Kgs 18:3), Josiah (2 Kgs 22:2).[124] Similarly, the Deuteronomist attributes the bad behavior of evil Judean kings to either extra-Israelite influence[125] or the king's father's behavior.[126]

Thus, according to the Deuteronomist, an inherited potentiality for virtue passed down through the Davidic line. To be sure, Judean kings occasionally followed the evil way of Israel and the other nations, and their sons occasionally followed in their footsteps. Nevertheless, their sons or grandsons could return to the righteous way of the dynastic founder and father of all Judean kings, David.[127] Moreover, good Davidic kings usually produced good successors, barring outside influence. Solomon is a mix of the two. Though he loved יהוה (YHWH) and built the temple, he eventually succumbed to outside influence (1 Kgs 11:1-8). 1 Kgs 3:3a, with its favorable evaluation of Solomon and comparison to David, anticipates the good first portion of Solomon's reign (1 Kgs 4-10). The qualification of praise in 1 Kgs 3:3b anticipates his apostasy (1 Kgs 11).

---

[124] The exception is Jehoash. The Deuteronomist disapproves of his father, Ahaziah, but explains his good behavior as the result of his instruction by the priest, Jehoiada.

[125] Jehoram (2 Kgs 8:18), Ahaziah (2 Kgs 8:27), Ahaz (2 Kgs 16:3), Manasseh (2 Kgs 21:2).

[126] Abijam (1 Kgs 15:3), Amon (2 Kgs 21:20).

[127] This is exemplified most of all by Hezekiah following Ahaz's reign and Josiah following Manasseh's reign.

Though the Deuteronomist carefully preserves the Vorlage, each of the Deuteronomistic additions significantly modifies the structure of the Gibeon story. This is particularly true of the addition of 1 Kgs 3:3. The structure of the Vorlage introduction ran as follows:

Dream Epiphany Report..1 Kgs 3:4-15*
I. Description of Circumstances of Epiphany.................................... 4
    A. Placement of Solomon at the Gibeon sanctuary............ 4aα
    B. Explanation of choice of the Gibeon sanctuary 4aβ-b
        1. Gibeon's General Importance.....................................4aβ
        2. Solomon's Specific Preference for Gibeon 4b

The addition of 1 Kgs 3:3 makes the Gibeon story into the introduction to a larger narrative. Now it introduces Solomon's reign by explaining both his success and the dependence of that success on God's favorable evaluation of him. This produces the following macro-structure for the Deuteronomist's description of Solomon's reign:

Solomon's Reign   ....1 Kgs 3:3-11:43
I. Introduction: Gibeon Story....................................... 3:3-15
II. Reign proper   3:16-11:40
    A. Positive Half: Reward for I. 3:16-10:29
    B. Apostasy and Downfall from Favor of I................... 11:1-40
III.   Concluding Notes 11:41-43

With the addition of 3:3, the regnal evaluation becomes the ethical context for Solomon's particular trip to Gibeon. The micro-structure of the Gibeon story's introduction now runs as follows:

Introduction to Solomon's Reign:
Dream Epiphany Report..3:3-15*
I. Description of Circumstances of Epiphany...............................3-4
    A. Regnal Evaluation:
       Solomon's Patronage of Sanctuaries in Context................ 3
        1. General Endorsement: Solomon like David................3a
        2. Qualification with Respect to Sanctuaries.................. 3b
    B. Location of Epiphany:
       Particular Trip to a Sanctuary 4
        1. Placement of Solomon at Gibeon Sanctuary 4aα

Solomon's Speech: 1 Kgs 3:6-9

Pre-Deuteronomistic Vorlage

1 Kgs 3:6aα

Solomon said, "You have acted with great faithfulness towards your servant, my father David.

First Deuteronomistic Edition

1 Kgs 3:6aα

Solomon said, "You have acted with great faithfulness towards your servant, my father David,

1 Kgs 3:6aβ

when he walked before you in total loyalty and in integrity of heart with you,

1 Kgs 3:6b

and you acted with great faithfulness toward him in the following way: you gave to him a son sitting on his throne as on this very day.

1 Kgs 3:7

and now, oh LORD my God, you have made your servant king after my father David, but I am a little youth. I do not know how to go out or come in.

1 Kgs 3:7

and now, oh LORD my God, you have made your servant king after my father David, but I am a little youth. I do not know how to go out or come in.

1 Kgs 3:8

Your servant is in the midst of your people whom you have chosen, a great people who can not be counted or numbered because of their multitude.

1 Kgs 3:9a

Give your servant a hearing heart in order to **govern** your people and to distinguish between **good** and **evil**.

1 Kgs 3:9a

Give your servant a hearing heart in order to **judge** your people and to distinguish between **right** and **wrong**.[128]

1 Kgs 3:9b

For who is able to judge this, your great people?"

---

[128] See the preceding redaction chapter in this study for discussion of the relationship between the redaction of this passage and the translation ambiguity in it.

The Deuteronomistic addition in 1 Kgs 3:6aβ continues the above discussed Deuteronomistic emphasis on the ethical aspects of the succession of David. As argued above in the previous chapter, the Vorlage merely noted God's past loyalty to David as a prologue to accusing God of putting Solomon in his place. This note then sets up a tension between God's proven loyalty to David and God's unproven loyalty to Solomon, David's successor by virtue of God's own action.

The Deuteronomist makes several additions to this prologue. First, in 6aβ he specifies that God was loyal to David because David was loyal to God. This specification undermines the royal ideology implicit in the Vorlage version. Solomon cannot expect loyalty from Yahweh simply because he is a legitimate member of the Davidic dynasty. Rather, he can only partake of the benefits of being a member of the Davidic dynasty if he copies David's righteousness. The Deuteronomistic God contradicts the royal ideology implicit in 6aα by having Solomon recognize that he must "ask not only what your God can do for you, but what you can do for your God." The conglomeration of Deuteronomistic phrases describing righteous behavior in 6aβ emphasize the kind of high standard which the Deuteronomist sees David as having set for his descendants.

Second, in 6b the Deuteronomist uses a phrase from the succession narrative to specify exactly how God was loyal to David; God made one of David's sons succeed him. By doing so, the Deuteronomist integrates the statement about God's loyalty in 1 Kgs 3:6aα into the new literary context of the Gibeon story. Once placed in the Deuteronomistic history, the Gibeon story follows the Nathan oracle promise to David of a successor (2 Sam 7:12-15) and the succession narrative description of the fulfillment of that promise. In 6b the Deuteronomist refers to the 6aα description of God's faithfulness to God's provision of a successor to David. This reference would only be possible given the Deuteronomist's own placement of the Gibeon story in its present position in the Deuteronomistic history.

This Deuteronomistic interpretation of 1 Kgs 3:6aα alters the force of Solomon's argument. The Vorlage used the reference in 6aα to underscore God's responsibility for dealing with the problem God created through making Solomon succeed David. But the Deuteronomistic 6b addition now presents God's placement of Solomon on David's throne as being the very act of loyalty described in 6aα. The Deuteronomistic addition in 6b, like the one in 6aβ, establishes God's freedom. Just as God is not required to help Solomon because he is the legitimate successor (6aβ), God's fulfillment of the promise to David of a successor does not necessarily obligate God to help Solomon with anything he wants (6b). In the Deuteronomistic version, all of these earlier implicit arguments to force a divine response become background information explaining why Solomon requested wisdom.

In 1 Kgs 3:8 and 9b the Deuteronomist redescribes the difficulty of Solomon's job in terms of Moses' account of his request for legal assistance in Deut 1:9-10. These additions both emphasize that Solomon is in special need because God has placed him over God's great, chosen people. The additions heighten the implication, already in the Vorlage, that kingship is a job which an inexperienced youth could not do well. But now the difficulty lies not only in God's placement of Solomon on the throne, but also in God's multiplication of God's chosen people. Moreover, as with God's protection of David's succession, God's multiplication of the chosen people is the fulfillment of a promise, this time to Israel's ancestors. *Both* aspects of Solomon's dilemma, the difficulty of the job and his placement in it, are the results of God's conscious behavior, God's fulfillment of promise.

Though the terminology of Solomon's request does not change, the associations with Deut 1:9-18 already established by the additions of 3:8 and 9b suggest a legal cast to phrases originally meant to refer to general wisdom. Now, just like Moses, Solomon has been placed in a position where he must judge God's great, chosen people. But whereas Moses requested wise men from among his people, the Deuteronomist's Solomon petitions God for *legal* wisdom, a capacity essential for his successful fulfillment of the Deuteronomistic kingship ideal. This emphasis on the legal aspects of Solomon's request becomes explicit in the Deuteronomistic addition in 3:11. As mentioned in the redaction analysis, Solomon's request as read by the Deuteronomist exactly corresponds to the Deuteronomist's kingship ideal. Kings must seek the Torah first.

This reconstrual of Solomon's situation and resulting request introduces some shifts in the structure of Solomon's speech. As argued in the preceding chapter, the Vorlage version of Solomon's prologue implies God's responsibility to fulfill Solomon's petition by juxtaposing God's loyalty to David with God's creation of a problem by having Solomon succeed David. The Deuteronomistic additions, however, neutralize this presentation. Now the prologue to his petition shows how the circumstances leading up to his petition are the results of God's conscious behavior toward the chosen king (David) and chosen people (Israel). This implies that Solomon can also count on God to be faithful to him if he is faithful like David. Moreover, Solomon's petition is recontextualized (through references to Deut 1:9-18) so that he now demonstrates his faithfulness through requesting legal wisdom, an item essential to fulfilling the Deuteronomistic kingship ideal.

The resulting structure may be diagrammed as follows:

The Divine Speech Prologue: 1 Kgs 3:11aα4-b

Pre-Deuteronomistic Vorlage	*First Deuteronomistic Edition*
1 Kgs 3:11aα1-3	1 Kgs 3:11
And God said to him,	And God said to him, "because you asked this thing, and did not request many days or riches for yourself, nor did you request the life of your enemies, but you requested discrimination to hear cases, . . . "

---

[129] The division of the "Speech Proper" into three parts is based on Gerstenberger's study of the Old Testament petition form (Erhard Gerstenberger, *Der Bittende Mensch: Bittritual und Klagelied des Einzelnen im Alten Testament*, WMANT, no. 51 (Neukirschen-Vluyn: Neukirschener Verlag, 1980), 39-42; cf. examples in his note 60). Long, *1 Kings*, 65 cites Gerstenberger to support his division of Solomon's speech into two parts. This is not Gerstenberger's position and does not conform to the final form of the text.

The above outline, however, does not follow Gerstenberger in seeing a more specific function of the third part (his *"Begrundung"*) over against the first part (his *"Situationsschilderung"*). For detailed discussion of the reasons for this divergence see Carr, "Royal Ideology and the Technology of Faith," 186-187.

As argued in the second chapter, most of verse 3:11 is the Deuteronomist's explanation of God's extra gifts to Solomon. Against the anti-Solomonic traditions such as those in Deut 17:16a, 17 and 1 Sam 8:11b-17*, the Deuteronomist claims that Solomon's wealth and honor came to him for two reasons: 1) because he fulfilled the Deuteronomistic kingship ideal by putting his priority on legal wisdom and 2) because he thus rejected things valued by the kings of "the nations:" long life, wealth, and honor. This argument is part of a larger Deuteronomistic presentation of Solomon which decontextualizes the anti-Solomonic traditions in Deut 17:16a, 17 and 1 Sam 11b-17* and portrays Solomon as pious up through his construction of the temple. Only after he has finished the temple and enjoyed some of his wisdom, wealth, and honor, does Solomon succumb to the extra-Israelite influences of his foreign wives and build cultic centers for their gods.

Without 1 Kgs 3:11, the Vorlage builds on royal ideology in its emphasis on the great favor which God showed Solomon, first in offering him anything he wanted and then in fulfilling his request and giving him things he did not request. As previously argued, the Vorlage shaped the story in order to imply that worship at the great Gibeon sanctuary, not study in the wisdom academy, is the way to royal riches and honor.

Apparently the Deuteronomist was sensitive to the subtle argument at work throughout the Vorlage, hence the introduction in 1 Kgs 3:3. Against the Vorlage's attempt to imply that Solomon received favor *because* of his faithful practices at Gibeon, 1 Kgs 3:3 endorses Solomon *in spite of* his patronage of non-Jerusalemite sanctuaries. This introduction then sets the stage for the Deuteronomistic explanation of Solomon's favor in 1 Kgs 3:11. Similarly, the Deuteronomistic additions in 1 Kgs 3:6aβb, 8, and 9b establish God's freedom over against Solomon's claims in the Vorlage (1 Kgs 3:6aα, 7).

Thus, Deuteronomistic additions to the Vorlage in 3:3 and 6-9 set the stage for the Deuteronomistic explanation of God's favor in 3:11. According to the Deuteronomistic perspective, Solomon already had a predisposition to be faithful by being David's son. Nevertheless, God did not provide him with gifts because of this predisposition, because he was king (royal ideology), because he worshipped at Gibeon (epiphany genre), or because of an indirect argument that God was responsible for clearing up the mess which God had caused by being faithful to David (3:6aα, 7). According to the Deuteronomistic version, God gave Solomon extra gifts because Solomon fulfilled the Deuteronomistic kingship ideal through his request.[130]

Incomparability Formulae: 1 Kgs 3:12b$\beta\gamma$, 13b

Pre-Deuteronomistic Vorlage	*First Deuteronomistic Edition*
1 Kgs 3:12abα	1 Kgs 3:12abα
"Behold, I act according to your words. Behold I give you a wise and intelligent heart	"Behold, I act according to your words. Behold I give you a wise and intelligent heart
	1 Kgs 3:12b$\beta\gamma$
	so that no one like you will have existed before you, nor after you will one arise like you.
1 Kgs 3:13a and 13bβ	1 Kgs 3:13a
Also that which you did not request I give you, both riches and honor	Also that which you did not request I give you, both riches and honor,
	1 Kgs 3:13b
	so that no one among the kings will
all your days,	be like you all your days.

The Deuteronomistic incomparability formulae have no counterparts in the pre-Deuteronomistic Vorlage. Instead, in the Vorlage God merely promises wisdom and then wealth and honor along with a long life in which to enjoy them. The Deuteronomist, however, uses incomparability formulae to place Solomon's wisdom, wealth, and honor in relationship with wisdom, wealth and honor enjoyed by others.

The Deuteronomistic incomparability formula used to describe Solomon's wisdom (1 Kgs 3:12b$\beta\gamma$) corresponds to older descriptions of Solomon's wisdom as incomparable (1 Kgs 5:10-11; 10:23). 1 Kgs 3:12b$\beta\gamma$ integrates these older incomparability claims about Solomon's wisdom into the Gibeon story. The older descriptions, however, assert that Solomon's wisdom was greater than any of his pagan contemporaries, i. e. the Easterners (בני־קדם) Egyptians, all the kings of the earth (כל מלכי הארץ) and famous sages such as Ethan the Ezrahite and the sons of Mahol (Heman, Calcol and Darda). In order to emphasize the

---

[130] The discussion of the structural shifts introduced by this Deuteronomistic explanation will come after discussion of other Deuteronomistic additions to 1 Kgs 3:11-14.

distinctiveness of Solomon's wisdom, the Deuteronomist expands the comparison to include non-royalty and Israelites, all who lived before and after Solomon.

Through expanding the time reference of the incomparability formula, the Deuteronomist places Solomon's wisdom in the scheme of a history which extends before and after Solomon. In other words, just like the Deuteronomistic reference to the fulfillment of the Nathan oracle (1 Kgs 3:6b), the Deuteronomistic description of the incomparability of Solomon's wisdom is part of the placement of the Gibeon story in the larger literary context of the Deuteronomistic history. This intensification of the description of Solomon's wisdom is particularly significant since the Deuteronomist has taken care throughout the story to characterize Solomon's wisdom as judicial knowledge, the kind of Torah learning which the Deuteronomist values so highly in an Israelite king.

Just as in the case of 1 Kgs 3:12b$\beta\gamma$ the Deuteronomistic incomparability formula in 1 Kgs 3:13b is a reformulation of similar claims in older materials (1 Kgs 10:10b, 12b, 20b, and especially 23). Unlike 3:12b$\beta\gamma$, however, 1 Kgs 3:13b preserves the earlier formulae's exclusive emphasis on Solomon's distinctiveness over against pagan royalty. This is part of the picture begun in 1 Kgs 3:11 of Solomon in contrast to the pagan kings. That verse portrays God as rewarding Solomon for not choosing the things valued by them. Within this context, Solomon's incomparable wealth and honor gain new significance. By choosing legal wisdom above the things valued by his pagan contemporaries, he surpassed his contemporaries even in things which they chose first.

1 Kgs 3:13b also preserves the earlier formulae's exclusive emphasis on Solomon's greatness over against his contemporaries. Apparently the Deuteronomist sees no need to claim Solomon's distinctive wealth and honor over against preceding and following generations. By using different incomparability formulae, the Deuteronomist portrays legal knowledge as the biggest gift bestowed by God on Solomon at Gibeon. Next, the Deuteronomist stays closer to the early incomparability formulae in presenting Solomon's wealth and honor as auxiliary gifts. The promise of long life appears last.

The Promise of Long Life: 1 Kgs 3:14

Pre-Deuteronomistic Vorlage	*First Deuteronomistic Edition*
	1 Kgs 3:14a
	And if you walk in my ways, observing my norms and commandments like your father David,
1 Kgs 3:14b	1 Kgs 3:14b
and I will lengthen your days.	(and) I will lengthen your days.

The Vorlage had an unconditional promise of long life, one which built upon and completed the previous promise of riches and honor throughout Solomon's days. Together with those other promises, the promise of long life underlined the divine favor which Solomon enjoyed as a result of his royal status and patronage of the sanctuary at Gibeon.

The Deuteronomist undermines the Vorlage's picture of God's unreserved approval for Solomon by adding a condition to the Vorlage's originally unconditional promise of long life. Back in 1 Kgs 3:11 the Deuteronomist explained God's promise of wisdom, riches, and honor as the result of Solomon's choice of wisdom and rejection of things valued by pagan kings. This explanation, however, is not sufficient justification for a promise of long life. The Deuteronomist devotes particular attention to this promise because long life is a particularly important theme in the Deuteronomistic law. That law describes long life in the land as a major reason for the people of Israel to obey the law, and long rule as a major reason for the king to obey the law.

The addition in 14a now combines with the Deuteronomistic additions in 1 Kgs 3:3, 6aβb, 11 in the emphasis on the ethical succession of Solomon to David. God only favors Solomon in so far as he is righteous like his father David. Nevertheless, the Deuteronomistic addition in 3:14a has its own contribution to make to this overall picture. Whereas the Deuteronomistic additions in 1 Kgs 3:3, 6aβb and 11 describe either Solomon's present righteousness (1 Kgs 3:3, 11) or David's righteousness and resulting divine reward (1 Kgs 3:6aβb), the Deuteronomistic addition in 1 Kgs 3:14a explicitly unites these reflections and applies them to Solomon's future, specifically the promise of long life. This topic is unusually well suited for such a summary since the Deuteronomist sees long life as the reward for obedience.[131]

The Deuteronomistic additions of the prologue in 11, incomparability formulae, and 1 Kgs 3:14a dramatically reshape God's reply to Solomon. Originally, the Vorlage version of the reply was structured in the following way:

3. Speech Report: Petitioned's Response 11-14*
   a. Speech Report Introduction... 11aα1-3
   b. Speech Proper... 12abα, 13a, 13bβ, 14b
      1) Granting of Requested Item 12abα
      2) Granting of Items not Requested............................ 13a, 14b
         a) Riches + Honor all Solomon's life.................... 13a,13bβ
         b) Long life to Enjoy Riches and Honor 14b

The structure of the Deuteronomistic version of the reply now runs as follows:

3. Speech Report: Petitioned's Response 11-14
   a. Speech Report Introduction... 11aα1-3
   b. Speech Proper... 11aα4- 3:14
      1) Prologue: Reasoning Behind 2)............................... 11aα4-b
      2) Divine Promises 12-14
         a) Requested Item... 12
         b) Items not Requested 13-14
            α. Unconditional..13
            β. Conditional 14

---

[131] Some have proposed that in adding the condition the Deuteronomist subtly anticipates Solomon's apostasy described in 1 Kgs 11:1-8. As mentioned in the above redaction analysis (chapter two), the pre-Deuteronomistic traditions about Solomon do not include descriptions of an unusually long life. According to this theory, 1 Kgs 3:14a is the Deuteronomist's subtle implication that Solomon did not live an unusually long time because he did not remain faithful to Yahweh. There are two main problems with this theory: 1) 1 Kgs 3:14 does not promise Solomon an incomparably long life but just a longer life than he might otherwise have enjoyed and 2) the Deuteronomist does not elsewhere emphasize that Solomon did not live an unusually long life, thus fulfilling the conditional aspect of 1 Kgs 3:14. As seen in other parts of the Gibeon story itself, the Deuteronomist puts great emphasis on the fulfillment of the divine word.

The addition of the prologue (3:11*) adds another hierarchical level to the structure of the speech, 3.b.1) and 3.b.2) of the above diagram. Placement of the incomparability formula between the promise of riches and honor (13a) and כל־ימיך ("all your days" at the end of 13b) results in the separation of the promise of riches and honor from the promise of long life. Now, with the addition of the condition in 14a, verse 13 is the unconditional set of promises of items not requested (riches and honor), while verse 14 is the conditional promise of another item not requested, namely long life.

Concluding Summary

Context, Themes and Theology of the Redaction

By the time the first Deuteronomistic redaction was written, many of the original factors behind the story were ancient history. The Josianic editor confronted a variety of traditions, both pro-Solomonic (such as the Vorlage to this story) and anti-Solomonic (such as Deut 17:16a, 17; 1 Sam 8:11b-17). Engaged in legitimating a nationalistic program of unification of the kingdom and centralization of its cult, he must have felt a certain ambivalence toward this worldly king. On the one hand, Solomon built the Jerusalem temple, the only legitimate cult place according to Deuteronomistic theology. Moreover, his kingdom was the political highpoint of the history of Israel. Within the act-consequence Deuteronomistic perspective, this required some kind of explanation, particularly since the kingdom held together until after Solomon's death. On the other hand, Solomon was reputed to have been a less than ideal king in some crucial ways: he built extra-Jerusalemite sanctuaries for his foreign wives and oppressed the people of the land in order to build his great kingdom. Indeed, his rich and powerful kingdom was indistinguishable from those of his neighbors in many of the ways which mattered most to the anti-pagan Deuteronomists.

In sum, the Deuteronomist faced a tension between factors dictating a positive evaluation of Solomon and factors dictating a negative evaluation. In the editing of the Gibeon story, this editor introduces Solomon's reign by showing the terms on which he would rule. The approach is two-pronged. On the one hand, he neutralizes any element in the Vorlage which implies that God owed Solomon his wisdom, riches and honor. On the other hand, he adds an ethical component at four important junctures of the story, the introduction (3:3), Solomon's petition (3:6-9), and the beginning and end of God's reply (3:11 and 14a).

Specifically, the introduction in 3:3 rules out any implication that Solomon's practices at Gibeon may have played a role in his good fortune there. The additions to Solomon's speech portray divine favor as not just dependent on legitimate succession, but also on righteous behavior in accordance with the behavior of the dynasty's founder, David. Moreover, the Deuteronomistic version of Solomon's speech no longer accuses God of having caused the problem. Instead, it portrays both poles of the problem - Solomon's being in his position and the large size of the people - as the results of God's conscious behavior toward God's chosen king and people.

The prologue to the divine speech specifies that Solomon's rejection of pagan values and priority on legal wisdom were the reasons for the divine gifts of both requested and non-requested items. The added incomparability formula used for Solomon's wisdom places his wisdom in the scheme of the overarching Deuteronomistic history, and the incomparability formula used for his riches and honor shares the Deuteronomistic prologue's emphasis on Solomon over against his contemporaries. Finally, the addition of the condition on the promise of long life applies all of the earlier ethical emphases directly to Solomon's future behavior.

These changes produce notable theological shifts. The neutralization of many of the royal ideological elements in the story sharpen the focus on God's initiative. According to the Deuteronomistic version of the Gibeon story, God does not just initiate the encounter at Gibeon, begin the petition situation, and offer extra-gifts. In addition, God produces Solomon's problem through multiplying the chosen people and fulfilling the promise to David. Moreover, this God is not a creature of the monarchy, but claims sovereignty over Solomon's priorities and regulates his behavior. Despite these changes, the Deuteronomistic version portrays Solomon quite positively. Through doing so, the Deuteronomist can maintain the overall system of retribution and reward, while acknowledging that Solomon, the temple builder, built a kingdom indistinguishable in many important respects from those of his neighbors. In short, the solution—articulated in the Deuteronomistic edition of the Gibeon story—claims that he was able to build such a kingdom only because he rejected the values of his neighbors and put legal wisdom first.

Stability and Adaptability in Use of Earlier Tradition

As we turn to consider the Deuteronomist's stance toward earlier traditions it is clear that the Deuteronomistic interpretation of the

Vorlage is different in kind from the Vorlage's interpretation of traditions prior to it. The Vorlage merely built on the content of preceding traditions about Solomon's wisdom, wealth and honor, his practices at Gibeon, and the plot that wisdom leads to wealth, long life and honor. The long life promise is the only part of the Vorlage which may have been built on the wording of a previous text.

In contrast, the Deuteronomistic redaction of the Vorlage scrupulously preserves the wording of the Vorlage, even at points—such as 3:4— where the intent of the Vorlage is at odds with the Deuteronomistic program. Rather than eliminating such texts, the Deuteronomist confronts and recontextualizes them. Whereas 3:4 implies that the sanctuary at Gibeon is great because Solomon sacrifices at it, the Deuteronomistic addition in 3:3 describes Solomon's patronage of local sanctuaries (like that at Gibeon) in order to *qualify* its praise of him. The Vorlage version of Solomon's speech in 3:6aα subtly implies that God should show Solomon the same unconditional favor that God showed his father David, and 3:7 accuses God of being responsible to equip Solomon for the job in which God placed him. In contrast, the Deuteronomistic addition in 3:6aβ claims that God's favor to David was conditional on his obedience. Then 3:6b restates 3:6aα, asserting that Solomon's placement on the throne was proof of God's loyalty, a loyalty which Solomon can also enjoy if he is obedient like David.

These and other Deuteronomistic additions neutralize both explicit and implicit claims in the Vorlage that God favored Solomon at Gibeon 1) because he was king, David's legitimate successor, and 2) because he was at Gibeon, the great sanctuary. The Deuteronomist counters such ancient cultic and royal ideology with a theory of ethical succession: God favors Solomon only in so far as he obeys God and thus actualizes his propensity toward good inherited from David. Within the story itself, Solomon's faithfulness consists of rejecting the priorities of the non-Israelite kings and affirming the prime value of Deuteronomistic royal ideology, legal knowledge.

In each case, the Deuteronomist not only allows the wording of the Vorlage to stand, but he also incorporates part of the content of the Vorlage verse into his rereading of it. Thus, the Deuteronomistic regnal introduction (3:3) recontextualizes the Vorlage introduction (3:4), but both presuppose Solomon's reputation as a great Israelite king. The Vorlage text in 3:6aα and Deuteronomistic additions in 3:6aβ and 6b share an emphasis on David. 3:6b (Deuteronomistic) and 3:7 (Vorlage) both focus on God putting Solomon on the throne. The latter (Vorlage) portrays God as putting Solomon in an impossible situation, while the former (Deuteronomistic version) presents God as fulfilling a promise to David. The Deuteronomistic addition in 3:11 builds on suggestions throughout the Vorlage that God favors Solomon, while explicitly countering suggestions that God favors Solomon because he is king and worships at Gibeon. Finally, the cultic formula in Vorlage version of the long life promise originates in contexts where long life and rule are seen as rewards for cultic piety. The Deuteronomist portrays long life as a reward for Solomon following the good ethical example of his father David.

The most significant example of this hermeneutic of preservation (stability) and recontextualization (adaptability) is the Deuteronomist's treatment of Solomon's request. Here, the Deuteronomist modifies Solomon's request for general wisdom in 3:9a without any addition in wording to the request itself. Instead, he adds the legal implications by the allusions to Deut 1:9-18 in 1 Kgs 3:8 and 3:9b and the description of Solomon's request in 3:11. As we will see, the characterization of Solomon's request is a pivotal point in later interpretations of the Gibeon story. This is the point in the story where each interpreter presents what each considers to be the value which brings all other benefits with it. Thus it is significant that at this point the Deuteronomist was able to resonate so much with the wording of Solomon's request, that he preserved it without additions.

Inter-textuality and Counter-textuality in the Redaction

One significant component of the Deuteronomistic adaptation of the Gibeon story is its integration of the story with other texts in the Deuteronomistic history. This contrasts with the interpretation implicit in the Vorlage. For, though the Vorlage may have been part of a larger text (it is difficult to say at this point), it can stand alone. It does not require knowledge of specific traditions in a larger literary context. Though it builds on Solomon's reputation to build up that of the sanctuary, no specific description of that reputation is presumed. This emerges yet more clearly in comparison with the Deuteronomistic redaction of the Gibeon story.

The Deuteronomistic introduction to the story (3:3) presupposes Deuteronomistic cultic centralization regulations (Deut 12) and the corresponding Deuteronomistic royal ideology of ethical succession. The Deuteronomistic addition in 3:6b quotes from dynastic promises in the preceding succession narrative. The Deuteronomistic additions in 3:8 and

9b allude to Deut 1:9-18 to redescribe the difficulty of Solomon's job. In addition, the description of Israel in 3:8 alludes to the promises to the patriarchs. The incomparability formulae in 1 Kgs 3:12b$\beta\gamma$ and 3:13b build on pre-Deuteronomistic incomparability formulae in 1 Kgs 5:10-11; 10:23. The first incomparability formula emphasizes the distinctiveness of Solomon's wisdom by placing Solomon's wisdom in the scheme of the Deuteronomistic history extending before and after him. The second incomparability formula stays closer to its non-Deuteronomistic proto-types in comparing Solomon's riches and honor with that of his pagan contemporaries. Finally, the Deuteronomistic explanation of God's extra gifts in 3:11 builds on the Deuteronomistic kingship ideal (Deut 17:14-20, etc.) and counters (Deuteronomistic perceptions of) extra-Israelite royal values.

Coming right after the succession narrative, this Deuteronomistic introduction to Solomon's reign stands in particularly pointed contrast to a succession narrative tale which stands near the beginning of David's reign, the Bathsheba story. Through this placement of the Gibeon story, the Deuteronomist achieved a striking contrast between David's early folly and Solomon's early wisdom. The Bathsheba story ends in a scene of judgment against David, resulting death of his first child by Bathsheba, and subsequent birth of Solomon (2 Sam 12:1-25). In contrast, the Gibeon story ends in a scene of wise judgment by Solomon regarding a dead and a living child (1 Kgs 3:16-28).[132]

One example of Deuteronomistic inter-textuality, that regarding extra-Israelite royal values, can be more specifically described as an example of "counter-textuality." For the Deuteronomist appropriates traditions only to subvert them. The same is true of the Deuteronomistic stance toward originally anti-Solomonic traditions, such as those in Deut 17:16a, 17; 1 Sam 8:11b-17. The Deuteronomist neutralizes these anti-Solomonic tradi-tions through having them characterize not Solomon, but "kingship like the nations." According to the Deuteronomistic account of Solomon's

---

[132] I am indebted for the basic insights of this paragraph to Carole Fontaine, "The Bearing of Wisdom on the Shape of 2 Sam 11-12 and 1 Kgs 3," *JSOT* 34 (1986): 61-77. Note that I do not follow her more specific arguments regarding the importance of dame wisdom in the Gibeon story. As we will see in a later chapter, Fontaine's inser-tion of "dame wisdom" into 1 Kgs 3:2-15 parallels a similar move by the Wisdom of Solomon. Her reading is a possible interpretation of 1 Kgs 3:2-15 in its present canonical juxtaposition with Proverbs. Nevertheless, such a reading does not repre-sent the text's original intent and thus cannot be used to contrast the Deuteronomistic version of the story with later interpretations of it.

reign, only in the *post-temple* part of his rule does Solomon fail to follow the example of his father David and deserve rejection by God (1 Kgs 11:6). The Gibeon story introduces the terms for both God's favor for him in 1 Kgs 3-10 and rejection of him in 1 Kgs 3:11. At this early point in the narrative the young Solomon is presented as one worthy to succeed David and build a temple in "the place where the Lord, your God, will choose to make his name dwell there" (Deut 12:11; cf. 12:5).

In sum, the Deuteronomistic redaction of the Vorlage is an example of intense inter-textuality, even (more specifically) counter-textuality. The Deuteronomist allows the wording of the Vorlage to stand and often appropriates the content of the Vorlage even while undermining it. The Deuteronomistic additions integrate the story with a larger literary context, the Deuteronomistic history, so that the story's qualified positive portrayal of Solomon contrasts with 2 Sam 11-12 and builds on preceding cultic centralization regulations, Moses' request for legal assistance (Deut 1:9-18), and descriptions of God's promises (to the patriarchs and to David), while looking forward to pre-Deuteronomistic traditions regarding Solomon's incomparable wisdom, wealth, and honor. Deuteronomistic models are followed for the introductory regnal formula (3:3), description of David's virtue (3:6aβ, 14a), and incomparability formulae. Finally, anti-Solomonic traditions are contradicted, at least for the pre-temple and temple portions of Solomon's reign, by this characterization of Solomon as David's worthy successor.

Yet, all of this inter-textuality is not an end in itself. Indeed, the Deuteronomist takes decisively different stances toward material depending on how it conforms with the Deuteronomist's perspective. Textual traditions which conflict with the Deuteronomist's perspective—both within and outside of the Vorlage—are preserved yet neutralized. One part of this process of neutralization is the recontextualization of non-Deuteronomistic traditions through references to traditions elsewhere in the Deuteronomistic history. The aim and result of this complex process of inter-textuality is a cohesive statement of the true origins of Solomon's greatness, a statement which encompasses and neutralizes its opposition.

The Structure of the Deuteronomistic Gibeon Story

This cohesive statement has its own structure, one different in many respects from that of its Vorlage. The macro-structure of the Vorlage, however, is preserved unchanged. Instead, the Deuteronomist works within this macro-structure, producing micro-structural changes while reframing the overall focus of the story. The final structure of the first Deuteronomistic edition of the Gibeon story runs as follows:

As discussed above, this story is now the introduction to the Deuteron-omistic account of Solomon's reign.

THE ADONAI DEUTERONOMISTIC EDITION

First Deuteronomistic Edition	*Deuteronomistic Edition with Adonai Editor's Additions*
	1 Kgs 3:10
	The thing pleased Adonai, that Solomon had asked this thing,
1 Kgs 3:11	1 Kgs 3:11
And God said to him, "because you asked this thing, and did not request many days or riches for yourself, nor did you request the life of your enemies, but you requested discrimination to hear cases,..."	And God said to him, "because you asked this thing, and did not request many days or riches for yourself, nor did you request the life of your enemies, but you requested discrimination to hear cases,..."
[Intervening promises (3:12-14)]	[Intervening promises (3:12-14)]
1 Kgs 3:15a	1 Kgs 3:15a
Solomon awoke, and behold, it was a dream.	Solomon awoke, and behold, it was a dream.
	1 Kgs 3:15bα1-6
	He went to Jerusalem, stood before the ark of the covenant of Adonai,
1 Kgs 3:15bα7-10β	1 Kgs 3:15bα7-10β
and he offered burnt offerings, performed communion sacrifices, and held a banquet for all his servants.	and (he) offered burnt offerings, performed communion sacrifices, and held a banquet for all his servants.

The contributions of the Adonai editor are quite different from those of the first Deuteronomist. Whereas the first Deuteronomist intervened extensively throughout the Gibeon story, the Adonai editor merely adds two transitions. Both of these transitions are at major junctures in the story, between parts II.B.2 and II.B.3 and between parts II. and III. of the structure diagram given above. Because they occur at such major junctures, the transitions introduce major changes on the higher levels of the structure of the story.

Before the addition of 3:10, the first Deuteronomistic edition of the Gibeon story had the following structure for God's response to Solomon's petition:

3. Speech Report: Petitioned's Response 11-14
   a. Speech Report Introduction 11aα1-3
   b. Speech Proper 11aα4- 3:14

Some other Biblical reports of the response of the petitioned include descriptions of the petitioned's affective response prior to the quote of their verbal response.[133] 1 Kgs 3:10 adds such a component to God's response in 1 Kgs 3:11-14. With this addition, God's response is no longer just a speech report. Instead, the speech report is now the second part of God's response, the verbal part. The structure runs as follows:

3. Petitioned's Response 10-14
   a. Affective 10
   b. Verbal: Speech Report 11-14
     1) Speech Report Introduction 11aα1-3
     2) Speech Proper 11aα4- 3:14

As mentioned before, this addition stresses the value of Solomon's positive request for wisdom, while neglecting the earlier Deuteronomist's emphasis on the value of Solomon's rejection of pagan royal values. Thus, the Adonai editor did not merely add an affective component to

---

133 The verbs יטב and רעע are frequently used to describe positive and negative affective responses to all kinds of events and actions. Such descriptions typically use a third masculine singular converted imperfect Qal form of the verb in the following formula: (pronominal suffix)...וַיִּיטַב/וַיֵּרַע בְּעֵינֵי/עֵין. Particularly in petition scenes, the thing which pleased or displeased the person (or people) in question is referred to through the insertion of הדבר between the verb and the prepositional phrase, בעיני (Genesis 21:11; 2 Sam 8:6; Esther 1:21; 2:4; 5:14). 1 Kgs 3:10 follows this form.

the divine speech, but used the generic option of "description of affective response" as a vehicle for his emphasis on the positive value of wisdom.

Similarly, the addition of 1 Kgs 3:15bα1-6 modifies both the divisions and the headings of the conclusion. Before the addition of this verse, its structure was the following:

> III.   Solomon's Response to Epiphany 15bα7-10β
>
> A. Offerings...15bα7-10
>
> B. Banquet... 15bβ

1 Kgs 3:15bα1-6 describes Solomon's return to the Jerusalem sanctuary, the only legitimate cultic center according to the Deuteronomistic perspective. Specifically, the Adonai editor places Solomon before the "ark of the covenant of Adonai." The structure of the conclusion now runs as follows:

> III.   Solomon's Response to Epiphany: Jerusalem 15b
>
> A. Return to the Proper Place for Sacrifice...................15bα1-6
>
> B. Response Proper.. 15bα7-10β
>
> 1. Offerings..15bα7-10
>
> 2. Banquet.. 15bβ

With this addition, the story moves from Solomon's habit of sacrificing great amounts at Gibeon (1 Kgs 3:4b) to his response to the Gibeon epiphany by sacrificing in the proper cultic center in Jerusalem (3:15bα1-6). The implication is that not only did Solomon receive wisdom, wealth, honor, and long life at Gibeon, but he also realized the proper place for offering sacrifices to God.[134]

With both of these additions the Adonai editor respected the integrity of the larger structural units. The "stability of the tradition" has extended from its wording (the first Deuteronomistic edition) to the integrity of its structural units. Where the first Deuteronomistic editor incorporated content of the Vorlage in the process of undermining it, the Adonai editor extends and only slightly modifies the content of the first Deuteronomistic edition. By adding 1 Kgs 3:10, the Adonai editor stressed one half of the Deuteronomistic message in the prologue to the divine speech (1 Kgs 3:11*). With its emphasis on the Jerusalem sanctuary, the addition in

---

134 Kenik, *Design for Kingship*, 182-197.

1 Kgs 3:15bα is even more clearly consistent with the earlier Deuteron-omist's perspective (1 Kgs 3:3).

Despite the similarities to the first Deuteronomist's contributions, the additions of the Adonai editor nevertheless show certain shifts in theo-logical perspective. Later additions to the Deuteronomistic history, such as those by the Adonai editor, were probably done during the exilic and post-exilic periods. Solomon and his kingdom no longer stand as models for traditional (Vorlage) or reforming (the first Deuteronomist) royal ideology. Instead, the people of Israel begin to look to him in two new ways. On the one hand, as the ruler during the height of the Israelite empire, Solomon becomes the symbol of a kingless people's glorious past. On the other hand (distinct but not separate from the above), stories about Solomon become models for individual behavior.

The above statements are made in part on the basis of trends in inter-pretations which will not be discussed until the next chapter. Nevertheless, by describing Solomon's return to Jerusalem, the Adonai editor already seems to show a concern for positively portraying Solomon, providing a more forgiving picture of him than the mixed evaluation of him in 1 Kgs 3:3. Solomon learns from his experience at Gibeon, and goes to Jerusalem instead. The extra emphasis on God's positive response to Solomon's prayer, similarly magnifies Solomon. Moreover, it does so in terms which could be appropriated by the exilic and post-exilic readers of the story. They would not be so concerned about Solomon's rejection of pagan royal values, but his choice of wis-dom was something anyone with access to the growing Israelite educa-tional establishment could emulate.

In sum, the Adonai editor merely adds minor transitions at major junctures, respecting both the structure and intent of the earlier edition, but adapting it to portray Solomon more positively and as an example for people who are not kings. As a result of these adaptations, the larger units of the structure alter into the following form:

Introduction to Solomon's Reign:

Dream Epiphany Report 3:3-15

I. Description of Circumstances of Epiphany: Gibeon 3-4

II. Dream Epiphany Proper 5-15a

      A. Dream Epiphany Introduction Formula 5a

      B. Petition Scene Initiated by the Petitioned 5b-14

            1. Speech Report: Petitioned's Open Ended Offer 5b

THE SUPPLEMENT TO THE INTRODUCTION

First Deuteronomistic Edition	*Marginal Gloss*
1 Kgs 3:3	
Solomon loved the LORD, living according to the norms of David, his father,	1 Kgs 3:2
only he sacrificed and made smoke offerings in the local sanctuaries.	only the people sacrificed at the local sanctuaries outside Jerusalem because the temple had not yet been built to the name of the LORD in those days.

1 Kgs 3:2 is a correction of the first Deuteronomist's criticism of Solomon (1 Kgs 3:3b) for sacrificing at non-Jerusalemite sanctuaries. Whereas 1 Kgs 3:3b qualified the praise of Solomon by mentioning his sacrificing at non-Jerusalemite sanctuaries, 1 Kgs 3:2 excuses Solomon for such sacrifice. 3:2 implies that Solomon had to sacrifice at the non-Jerusalemite sanctuaries because everyone had to sacrifice outside Jerusalem before the temple was built. Thus first and foremost, 1 Kgs 3:2, like the Adonai editor's addition in 1 Kgs 3:15bα1-6, is a justification of Solomon.

This justification, has a special relationship with its literary context in the Deuteronomistic history. The author evidently saw the relationship between 1 Kgs 3:3 and the later Deuteronomistic qualified positive evaluations of Judean kings,[135] so he formulated the first half of his correction of 1 Kgs 3:3 to match the second half of those formulations. He wrote this

---

[135] 1 Kgs 22:44; 2 Kgs 12:4; 14:4; 15:4, 35.

correction "Biblically," thus invoking the authority of his Biblical models to support the authenticity of his own addition.

This addition, however, makes a very different point from the regnal evaluations which were the model for it. Whereas those evaluations qualified the Deuteronomist's otherwise positive evaluation of a king, the supplement in 1 Kgs 3:2 implicitly justifies Solomon over against the first Deuteronomist's later qualification of praise for him (1 Kgs 3:3b). Thus the supplement's author takes the form of other Deuteronomistic qualifications of praise to undermine the Deuteronomistic qualification of praise in 1 Kgs 3:3b. This adds a new dimension to the borrowing which occurs in 1 Kgs 3:2a. The supplement's author did not just borrow the style of the other regnal evaluations, but used part of their formulation to indicate the following: Before the temple was built, Solomon was justified in sacrificing in the non-Jerusalemite sanctuaries *even according to the standards used to qualify the praise of later Judean kings*. In sum, the supplement is a subtle inter-textual argument.

Like both the first Deuteronomistic editor and Adonai redactor, the author of the supplement is preoccupied with the problem that Solomon frequented non-Jerusalemite sanctuaries, even receiving his wisdom, riches, and honor at one. The first Deuteronomistic editor indicated that Solomon's patronage of non-Jerusalemite sanctuaries was not why he was rewarded. The Adonai redactor adds a trip to Jerusalem before Solomon's sacrifice, thus implying that Solomon reformed his ways upon seeing God and receiving wisdom, riches, honor and long life. In contrast, the supplement looks forward to the building and dedication of the temple in 1 Kgs 6-8 and limits the Deuteronomistic norm of centralized worship to the time when the temple existed.

Thus, the supplement implies the anachronistic character of the qualification of Solomon's praise in 1 Kgs 3:3b, an anachronistic character only evident from the literary context of the Gibeon story, i.e. at the beginning of Solomon's reign. Whereas the Adonai editor added a geographical component to the story in order to excuse Solomon, the author of the supplement adds a chronological component to the regulations used to criticize him in 3:3b.

The 1 Kgs 3:2 supplement establishes its link with the half verse which it corrects by beginning with the particle רק ("but, only"). As argued above, this particle is so difficult to interpret in context that we must suppose that the supplement originally stood in the margin next to 1 Kgs

3:3b.[136] Later in the manuscript tradition, the supplement was incorporated into the text itself. Significantly, the supplement was not put next
to the half-verse which it corrects, but instead was put at the very beginning of the story. This may indicate that by this time, the story was seen
as having a kind of literary integrity which could not be violated by the
introduction of supplements like 1 Kgs 3:2. The placement of 1 Kgs 3:2 at
the very beginning was also facilitated by the fact that the half-verse it
supplements is toward the beginning of the story.

Thus the stability of the tradition has extended from its wording (first
Deuteronomistic edition) and the integrity of its larger structural units
(Adonai edition) to the integrity of the story as a whole. Moreover, the
supplement preserves the content of its precursor tradition, particularly
the first Deuteronomist's value on cultic centralization. Whereas the first
Deuteronomistic edition of the story involved a fundamental reorientation of the precursor tradition, both the Adonai additions and the
Supplement work within the Deuteronomistic presuppositions of their
precursor tradition, using elements within that tradition to improve the
picture of Solomon in the Gibeon story. The first Deuteronomistic edition
has reconceptualized the terms on which Solomon could be praiseworthy
at all. The Adonai edition and Deuteronomistic supplement show how
Solomon can be even more praiseworthy *on those terms*.

With the addition of 1 Kgs 3:2, the structure of the Gibeon story shifts
yet again. Prior to the addition of the supplement, the structure of the
introduction ran as follows:

I. Description of Circumstances of Epiphany: Gibeon 3-4
    A. Regnal Evaluation: Solomon's Patronage
        of Sanctuaries in Context 3
        1. General Endorsement: Solomon like David 3a
        2. Qualification: Patronage of Sanctuaries 3b
    B. Location of Epiphany: Particular Trip to a Sanctuary 4

The supplement's history of formation in the margin and later insertion
creates some structural irregularities. The supplement shares the conjunction רק and focus on sacrificing at non-Jerusalemite sanctuaries with
1 Kgs 3:3b, but it serves the same function as 1 Kgs 3:3a. Both 1 Kgs 3:2
and 3:3a place Solomon's patronage of non-Jerusalemite sanctuaries in
context. With the addition of 1 Kgs 3:2, 1 Kgs 3:3a also begins to serve as

---

[136] See above, in the redaction chapter, p.27.

a justification of Solomon and counterbalance to 1 Kgs 3:3b. A diagram of the structure of the introduction with the supplement follows:

I. Description of Circumstances of Epiphany: Gibeon............ 2-4

    A. Regnal Evaluation: Solomon's Patronage of
    Sanctuaries in Context.. 2-3

        1. Context.. 2-3a

            a. General Pre-Temple Practices 2

            b. Solomon's Overall Faithfulness 3a

        2. Patronage of Sanctuaries.. 3b

    B. Location of Epiphany: Particular Trip to a Sanctuary 4

CONCLUDING DIAGRAM AND DISCUSSION

Looking back on the interpretation involved in the growth of 1 Kgs 3:2-15, we can see how its growth has effected its structure on both higher and lower levels. The following is a diagram of the structure of the story's final form.

Introduction to Solomon's Reign:
Dream Epiphany Report.. 3:2-15

I. Description of Circumstances of Epiphany: Gibeon 2-4

    A. Regnal Evaluation: Solomon's Patronage of
    Sanctuaries in Context.. 2-3

        1. Context.. 2-3a

            a. General Pre-Temple Practices 2

            b. Solomon's Overall Faithfulness 3a

        2. Patronage of Sanctuaries.. 3b

    B. Location of Epiphany: Particular Trip to a Sanctuary 4

II. Dream Epiphany Proper.. 5-15a

    A. Dream Epiphany Introduction Formula......................... 5a

    B. Petition Scene Initiated by the Petitioned................... 5b-14

        1. Speech Report: Petitioned's Open Ended Offer 5b

        2. Speech Report: Petitioner's Petition 6-9

            a. Speech Report Introduction............................ 6aα1-2

            b. Speech Proper... 6aα3- 3:9

                1) Prologue: Problem Situation 6aα3- 3:7

                    a) Past: Background to b) 6aα3-b

                      α. God's Loyalty to David.................. 6aα3-7

The story began as a royal ideological text promoting Solomon and the sanctuary at Gibeon, but it is now the introduction to the account of his reign in the Deuteronomistic history. Whereas the Vorlage originally explained Solomon's wisdom, wealth, and honor as the results of unequivocal divine favor, the Gibeon story now gives the ethical dimensions of the monarchy in general, and God's initiative is emphasized throughout, both to give *and* to command. The positive picture of Solomon, however, is maintained throughout most of the growth of the story, and the later redactional layers merely refine and extend this positive focus. Throughout the history of the development of the story, the editors focus ever more exclusively on describing the nuances of God's relationship with Solomon and vice-versa. As a result, the present version of the Gibeon story describes a Solomonic change of heart about extra-Jerusalemite sanctuaries after the divine epiphany, and it excuses his earlier practices as in accordance with pre-temple custom.

Though the first Deuteronomist's additions only produced low level structural shifts in the story, they fundamentally reoriented the story. Clearly, the first Deuteronomistic edition of the Gibeon story set the stage for later additions to it. First, whereas the Gibeon story was probably just a local sanctuary legend prior to the Deuteronomist's appropriation of it, now the Gibeon story is part of Israel's normative history. Its positive picture of Solomon, a culture hero for later Israelites, thus was important for later readers, important enough to refine and extend it. This leads to the second way the Deuteronomistic edition set the stage for later additions; it decisively reoriented the evaluation of Solomon to focus exclusively on ethical categories. All of the subsequent additions merely modify the application of ethical categories to Solomon, not questioning their primacy. Third, the most important royal norm for the first Deuteronomist was cultic purity and centralization (1 Kgs 3:3). This too, is presupposed in the additions by the Adonai editor and supplementer.

Chapter Five

INTERPRETATIONS IN HISTORIES
OF ISRAEL

According to Jewish tradition, Solomon was the sage, par excellence. In the Hellenistic period a number of traditions collected around Ancient Near Eastern wise men.[137] Such men could supply the deeper wisdom missing in the contemporary scene and provide their respective ethnic sub-groups with a hero who predated the Greek wise men. Solomon was one such Ancient Near Eastern wise man. During this period Proverbs and the Song of Songs were ascribed to him, and Qohelet was written in his name. Later books connected to him include the Psalms of Solomon, and the Odes of Solomon.[138] The less mainstream traditions about Solomon are just as important, especially innumerable magic spells ascribed to him,[139] but also other references such as those in Josephus,[140] the Pseudepigrapha,[141] and the Nag Hammadi literature.[142]

---

[137] See Martin Hengel, *Judaism and Hellenism*, trans. J. Bowden (Philadelphia: Fortress, 1974), 1:129-130, for fuller discussion.

[138] See also Sir 47:12-22.

[139] Including incantation bowls cited by D. C. Duling, "Testament of Solomon," *The Old Testament Pseudepigrapha*, ed. James H. Charlesworth, vol. 1, *Apocalyptic Literature & Testaments* (Garden City: Doubleday, 1983), 948.

[140] *Antiquities* VIII:1-210.

[141] Sib. Or. 11:80-103; T. Solomon; 2 Bar 61; Life of Adam and Eve, Appendix (quite late). Brief references occur in Bib. Ant. 26:12, 60:3; Lives of the Prophets 1:10-12; 18:2, 4; Eupolemus in Eusebius, *Preparatio Evangelica* 9:34:20.

[142] Apoc. Adam (V 5), 78:30, 79:3, 10; Treat. Seth (VII 2), 63:11; Testim. Truth (IX 3), 70:6, 25.

It is within this overall context that traditions about Solomon such as the Gibeon story were interpreted. With this emphasis on Solomon as a sage and culture hero, the Gibeon story gained importance as an etiology of the wisdom which made Solomon famous. The story has two sets of Second Temple Jewish interpretations. The first set consists of the narrative retellings of the Gibeon story. This set includes 2 Chronicles 1:1-13 and Josephus VIII:22-25. The second set consists of those instructional (wisdom) texts which reflect on the Gibeon story. The members of this second set of interpretations are Qohelet 1:12-2:26, Wisdom of Solomon 7-9, and Q 12:22-31.[143] These two sets interpret the Gibeon story quite differently. Therefore, these sets of interpretations are treated separately in this (narratives) and the following chapter (instructions), each set of interpretations being discussed in rough chronological order.

2 CHRONICLES 1:1-13

Recent studies of the Chronicler's historical viewpoint have substantially altered our perspective on the Chronicler's interpretation of 1 Kgs 3:2-15 in 2 Chr 1:1-13. To be sure, some scholars have argued that 2 Chr 1:1-13 relies on sources other than 1 Kgs 3:2-15, sources perhaps more historically accurate.[144] The vast majority, however, have been able to plausibly account for the shape of 2 Chr 1:1-13 without assuming sources other than 1 Kgs 3:2-15. In particular, studies such by Caquot, Mosis, Braun, Williamson, Japhet, Peterca, and Abramsky have shown how the Chronicler's overall historical perspective has shaped his picture of Solomon.[145] Some aspects of the story are clearly shaped to portray an

---

[143] Here and elsewhere the convention of giving Luke's versification in citing Q is followed.

[144] Cf. William Emery Barnes, *The Books of Chronicles*, Cambridge Bible for Schools and Colleges (Cambridge: At the University Press, 1899), 143; Peter R. Ackroyd, *I & II Chronicles, Ezra, and Nehemiah*, Torch Bible Commentaries (London: SCM, 1973), 100-101; Baruch Halpern, "Sacred History and Ideology: Chronicles' Thematic Structure —Indications of an Earlier Source," in *The Creation of Sacred Literature*, ed. Richard E. Friedman, University of California Publications: Near Eastern Studies 22 (Berkeley: University of California Press, 1981), p. 38; and Steven McKenzie, *The Chronicler's Use of the Deuteronomistic History*, HSM 33 (Atlanta: Scholars Press, 1984), p. 106.

[145] André Caquot, "Peut-on parler de messianisme dans l'oevre du Chroniste?" *RTP* 16 (1966): 110-120; Rudolph Mosis, *Untersuchungen zur Theologie des chronistischen Geschichtswerkes*, Freiburger theologische Studien 92 (Freiburg: Herder, 1967), 82-163; Roddy L. Braun, "The Message of Chronicles: Rally Round the Temple," *CTM* 42 (1971): 507-509; idem. "Solomonic Apologetic in Chronicles," *JBL* 92 (1973): 503-516; idem. "Solomon the Chosen Temple Builder: The Significance of 1 Chronicles 22, 28,

unblemished Solomon, but such modifications merely serve the larger purpose of presenting Solomon as the reviver of Moses traditions and divinely equipped temple builder. In addition, the Chronicler portrays his reign as inextricably linked to David's along the model of Moses and Joshua, so that the entire period of the United Monarchy culminates in their common work, the building of the temple. This study's discussion of the Chronicler's Gibeon story continues the process of seeing the Gibeon story in Chronicles within this overall context.

Structure

The Chronicler's historical perspective radically shifts in the macro-structure of the account of Solomon in general and of the Gibeon story in particular.

Structure Diagram

and 29 for the Theology of Chronicles," *JBL* 95 (1976): 581-590; H. G. M. Williamson, "The Accession of Solomon in the Book of Chronicles," *VT* 26 (1976): 351-361; idem. "Eschatology in Chronicles," *Tyndale Bulletin* 28 (1977): 133-154; Sarah Japhet, אמונות ודעות בספר דברי־הימים ומקומן בעולם המחשבה המקראית (Jerusalem: Bialik Institute, 1977), 401-410; Vladimer Peterca, *L'Immagine di Salomone nella Bibbia Ebraica e Greca* (Rome: Pontificia Universitas Gregoriana, 1981), 40-76; Samuel Abramsky, "שלמה המלך בעיני בעל דברי הימים" *EI* 16 (1982): 3-14.

The Chronistic Context for the Gibeon Story

The Chronistic version of the Gibeon story has an almost identical structure to that of the Deuteronomistic version.[146] The most dramatic structural shifts occur not within the story itself, but in its context. The Chronistic account of Solomon's reign is fundamentally different from the Deuteronomistic account. As mentioned above,[147] the body of the Deuteronomistic account of Solomon's reign has two parts. The first part of the account portrays Solomon positively, focusing particularly on his construction and dedication of Yahweh's temple in Jerusalem. The second part of the Deuteronomistic account portrays Solomon negatively, opening with his construction of pagan shrines (1 Kgs 11:1-10—Verses 1-6 are secondary). Within its Deuteronomistic context, the Gibeon story presents God's rules for dealing with Solomon: while Solomon is faithful (as at Gibeon) he will enjoy God's favor (1 Kgs 4-10), but when he is unfaithful, he will incur God's judgment (1 Kgs 11).

In Chronicles, however, Solomon's entire reign is positively viewed. Everything focuses on Solomon's role in building the temple, and there is no Chronistic counterpart to 1 Kgs 11.[148] Now, this Chronistic account of Solomon's reign focuses almost exclusively on the establishment of the temple cult (7 out of 8 1/2 chapters). The Gibeon story now functions to introduce a reign primarily characterized by Solomon's establishment of the cult. This focus on cult is reflected in the Chronistic sequel to the Gibeon story. In the Deuteronomistic account, Solomon's *legal* expertise is emphasized by the story of Solomon's wise decision in the matter of the two prostitutes (1 Kgs 3:16-28). The Chronicler replaces the story of the two prostitutes with a description of God's fulfillment of God's promise of overwhelming wealth at Gibeon. In this way God provides Solomon the riches he needs to initiate the building of the temple (2 Chr 2:1).

---

[146] The most important shift is the elevation of the description of Solomon's practices at Gibeon (1 Kgs 3:2-4) to the status of an independent (though related) account.

[147] See p. 61.

[148] So Mark A. Throntveit, *When Kings Speak: Royal Speech and Royal Prayer in Chronicles,* SBLDS 93 (Atlanta: Scholars Press, 1987), 115 (commenting on 2 Chr 1:8-12).

Interpretation of the Gibeon Story

Solomon's First Cultic Act: 2 Chr 1:2-6

Whereas 1 Kgs 3:2-4 merely introduced an epiphany report, the story in 2 Chr 1:2-6 is a narrative in its own right. As seen in previous chapters, 1 Kgs 3:2-4 contains three traditio-historically distinct notes, each providing their own introduction to the epiphany at Gibeon:

1)   The note about the people's pre-temple worship practices (1 Kgs 3:2).

2)   The first Deuteronomist's positive evaluation of Solomon qualified by a mention of his worship outside Jerusalem (1 Kgs 3:3).

3)   The pre-Deuteronomistic description of his trip to Gibeon because of the greatness of the sanctuary there (1 Kgs 3:4).

The Chronicler weaves elements from each of these three notes into a unified account of Solomon's first royal act.

- *2 Chr 1:2-3a*

Deuteronomistic Gibeon Story	Chronistic Gibeon Story
1 Kgs 3:2	2 Chr 1:2
Only, the people were sacrificing at the local sanctuaries outside Jerusalem because the temple had not yet been built to the name of the LORD in those days.	And Solomon called to all Israel, to the officers over the thousands, the hundreds, to the judges, to every prince of all Israel, the heads of the families.
1 Kgs 3:3	
Solomon loved the LORD, living according to the norms of David, his father, but he sacrificed and made smoke offerings in the local sanctuaries.	
1 Kgs 3:4aa	2 Chr 1:3
The king went to Gibeon to sacrifice there	And Solomon and all the assembly of his people went to the sanctuary which was at Gibeon

1 Kgs 3:2 mentions the people's sacrificing outside Jerusalem in order to justify Solomon's sacrificing outside Jerusalem, a practice criticized in 1 Kgs 3:3. The Chronicler, however, combines information from 1 Kgs 3:2-4a, integrating the people into a positive description of Solomon's trip to Gibeon. Moreover, in contrast to the mere mention of הַעָם "the peo-

ple") in 1 Kgs 3:2, the Chronicler stresses the comprehensiveness of Israel's participation in this event. Not only does he say that Solomon commanded כל־ישראל ("all Israel"), but he goes on to specify all the leadership groups included in that expression. Now Solomon inaugurates his reign with an assembly and sacrifice similar to David's inauguration of his reign with the ark procession and celebration (1 Chr 13-16). Both events, David's procession with the ark and Solomon's sacrifice at Gibeon, are cultic inaugurations of the rule of the two kings of the United Monarchy. Moreover, the Chronicler emphasizes the participation of all of Israel in both (1 Chr 13:1-4, 5, 6; 15:3-11, 28; 16:43 and 2 Chr 1:2).[149]

- *2 Chr 1:3b-4*

Deuteronomistic Gibeon Story	*Chronistic Gibeon Story*
1 Kgs 3:4a	2 Chr 1:3
The king went to Gibeon to sacrifice there	And Solomon and all the assembly of his people went to the sanctuary which was at Gibeon
because it was the greatest of the sanctuaries.	because the Tent of Meeting of God, which Moses the servant of the LORD had made in the wilderness, was there.
	2 Chr 1:4
	But David had brought up the ark of God from Kiryat Yearim to the place which David had established for it for he set up a tent for it in Jerusalem.

Having linked "all Israel" with Solomon on his way to Gibeon, the Chronicler extensively expands and revises the ancient Vorlage notice in 1 Kgs 3:4aβ that Solomon went to Gibeon because it was הבמה הגדולה ("the great sanctuary"). The Gibeonite Vorlage expanded on the greatness of the sanctuary at Gibeon by describing Solomon's patronage of it (1 Kgs 3:4b). In contrast, the Chronicler picks up on previous Chronistic references to the tent's placement at Gibeon (1 Chr 16:39; 21:29) and reminds the reader of its location there. Now, Solomon (and all the assembly with him) go to the sanctuary in Gibeon because *the tent of meeting* was there. This is a crucial reconstrual of the greatness of the sanctuary at Gibeon. Now Gibeon is important because it has cultic items

---

[149] H. G. M. Williamson, 1 & 2 Chronicles, NCB Commentary (Grand Rapids: Eerdmans, 1982), 193-194. Cf. also Abramsky, "שלמה המלך" 6.

from the wilderness period. This then becomes an opportunity to unite the Mosaic and Davidic traditions, portraying Solomon as the founder of the new tent of meeting and restorer of wilderness traditions. Again there are important connections to the Chronicler's similar focus on David's procession with the ark to Jerusalem (1 Chr 13-16). Together, David's and Solomon's acts encompass the cultic items which figure highly in the Pentateuchal tabernacle traditions: the ark, tabernacle, and altar. In order to underscore this picture, the Chronicler adds a parenthesis in 2 Chr 1:4 about the location of the ark in Jerusalem and David's role in placing it there.[150]

- *2 Chr 1:5-6*

Deuteronomistic Gibeon Story	*Chronistic Gibeon Story*
1 Kgs 3:4b	2 Chr 1:5
	And he placed[151] the bronze altar which Bezalel, son of Uri, son of Hur, had made, before the Tabernacle of the LORD and sought him, Solomon and the assembly.
	2 Chr 1:6
Solomon used to offer a thousand burnt offerings on that altar.	And Solomon offered up a thousand burnt offerings. there on the bronze altar before the LORD[152]

Having explained (at length) why Solomon went to Gibeon, the Chronicler describes three things that he did there: he placed Bezalel's bronze altar before the Tabernacle, he and the assembly sought the Lord,

---

[150] Mosis, *Untersuchungen*, 125-135, 162-163. Cf. also Caquot, "Peut-on parler de messianisme?," 117; Henri Cazelles, *Les livres des Chroniques*, La Sainte Bible (Paris: Les Éditions du Cerf, 1961), 129; and Abramsky, שלמה המלך, 5-6.

[151] The Old Greek, Vulgate (possibly dependent on the Old Greek), and a Massoretic tradition read שָׁם ("there") at this point rather than reading שָׂם ("he placed"), a reading found in the Peshitta, Targum, and a second Massoretic tradition. See Dominique Barthélemy, *Critique textuelle de l'Ancien Testament*, OBO 50, vol. 1, *Josué, Juges, Ruth, Samuel, Rois, Chroniques, Esdras, Néhémie, Esther* (Göttingen: Vandenhoeck & Ruprecht, 1982), 474-475. The reading of שָׁם, however, is easily explained as an assimilation to the context (cf. 2 Chr 1:3b, 6a). Not only are such assimilations well known in textual transmission, but this particular assimilation avoids a mild contradiction between the reading שָׂם ("he placed") and the gloss in 1:6 ([the bronze altar] "which belonged to the Tent of Meeting)."

[152] For discussion of the phrase אשר לאהל מועד ("which belonged to the Tent of Meeting") see the discussion of the gloss below.

and he offered burnt offerings on the bronze altar. Once again we see the Chronicler's focus on Solomon's relationship to cultic items (specifically worship items from the wilderness period) in contrast to the 1 Kgs 3:4-5 focus on Solomon's relationship to a place (the sanctuary at Gibeon). This note on Bezalel's construction of the bronze altar corresponds to the preceding notice about Moses' construction of the Tent of Meeting (2 Chr 1:3bβ). Both notes serve to emphasize the wilderness connections of the cultic items Solomon used at Gibeon. The former note (2 Chr 1:3bβ) corresponded to the 1 Kgs 3:4aβ explanation of Solomon's trip to Gibeon and established the wilderness connections of the sanctuary by claiming that the "Tent of Meeting" was there. The present note corresponds to the 1 Kgs 3:4b note that Solomon sacrificed a thousand burnt offerings *on that altar* (על המזבח ההוא). Here the Chronicler establishes the wilderness connections of "that altar" by claiming that it was a *bronze* altar, the one made by Bezalel.

Perhaps yet more importantly, the Chronicler describes how Solomon placed Bezalel's bronze altar before the Tabernacle at Gibeon. Thus Solomon not only initiates his reign by sacrificing at a cult place with wilderness connections, but he himself plays a role in setting up that cult place prior to his sacrifice. This role in setting up the temporary wilderness sanctuary at Gibeon then prefigures his all important role in constructing and dedicating the permanent sanctuary in Jerusalem.

In the Chronistic account, Solomon sacrifices a thousand burnt offerings in the context of his and the assembly's "seeking the Lord." The insertion of "sought the Lord" before Solomon's sacrifice makes his sacrifice into a purposeful act. This emphasis on Solomon's initiative contrasts with the picture in the 1 Kgs account. 1 Kgs 3:4-6 presents Gibeon as a "great sanctuary" continually patronized by important people like Solomon, a place where God appeared to Solomon at God's own initiative. The mention of Solomon's *ongoing* practices is used to render a *place*. In contrast, 2 Chr 1:2-6 describes Solomon's inauguration of his reign with a *specific* assembly and sacrifice. Now the story of Solomon's first royal sacrifice renders a *character*.[153]

---

[153] Context may be an additional factor in this shift. The description of Solomon's ongoing practices in 1 Kgs 3:4b is part of the explanation of Solomon's trip to Gibeon, explaining what a great sanctuary Gibeon was (1 Kgs 3:4aβ). In contrast, by 2 Chr 1:6 Solomon's trip to Gibeon has already been explained. He went to Gibeon because the tent of meeting was there (2 Chr 1:3b). This explanation (2 Chr 1:3b) opens the way to another function for the Chronistic description of his practices there.

All of these shifts indicate that the Chronicler's modifications to the Gibeon story introduction (1 Kgs 3:2-4) are more than an attempt to excuse Solomon for sacrificing outside Jerusalem.[154] The assembly of "all Israel," the repeated focus on cultic items from Israel's wilderness traditions, the resulting parallels to David's inauguration of his reign, the description of his placement of the bronze altar in front of the Tabernacle, the transformation of the 1 Kgs 3:4b description of Solomon's general practices into a description of a concrete sacrifice by Solomon at Gibeon, and the recontextualization of that sacrifice as an effort to seek Yahweh: all of these elements combine to characterize Solomon and set the tone for his subsequent reign.

As a result of these shifts, the Gibeon story is enclosed, before and after, with narratives focusing on Solomon's participation in the cult. The Chronistic Gibeon story is preceded by this description of Solomon's first royal act: an assembly at the tent of meeting and sacrifice there. The Chronistic Gibeon story is followed by a description of God's fulfillment of the promise of riches (2 Chr 1:14-17) and Solomon's initiation of construction of the temple (2 Chr 2:1ff.). After a brief look at a later insertion into the Chronistic account of Solomon's sacrifice, we will turn to look at the story in between the cultic events, the epiphany where God provides for Solomon's temple building reign (2 Chr 2:7-12).

A Gloss in 2 Chr 1:6

The final form of the first sentence in 2 Chr 1:6 is almost unintelligible. The following is a translation slavishly following the existing word order of the sentence: "Solomon offered there on the bronze altar before the LORD which belonged to the Tent of Meeting." The relative clause "which belonged to the Tent of Meeting," would ordinarily modify the noun immediately preceding it, in this case "the LORD." But given the emphasis throughout the Hebrew Bible on God's transcendence of any cult place, it is much more likely that this relative clause was not meant to assert that God belonged to the Tent of Meeting, but that the bronze altar belonged there.

This irregularity suggests that some process of traditio-historical growth has separated the relative clause from its referent. The phrase "before the LORD" is the first candidate to be the cause of the problem,

---

154 For the Chronicler, the appropriate cultic items take precedence over place. Although offerings are offered in Jerusalem on the occasion of the delivery of the ark (1 Chr 16:1-2), the ongoing burnt offerings by Zadok and his brethren are done at Gibeon (1 Chr 16:39-40). Japhet, אמונות ודעות בספר דברי־הימים, 196-197.

since it now separates the relative clause from its referent. It could have been misplaced from an earlier point in the sentence or added on analogy to לפני משכן יהוה ("before the tabernacle of the LORD") in the preceding verse (2 Chr 1:5). But it is not clear why a glossator would make such an insertion, particularly since this insertion would divide an originally coherent phrase into unintelligible halves. Moreover, if a glossator added the phrase on analogy to "before the Tabernacle of the LORD," it is not clear why they chose the term "Tent of Meeting" at this point rather than "Tabernacle of the LORD."

Rather, the phrase אשר לאהל מועד ("which belonged to the Tent of Meeting") is more likely the later addition, added after the original clause in order to re-emphasize the stress in 2 Chr 1:3b on the Tent of Meeting. 2 Chr 1:3b stated that Solomon and the assembly traveled to Gibeon because the Tent of Meeting was there. Without the relative clause "which belonged to the tent of meeting," the original description of his activities at Gibeon did not mention the "Tent of Meeting." Therefore, the glossator made the connection explicit, claiming that the bronze altar "belonged" to the Tent of Meeting. At this point (2 Chr 1:6), however, the gloss mildly conflicts with the preceding verse (2 Chr 1:5a). Not only is the terminology different ("Tent of Meeting," "Tabernacle of the LORD"), but 2 Chr 1:5a implies that Solomon had *only recently* placed the bronze altar "*before*" the Tabernacle.

These syntactic and thematic tensions indicate the secondary character of the phrase אשר לאהל מועד ("which belonged to the Tent of Meeting"). The addition of this phrase disrupted the flow of the sentence into which it was inserted. Therefore, the glossator repeated the verb, preposition, and pronoun referring to the altar before giving the description of the extravagant number of burnt offerings which he offered there: ויעל עליו עלת אלף ("and he offered on it a thousand burnt offerings"). Despite the syntactic interruption (requiring *Wiederaufnahme*) and thematic tensions, the gloss is an extension of the Chronicler's own tendency to expand the Gibeon story at each juncture where it was possible to re-emphasize Solomon's link with the cultic implements of the wilderness period.

Initiation of the Epiphany and Petition Scene: 2 Chr 1:7

Deuteronomistic Gibeon Story	Chronistic Gibeon Story
1 Kgs 3:5	2 Chr 1:7
At Gibeon the LORD appeared to Solomon in a dream of the night and God said, "Ask what I should give you."	On that night God appeared to Solomon and said to him, "Ask what I should give you."

In contrast to the preceding section, the Chronicler's epiphany introduction is quite similar to that in 1 Kgs 3:5, and God's initiation of the petition scene is almost identical in both accounts. The most striking difference in the Chronistic epiphany introduction is its emphasis on the time when God appeared to Solomon. The 1 Kgs Gibeon story begins with an explicit emphasis on the *place* where the epiphany occurred, only mentioning the time at the end of 1 Kgs 3:5. This emphasis on place builds on the preceding description of the greatness of Gibeon (1 Kgs 3:4aβb). In contrast, the Chronicler begins by mentioning the time God appeared to Solomon—"in *that* night"— and does not mention the place. This emphasis on the idea that God appeared "that night" builds on the preceding description of Solomon's cultic activities: Solomon placed Bezalel's bronze altar before the tabernacle (2 Chr 1:5a), sought the LORD with the assembly (2 Chr 1:5b), and offered a thousand burnt offerings on that altar (2 Chr 1:6), and God appeared to him that very night.[155]

This mention of night is the only Chronistic reflection of the 1 Kgs 3 dream theme (cf. 1 Kgs 3:5a, 15a). Many have explained the absence of a dream notice in 2 Chr 1:7 as a reflection of the disrepute into which dreams fell in the post-exilic period. Beginning in the seventh century, prophets class dreams among the various types of foreign divination,[156] and later Biblical literature often uses dreams to symbolize that which is temporal and illusory[157] or frightening.[158] Given this background, the

---

[155] Ehrlich uses this half-verse to argue that the Gibeon story is an incubation account (*Der Traum im Alten Testament*, 21-22). Though the Chronicler connects a sacrifice by Solomon with God's appearance to him, the initiative remains God's in the Chronistic account. Moreover, the connection of epiphany and sacrifice are part of the Chronicler's overall emphasis on the cult. The Chronistic Gibeon story is not an incubation account.

[156] Deut 13:2-6; Jer 23:25-32; 27:9-10; Zech 10:2. Joel 3:1 presents the only clearly positive view of dreams among the later prophets. Cf. Gnuse, *The Dream Theophany of Samuel*, 85-88, for the texts and discussion.

[157] Job 20:8; Pss 73:20; 126:1. Also cf. Is 29:7-9.

Chronicler may have omitted the dream aspect of Solomon's epiphany as part of his general program of portraying Solomon positively. A much simpler explanation, however, would be that the dream notice did not serve the Chronicler's purposes. This is the first of several places in the story where the Chronicler simply omits parts of the Deuteronomistic account which did not fit his program.

Solomon's Petition: 2 Chr 1:8-10[159]

- *2 Chr 1:8*

Deuteronomistic Gibeon Story	*Chronistic Gibeon Story*
1 Kgs 3:6	2 Chr 1:8
Solomon said, "You have acted with great faithfulness towards your servant, my father David, when he walked before you in total loyalty and in integrity of heart with you, and you acted with great faithfulness toward him in the following way: You gave to him a son sitting on his throne as on this very day	Solomon said to God, "You have acted with great faithfulness towards my father David, and you made me king after him.

The same disregard for elements unessential to his program appears in the Chronicler's omission of many Deuteronomistic elements of 1 Kgs 3:6. Ackroyd suggested that the Chronicler eliminated the 1 Kgs 3:6 reference to David's obedience in order to imply that David's virtue was never in doubt.[160] Japhet, however, has shown that the Chronicler was systematically opposed to portraying Solomon as having any faults, but open to seeing fault in David.[161] Therefore, the Chronicler probably omitted the reference to David's obedience because it is irrelevant.[162]

---

[158] Job 7:13-14; Qoh 5:2, 6; Sir 31:1; 40:5-7. See Gnuse, *The Dream Theophany of Samuel*, pp. 101-105; Caquot, "Les songes et leur intrprétation selon Canaan et Israel," 118-120 for more discussion of post-exilic views of dreams.

[159] On this speech cf. most recently Throntveit, *When Kings Speak*, 55-56 who agrees with Curtis' assessment that the Chronicler appropriates the Deuteronomistic version of Solomon's speech "with no significant theological changes."

[160] Ackroyd, *I & II Chronicles*, 101.

[161] Japhet, אמונות ודעות בספר דברי־הימים, 393-401.

[162] This is a similar position to that of Abramsky, "שלמה המלך" 6, who argues that the Chronicler eliminates references to David in order to magnify Solomon. He points out that the Chronicler does not share the Deuteronomist's apparent need to place Solomon under David.

Instead the Chronicler focused his version almost exclusively on Solomon. Whereas 1 Kgs 3:6b presents God as being faithful to David by putting a *son* on the throne in his place, 2 Chr 1:8 portrays God as being faithful by putting *Solomon* on the throne.[163]

- *2 Chr 1:9a and 10a*

Deuteronomistic Gibeon Story	*Chronistic Gibeon Story*
1 Kgs 3:7	2 Chr 1:9a
And now, oh LORD, my God, you have made your servant king after my father David, but I am a little youth. I do not know how to go out or come in.	Now, oh LORD God, may your promise to my father David be confirmed.
1 Kgs 3:9a	2 Chr 1:10a
Give your servant a hearing heart in order to judge your people and to distinguish between good and evil.	Now, give me wisdom and knowledge And I will go out before this people and come in.

The Chronicler adapts Solomon's comments in 1 Kgs 3:7 about his youth. In the 1 Kgs 3:7b version, Solomon contrasts the great role which God has put him in with his youthful inability to fulfill that role. Such an emphasis on youthful inability contradicts the Chronicler's attempt to magnify Solomon. Therefore the Chronicler does not mention Solomon's youth in the speech at Gibeon, but instead uses Solomon's youth to justify David's preparations for the temple (1 Chr 22:5; 29:1). Thus, just as in the case of the sacrifices at Gibeon, the Chronicler does not omit, but adapts elements foreign to his program in order to serve that program.[164] This is even true for the part of 1 Kgs 3:7b not included in 1 Chr 22:5 and 29:1, that is Solomon's description of himself as not knowing how "to go out or come in" (לא אדע צאת ובא). The Chronicler's Solomon now uses

---

[163] This Chronistic interpretation of the Nathan oracle appears earlier in the Chronistic history in 1 Chr 22:9.

[164] This explanation contrasts with the approach of those who argue that the mention of youth and long life promise were omitted in order to avoid the impression that Solomon failed to fulfill the condition for long life in 1 Kgs 3:14a (Abramsky, "שלמה המלך," 6, gives this sort of argument). Such an approach would be more persuasive if such a condition were included in the Chronicler's account. One can not assume that the Chronicler presupposed that his accounts would be read in conjunction with those in 1 Kgs. On this latter point see Michael Fishbane's persuasive arguments in *Biblical Interpretation in Ancient Israel* (Oxford: Clarendon, 1985), 380-383.

this phrase to describe the capacities which he will have when God grants him wisdom (2 Chr 1:10aβ).

Rather than referring to his youthful inability to do his job, the Chronicler's Solomon asks that God's "word" to David be affirmed (יאמן דברך עם דוד אבי). As Mosis points out, this "word to David" is the Chronicler's way of referring to the Nathan oracle. The expression occurs in 1 Chr 17:23, 24; 2 Chr 1:9, and again in Solomon's prayer of dedication of the temple. This distribution indicates that the Chronicler understood the Nathan oracle ("God's word to David") as an unconditional promise that Solomon would build a dwelling place for God. 2 Chr 1:9-10 is Solomon's request that God fulfill a proximate goal of that promise by granting Solomon wisdom, a wisdom which will enable him to build the temple.[165] Because of this emphasis on wisdom for temple building, the Chronicler uses the more general terms חכמה ("wisdom") and מדע ("knowledge") to describe Solomon's request (2 Chr 1:10) rather than the legally oriented phraseology of 1 Kgs 3:9, לב שמע לשפט את־עמך להבין בן־טוב לרע ("a hearing heart in order to judge your people to discriminate between good and evil").[166] This temple centered character of Solomon's wisdom emerges again in Hiram's praise of Solomon's wisdom in 2 Chr 2:11.

Beginning with 2 Chr 1:10 we can see how the Chronicler has eliminated some of the "gaps" which characterized his precursor text (1 Kgs 3:2-15). In 1 Kgs 3:9, 11 and 12 there was a movement from obscurity to clarity in the description of Solomon's request. The 1 Kgs version progressed from an ambiguous term Solomon himself uses in his request (לב שמע: "hearing heart") to terms where God reveals the true nature of Solomon's request: הבין לשמע משפט ("discrimination to hear cases") and לב חכם ונבון ("a wise and intelligent heart"). In contrast, the Chronicler consistently describes Solomon's request in the same clear terms, as a request for חכמה ומדע ("wisdom and intelligence"). The 1 Kgs artful progression from human expression to divine clarification is not central to the Chronicler's purposes. Therefore, the Chronicler flattens the story out in order to more directly reveal God's favor for Solomon as the chosen temple builder.

---

[165] Mosis, *Untersuchungen zur Theologie des chronistischen Geschichtswerkes*, 131; Williamson, *1 & 2 Chronicles*, 195.

[166] Cf. Abramsky, שלמה המלך, 6, who argues that the word מדע was added to further emphasis Solomon's uniqueness.

• *2 Chr 1:9b and 10b*

Deuteronomistic Gibeon Story	*Chronistic Gibeon Story*
1 Kgs 3:8	2 Chr 1:9b
Your servant is in the midst of your people whom you have chosen, a great people who can not be counted or numbered because of their multitude.	For you made me king over a people as numerous as the dust of the earth.
1 Kgs 3:9b	2 Chr 1:10b
For who is able to judge this, your great people?	For who will judge this, your great people?

In 2 Chr 1:9b and 10b the Chronicler again molds elements from 1 Kgs so that Solomon's greatness is magnified. In 1 Kgs 3:8 Solomon says that he is *in the midst* of God's great chosen people. This assertion is part of his argument that he is incapable of fulfilling his vocation without God's help. The Chronicler modifies this to have Solomon assert that he has been *made king over* this great people. This statement enhances his prestige. Even the rhetorical question following Solomon's petition is different. 1 Kgs 3:9b has Solomon ask "For who is able to judge this great people?," but in 2 Chr 1:10b Solomon merely asks "For who will judge this great people?" The 1 Kgs version of the question assumes that no one, not even Solomon, is able to judge the Israelite people, while the Chronicles version presupposes that Solomon is the only one suited to judge them.

In addition, the Chronicler modifies or omits Deuteronomistic elements which do not contribute to his program. Instead of using the Deuteronomistic metaphor for the greatness of the Israelite people (1 Kgs 3:8: "who can not be counted [or numbered because of their multitude]"), the Chronicler uses the description of Israel also used in Jacob's dream at Bethel (Gen 28:14: "as many as the dust of the earth"). Williamson's careful analysis of the genealogies establishes the importance Jacob-Israel had for the Chronicler.[167] The Deuteronomistic election theme of 1 Kgs 3:8a is irrelevant to the Chronicler's program and therefore dropped.

---

[167] Williamson, *1 & 2 Chronicles*, 40-45, 195-196.

God's Response to the Petition: 2 Chr 1:11-12

• 2 Chr 1:11

Deuteronomistic Gibeon Story	*Chronistic Gibeon Story*
1 Kgs 3:10	
The thing pleased the LORD, that Solomon had asked this thing,	
1 Kgs 3:11	2 Chr 1:11
And God said to him, "because you requested this thing, and did not request many days for yourself and did not request riches for yourself, and did not request the life of your enemies, but you requested for yourself discrimination to hear cases,...	And God said to Solomon, "Because this was **in your heart**, and you did not request riches, possessions, glory, and the life of your haters and even many days you did not request, but you requested for yourself wisdom and knowledge so that you could judge my people over whom I made you king

The Chronicles version of God's response to Solomon does not have the emphasis found in 1 Kgs 3:11 on God rewarding Solomon for his virtuous rejection of things valued by non-Israelite kings and choice of wisdom. 1 Kgs 3:11 lists those things Solomon did not request before describing his request. As discussed above, the dominant feature of the list of non-requested items is that the Deuteronomist saw all these things as the priorities of pagan kings. Through consistent repetition of clauses using second masculine singular perfect forms of שָׁאַל ("request") the Deuteronomist grouped the non-requested items (valued by pagan kings) together and then contrasts them with Solomon's request.

The Chronistic version of God's response softens the contrast through omitting the intensive repetition which occurs in 1 Kgs 3:11. Though second masculine singular perfect forms of שָׁאַל ("request") are used to describe Solomon's refusal to request certain items, two things which characterized the 1 Kgs prologue do not appear. First, whereas in 1 Kgs 3:11 there is a one to one correspondence between verb form and non-requested item, in 2 Chr 1:11 the second masculine singular perfect forms of שָׁאַל ("request") are not repeated for each non-requested item. There are only two verb forms corresponding to five non-requested items. Second, in 1 Kgs 3:11 parallel forms and words are used to describe Solomon's petition for wisdom and refusal to request other items. In 2

Chr 1:11 Solomon's request is first described without any request language (היתה זאת עם־לבבך: "This was in your heart"), and at the end a
converted imperfect form is used to describe his request rather than the
perfect forms used to describe his lack of petition for other items. This
Chronistic lack of emphasis on Solomon's priorities is further highlighted
by the lack of any description of God's positive affective response to
Solomon's petition, a description which would correspond to 1 Kgs 3:10.
Such concerns are not primary to the Chronicler.

To be sure, the distinction between what Solomon requested and did
not request still appears in 2 Chr 1:11, but the Chronicler adds a distinction to the prologue which did not exist in his 1 Kgs 3:11 precursor.
Through use of only two verb forms in a chiastic arrangement ("You did
not request x, y, and z, and v and w you did not request") the Chronicler
divides the description of Solomon's refusal into two parallel lines, sepa-
rating the non-requested items into two categories:

1) Those non-requested items which God granted to Solomon—עשר
   ונכסים וכבוד ("riches, honor and possessions")

2) Those non-requested items which God never gave to Solomon—
   נפש שנאיך וגם־ימים רבים("the life of your haters and even many
   days").

The latter list, that of non-requested and non-granted items, is simply
taken from the 1 Kgs 3:11 precursor text. The only potentially significant
shift is that from 1 Kgs 3:11 איביך ("your enemies") to 2 Chr 1:11 שנאיך
("haters\enemies)."[168] Though שנא can also refer to enemies, this switch
is unprecedented in the Chronicler's adaptation of Deuteronomistic
materials.[169] Therefore the change may reflect a democratization of the
more exclusively royal image of victory over military opponents so that
the term could refer to ordinary people's enemies.

In contrast, the Chronicler has made some more interesting changes in
the list of non-requested items which God granted to Solomon. The first
and last parts of the triad עשר ונכסים וכבוד ("riches, possessions, and
honor") appear not only in God's following promise to Solomon but also
in the Chronicler's descriptions of other kings whom he favorably

---

[168] נפש שנאיך 2 Chr 1:11 for נפש איביך in 1 Kgs 3:11.

[169] Examples of אויב preserved in Chr include 2 Sam 5:20 (preserved in 1 Chr 14:11);
1 Kgs 8:33 (preserved in 2 Chr 6:24); 1 Kgs 8:37 (preserved in 2 Chr 8:28); 1 Kgs 8:44
(preserved in 2 Chr 6:34) and I Kgs 8:46 (preserved in 2 Chr 8:26). I could not locate
examples of Joshua-2 Kgs אויב being replaced by שנא in Chronicles, except the
parallel between 1 Kgs 3:11 and 2 Chr 1:11.

evaluates.[170] Moreover, it is God's gift of these items (2 Chr 1:14-17) which prepares him to begin assembling labor and materials to build the temple (2 Chr 1:18-2:17).[171]

2 Chr 1:12

Deuteronomistic Gibeon Story	Chronistic Gibeon Story
1 Kgs 3:12	2 Chr 1:12
Behold, I act according to your words.	
Behold I **give** you a wise and intelligent heart so that no one like you will have existed before you, nor after you will one arise like you.	Wisdom and knowledge **are given** to you,
1 Kgs 3:13	
Also that which you did not request I **give** you, both riches and honor, so that no one among the kings will be like you all your days.	and riches, possessions, and honor I **will give** to you such as no one among the kings has had before you and none shall have after you.
1 Kgs 3:14	
And if you walk in my Chronistic ways, observing my norms and commandments like your father David, I will lengthen your days.	

The Chronicler introduces a temporal distinction between God's two promises which did not exist in the 1 Kgs precursor text. In 2 Chr 1:11-12 God uses a passive participle to declare that Solomon *is given* wisdom and knowledge, but uses a prefix form of the verb נתן, אֶתֶּן to promise riches, possessions, and glory *in the future*. The implication of the contrast between participle and prefix form is that Solomon is already wise by the time God responds to his request. The fact that the right request was "in

---

[170] David - 1 Chr 29:12, 28; Jehoshaphat - 2 Chr 17:5, 18:1, Hezekiah-2 Chr 32:27). Thomas Willi, *Die Chronik als Auslegung: Untersuchungen zur literarischen Gestaltung der historischen Überlieferung Israels,* FRLANT 106 (Göttingen: Vandenhoeck & Ruprecht, 1972), 141.

[171] Clearly riches and possessions play a more central role in Solomon's preparation for temple building (2 Chr 1:14-17) than honor. The Chronicler may have included honor in this list because its precursor text describes God as promising Solomon honor.

[Solomon's] heart," already reveals his wisdom.[172] The Chronicler reflects this perspective when he replaces the demonstration in 1 Kgs 3:16-28 of Solomon's judicial wisdom with the description in 1 Kgs 10:26-29 of his wealth and fame. Solomon's wisdom has already been demonstrated. The sequel focuses on God's fulfillment of the future oriented promises given in 2 Chr 1:11-12.

In general, the Chronicler puts more emphasis on Solomon's wealth and honor than on his wisdom. In the Chronicler's account of Solomon's reign, only 2 Chr 1:12 and 2:11 mention Solomon's temple building wisdom. Outside of these sections the Chronicler does not mention Solomon's wisdom again, omitting sections from 1 Kgs such as 5:9-14.

In the Chronistic Gibeon story, Solomon's wisdom is no longer unique. The Chronicler combines elements from the two 1 Kgs incomparability formulae to describe the great incomparability of Solomon's riches, possessions and honor. The use of the verb היה ("be") and reference to kings in 2 Chr 1:12 corresponds to the 1 Kgs 3:13bα incomparability formula describing Solomon's wealth and honor. But the description of Solomon's riches, possessions, and honor as *eternally* incomparable corresponds to the 1 Kgs 3:12bβγ incomparability formula describing Solomon's wisdom. This mix of elements heightens the praise of Solomon's riches, possessions, and honor. In 1 Kgs 3:12-13, Solomon's wisdom is eternally incomparable, while his riches and honor are only incomparable during his lifetime. In contrast, 2 Chr 1:12 reverses the emphases of his precursor text. Now it is Solomon's riches, possessions and honor which are eternally incomparable, not his wisdom.

This temple focused emphasis on Solomon's wealth, possessions and honor explains the Chronicler's omission of any promise of long life. To be sure, Solomon's reign was not unusually characterized by long life. Since Solomon was young upon his accession to the throne (1 Kgs 3:7) and ruled the same length of time as David, he probably was not as old as David when he died. The Chronicler may have omitted the long life promise in order to avoid any implication that disobedience caused Solomon not to live a long time.[173] But the best explanation of the Chronicler's omission is that long life would not contribute to building

---

[172] The Chronicles version emphasizes Solomon's thoughts, not his action. In contrast, 1 Kgs 3:11 reads "Because you asked this thing."

[173] Abramsky, "שלמה המלך," 6. Note that 1 Kgs 3:14 does not promise an incomparably long life, but merely a longer life than Solomon would otherwise have enjoyed. In addition, the Chronicler could easily have included the promise without the stipulation.

the temple. The Chronicler's Gibeon story is about how Solomon was equipped to build the temple. Therefore, the Chronicler did not include any promise of long life.

Concluding Departure and Assumption of Rule: 2 Chr 1:13

Deuteronomistic Gibeon Story	*Chronistic Gibeon Story*
1 Kgs 3:15	2 Chr 1:13
Solomon awoke, and behold, it was a dream. He went to Jerusalem, stood before the ark of the covenant of the LORD, offered burnt offerings, performed communion sacrifices, and held a banquet for all his servants.	And Solomon went from the sanctuary which is at Gibeon Jerusalem from before the tent of meeting[174] and ruled over Israel.

The textual witnesses to the Chronicler's description of Solomon's destination after the Gibeon epiphany are quite varied. Nevertheless, all of the relevant textual traditions preserve the following components in varying relationships to one another: במה ("sanctuary"), גבעון ("Gibeon"), and ירושלים ("Jerusalem"). In any case, the location of the sanctuary is not so important, because this time Solomon is not sacrificing. The sacrifice and banquet description—elements of the ancient message epiphany form in 1 Kgs 3:15b—are no longer relevant to the Chronicler's purposes. Instead, the Chronicler replaces the description of sacrifices and the banquet with a brief note indicating the Gibeon epiphany's macrostructural function (2 Chr 1:13b): as the introduction to Solomon's reign.

---

[174] This translation follows that of Yéfet ben Ely, Abulwalid, and others (See Barthélemy, *Critique textuelle*, 475) which translates the preposition ל here as "from" rather than the more common "to, for." This translation corresponds to that of the Old Greek and Vulgate, both of which should probably be seen as translation rather than textual variants at this point.

The resulting parallel phrases—

"from the sanctuary at Gibeon Jerusalem,
from before the tent of meeting"

—correspond to the reading in 2 Chr 1:3 which locates both the Gibeon sanctuary and the tent of meeting in the same place.

Concluding Reflections

Context, Themes and Theology

In the history of scholarship, Chronicles has proven to be one of most difficult (set of) books to locate institutionally and historically. Nevertheless, recent studies of Chronicles have narrowed the dating range for Chronicles to sometime in the Persian period.[175] Scholars current with this information generally take one of two routes in locating Chronicles historically, the early Persian period or the late Persian period. Those arguing for the very early Persian period focus primarily on macro-indicators, such as the presence of prophetic forms and emphasis on prophecy in Chronicles, the focus on the Davidic dynasty, and similarities in views of retribution and the cult between Chronicles and Haggai-Zechariah.[176] Those scholars who argue for a dating late in the Persian period focus on micro-indicators: particular verses in Chronicles which must be dated late and thus require a late dating for the work as a whole. The two major indicators adduced for later datings are the genealogy in 1 Chr 3:17-24 and the reference to אדרכנים ("Darics") in 1 Chr 29:7.[177]

---

[175] William F. Albright, "The Date and Personality of the Chronicler," *JBL* 40 (1921): 104-124; Sara Japhet, "The Supposed Common Authorship of Chronicles and Ezra-Nehemiah Investigated Anew," *VT* 18 (1968): 330-371; H. G. M. Williamson, *Israel in the Books of Chronicles*; James D. Newsome, Jr., "Toward a New Understanding of the Chronicler and his Purposes," *JBL* 94 (1975): 201-215; David L. Petersen, *Late Israelite Prophecy: Studies in Deutero-Prophetic Literature and in Chronicles*, SBLMS 23 (Missoula, MT: Scholars Press, 1977), 57-58; J. R. Porter, "Old Testament Historiography," in *Tradition and Interpretation: Essays by Members of the Society for Old Testament Study*, ed. G. W. Anderson (Oxford: Clarendon, 1979), 152-154; William J. Dumbrell, "The Purpose of the Books of Chronicles," *Journal of Evangelical Theology* 27 (1984): 257-266. See the survey of literature in Roddy L. Braun's, "Chronicles, Ezra, and Nehemiah: Theology and Literary History," in *Studies in the Historical Books of the Old Testament*, ed. J. A. Emerton, VTSup 30 (Leiden: E. J. Brill, 1979), 52-64.

[176] David Noel Freedman, "The Chronicler's Purpose," *CBQ* 23 (1961): 436-442; Frank Moore Cross, "A Reconstruction of the Judean Restoration," *JBL* 94 (1975): 12-13 (for his Chr1); Petersen, *Late Israelite Prophecy*, 58-60; Porter, "Old Testament Historiography," 153-154; Newsome, "Toward a New Understanding of the Chronicler and His Purposes," 215-217.

[177] For the main arguments and survey of literature on 1 Chr 29:7 see Williamson's detailed discussion in "Eschatology in Chronicles," 123-125. Throntveit, *When Kings Speak*, 89-93, uses his own analysis of royal prayer to support Mosis' arguments that 1 Chr 29:1-9 is secondary. On this basis he argues that the reference to Darics in 1 Chr 29:7 is only relevant for dating a hierocratic revision of Chronicles, not the first edition (99).

In sum, though the options have been narrowed (to the early or late Persian period), no conclusive and more specific decision can be made about the date of Chronicles. Nevertheless, whether one opts for an early or late Persian period dating, in both cases Chronicles emerges as a text aiming to legitimate the institution of the Second Temple. This is obvious not only in the massive reorientation of the description of David and Solomon's reigns, but also in the scope of the work: from the creation of the world to Cyrus' decree to rebuild the temple.

The narrative genre in which Chronicles is written is well suited for legitimation rather than proclamation. As discussed above, Ancient Near Eastern history writing tended to legitimate political programs. The idealization of Solomon must be understood in this context. Though both the Chronicler and Messianic movements drew on a growing idealization of David in the Second Temple period, there are no clear indicators of Messianic emphasis in Chronicles.[178] Neither a future Messianic figure is predicted, nor are present rulers told to follow Solomon's example (compare this with the explicit legal thrust of Deuteronomy and the Deuteronomistic history).[179] Instead, David's and Solomon's reputations are enhanced to serve another end: legitimation of an existing institution, the Second Temple. Indeed, Solomon's growing prestige in the Second Temple period is not only enhanced, but reconstrued to focus ever more on his role in building the temple.

In Chronicles we see a reciprocal relationship between the temple emphasis and picture of Solomon: the temple is built up through Solomon, while Solomon is built up by virtue of his connection with the temple. Solomon's significance is not the only item whose significance is reconstrued in this relationship. The relative lack of independent emphasis on the Moses period and corresponding constant focus on relating David and Solomon to wilderness traditions (including the Moses/

---

[178] I am indebted for this insight (a revision from the original thesis) to Simon J. De Vries' article, "Moses and David as Cult Founders in Chronicles," *JBL* 107 (1988): 619-639.

[179] If Chronicles was written in the early Persian period during times of Messianic hope centering on Zerubbabel, the completely whitewashed picture of Solomon might be a bit too idealized to serve as a good model for comparison with an actually existing human ruler. Zerubbabel might come off rather badly in such a comparison despite his best efforts! For a story about Zerubbabel with intriguing parallels to the Gibeon story, see 1 Esdras 3:1-5:6. Whether or not this story was originally part of the Chronicler's history (Cf. Cross, "Reconstruction of the Judean Restoration," p. 12, note 47) it is a testimony to the centrality of Zerubbabel in Second Temple Jewish traditions and picture of him as a wise temple builder.

Joshua model) implies a corresponding transferal of Mosaic legitimacy to the Judean heirs of David and Solomon. Ackroyd suggests that the context for this emphasis on David and Solomon might have been a claim by the Judeans to be the true bearers of Mosaic traditions. The Judeans would be making this claim in opposition to a Samaritan emphasis on Moses and attempts to claim legitimation of their non-Jerusalemite cult from him.[180]

The overall effect of this effort to legitimize the Judean cult is to reemphasize the divine initiative present in the Vorlage and to divest the story of the ethical component so important to the Deuteronomistic editors of 1 Kgs 3:2-15. This emphasis on the divine initiative places God squarely behind Solomon's temple building effort, and by analogy, implies God's provision for the Second Temple building enterprise. In an attempt to counter Samaritan claims on Mosaic tradition, the Chronistic emphasis on God's favor for the Second Temple is funneled through the account of David and Solomon's reigns, an account which frequently emphasizes their connections to the wilderness period through the overall Moses/Joshua model and through individual narratives like 2 Chr 1:2-6. According to this presentation, Solomon is not great and favored by God because of his wisdom, riches, and honor per se or because of his general virtue, but only in so far as all these things are tools to build the temple, the true extension of the Mosaic wilderness traditions and locus of Solomon's greatness.

Stability and Adaptability in the Use of Tradition

- *Adaptability*

As has become clear in the above discussions, the Chronicler molded the Gibeon story into an etiology about how Solomon was equipped to build the temple. Now it begins with the inaugural act of Solomon's reign, a great assembly of all Israel and sacrifice at the site of the tabernacle and altar. Now God's gifts to Solomon at Gibeon are the wisdom, wealth, and honor needed to construct the glorious temple in Jerusalem. And now the basis of God's favor is God's promise to David that Solomon would build a dwelling place for God in Jerusalem. All elements which are irrelevant to or might detract from the picture of Solomon as the flawless temple builder have been omitted or adapted to magnify him.

---

[180] Peter R. Ackroyd, "The Theology of the Chronicler," *Lexington Theological Quarterly* 8 (1973): 107.

This new separate edition of the Gibeon story makes more radical innovations in the story than the redactional additions by the Adonai editor, and Deuteronomistic glossator. With the exception of the localization of the story at Gibeon, all traces of the original Gibeonite dream epiphany Vorlage—including the description of Solomon's general practices there, the dream, the promise of long life, and the concluding sacrifices—all these traces disappear in the story's further transmission through Kings and Chronicles.

- *Stability*

Despite these changes, the Chronicler preserves and adapts many other elements of the original account, including the petition scene structure, epiphany report, description of Solomon's cultic practices at Gibeon, and many more minor parts of the story. Like the later additions to the story in Kings (Adonai editor and Deuteronomistic glossator), the Chronicler enhances the positive aspects of the story's portrayal of Solomon. But whereas the earlier additions coped with possible negative aspects in the earlier editions by supplementing them, the Chronicler completely recontextualizes the positive evaluation of Solomon, adapting or eliminating parts of the story which disagreed with this recontextualization. Solomon's positive reputation in post-exilic Judaism is harnessed to serve the Second Temple enterprise, and everything in the Chronicler's description of him and his reputation is adapted toward that end.

Inter-textuality and Counter-textuality

In many ways, the Chronicler appropriates and adapts inter-textual moves already made in his 1 Kings 3 precursor. As in 1 Kings 3, the Gibeon story inaugurates Solomon's reign, but now Solomon inaugurates his reign with a sacrifice at Gibeon before God appears to him. As in 1 Kgs 3:6, Solomon refers to God's promise of a successor to David, but now the Chronicler refers to God's present need to fulfill a "word to David" that his successor would build God's temple (2 Chr 1:9a). 2 Chr 1:12b$\beta\gamma$ resembles 1 Kgs 3:12b$\beta\gamma$, 13b in its comparison of Solomon's greatness with that of other kings. Nevertheless, the formula in 2 Chr 1:12b$\beta\gamma$ is a combination of those in 1 Kgs 3:12b$\beta\gamma$, 13b and applies only to God's gift of riches, possessions and honor to Solomon. In sum, the Chronicler's appropriation of Deuteronomistic inter-textual moves is as creative as his appropriation of other elements in 1 Kgs 3:2-15.

In addition, the Chronicler omits or softens other Deuteronomistic inter-textual and counter-textual moves. The Deuteronomist repeatedly related Solomon to his father David, emphasizing the need for Solomon to be faithful like his father David. The Chronicler minimizes references to David and omits the ethical emphasis of the Deuteronomistic account. Similarly, the Chronicler softens the contrast of pagan and Israelite royal values in 1 Kgs 3:11. This example of Deuteronomistic counter-textuality (both against anti-Solomonic traditions and pagan values) was not central to the Chronicler's program. On the other hand, in his description of Solomon's reign as a whole, the Chronicler extended and deepened the Deuteronomist's attempt to temporarily neutralize anti-Solomonic traditions. The Deuteronomist postpones Solomon's apostasy and God's disapproval of Solomon until after his construction of the temple. Now the Chronicler's Solomon is completely unblemished. He continues to be faithful and enjoy divine favor even in the latter part of his reign.

In addition to adapting Deuteronomistic intertextual moves, the Chronicler has introduced some moves of his own. These new intertextual moves are concentrated in the Chronicler's description of Solomon's assembly of "all Israel" at Gibeon and inauguration of his reign with an extravagant sacrifice there. First, through referring to the Tent of Meeting, ark, tabernacle, and Bezalel's bronze altar, the Chronicler relates Solomon's inauguration of his reign to the cult of the wilderness period. Second, the assembly of "all Israel" and mention of wilderness cultic implements make Solomon's regnal inauguration parallel to David's assembly of "all Israel" and procession of the ark to Jerusalem. As mentioned previously, this link between David and Solomon is part of a larger Chronistic intertextual tendency to portray their relationship along the model of that between Moses and Joshua.

Though the Chronicler is creative and even innovative in adapting the intertextual aspects of 1 Kgs 3:2-15 and introducing new ones, the overall effect is not as radical as those introduced by the Deuteronomist. The Deuteronomist radically undermined and reconstrued a cultic royal ideology text. In contrast, the Chronicler merely *extended* the Deuteronomist's reading, concentrating on adaptation of those elements which contributed to the Chronicler's legitimation program.

The gloss of unknown origin at the end of 2 Chr 1:6a displays a similar stance with respect to the original Chronistic Gibeon story. As a result of this addition, the Chronistic description of Solomon's inauguration of his reign mentions the Tent of Meeting as both the reason for his trip to Gibeon (2 Chr 1:3b) and the location of his sacrifice (2 Chr 1:6a). Through mentioning the Tent of Meeting in connection with Solomon's sacrifice, the gloss tidies up the story. Moreover, it *extends* the already existing Chronistic emphasis on wilderness cultic implements.

JOSEPHUS[181]

As we turn to Josephus it is clear that we can not build on the same wealth of previous studies of Josephus' *Antiquities*, his picture of Solomon, or his interpretation of the Gibeon story. Therefore, our treatment of Josephus will be relatively brief, focusing in particular on how he deals with the fact that he (unlike the Deuteronomist or the Chronicler) now has two versions of the Gibeon story with which to work.

Structure

Josephus' *Jewish Antiquities* VIII:1-210 corresponds to 1 Kings 1-11. A diagram of the structure of this section follows (intra-book references by paragraph):

---

[181] The text basis for this section is the edition by H. St. J. Thackeray and Ralph Marcus, *Josephus: with an English Translation*, vol. 5, *Jewish Antiquities, Books V-VIII*, LCL, (Cambridge: Harvard University Press, 1958), 582, 584.

As indicated in the above structure diagram, Josephus' Gibeon story develops the theme of Solomon's youth already implicit in his 1 Kgs 3-11 precursor text. Ostensibly, Solomon is considered to be younger in 1 Kgs 3-10 than in 1 Kgs 11. Moreover, in 1 Kgs 3:7 Solomon mentions his youth near the beginning of his rule.

Josephus goes beyond his precursors, however, in making Solomon's youthful competence the major theme of his introduction to the first part of Solomon's reign. Josephus begins his description of Solomon by stressing that Solomon was a good and just ruler *despite his youth*, fulfilling his responsibilities with a care *characteristic of those much older than him*. The Gibeon story is now a demonstration of this general description. At the high point of the story Josephus mentions that Solomon did not ask for riches *as a youth would have done*. Rather, he asked for intellectual ability, thus proving his competence to both God and the reader. His subjects, however, were not privy to this nocturnal demonstration of Solomon's ability. Instead, they made fun of Solomon *"as of a boy"* when he asked that both the dead and the living child be brought to him in the judgment between the two prostitutes. But when he wisely found the true mother, the multitude obeyed him henceforth, being convinced of his godlike prudence and wisdom. Now that Solomon has demonstrated his competence and established his rule, Josephus turns to a less thematically unified paraphrase of 1 Kgs 4-10, the early good part of Solomon's reign. Then—unlike Chronicles—Josephus follows 1 Kgs 11 in describing the later bad part of Solomon's reign.

Interpretation of the Gibeon Story

Solomon's Youthful Competence: Antiquities VIII:21

3 Kgdms 3:1-3	2 Par 1:1	Josephus Antiquities VIII:21[182]
Having taken possession of the kingdom,	And Solomon, son of David, gained strength over his kingdom, and the Lord, his God, was with him and made him great in height.	Solomon, now having come into possession of the kingdom and his enemies having been punished,
Solomon made a marriage treaty with the Pharaoh, king of Egypt, and took Pharaoh's daughter, and led her into the city of David until he finished building his house, the house of the Lord, and the city wall surrounding Jerusalem. But the people were sacrificing on the high places because a house had not been built to the lord until then.		married the Pharaoh, king of Egypt's, daughter, and rebuilt the city wall of Jerusalem much greater and stronger than it had been.
And Solomon loved the Lord		He directed the rest of the state affairs in complete peace, Neither being prevented by youth from both righteousness and preservation of the laws
going in the orders of David, his father,		and, lastly, remembrance of those things which his father commanded, But completing all things like those who have achieved advanced years and attained great perfection.
but he sacrificed and burned incense on the high places.		

This first part of Josephus' introduction to Solomon's reign is composed of two lengthy clauses. The first clause builds on 1 Kgs 3:1, men-

---

[182] This translation and those used in the following columns are modified from the translation by Thackeray and Marcus, *Josephus*, vol. 5, 583, 585.

tioning Solomon's marriage to Pharaoh's daughter. Notably, Josephus does not appropriate the comments in 1 Kgs 3:1b about Solomon bringing Pharaoh's daughter into the city. Moreover, Josephus' account does not include any mention of sacrifice outside Jerusalem. Such issues do not contribute to Josephus' apparent intent to emphasize Solomon's youthful ability to rule. Rather than focusing on Solomon's behavior toward Pharaoh's daughter or on worship practices during his time, Josephus concentrates on how Solomon's success in domestic politics was followed by success in international politics.

The second of Josephus' two introductory clauses implicitly continues the theme of international politics by emphasizing the peaceful character of Solomon's rule:

> "Having rebuilt Jerusalem's wall to be much greater and stronger than it was before, he directed the rest of state affairs in complete peace..."

Similarly, Chronicles attributed Solomon's worthiness to build the temple to the peacefulness of his rule.[183] Such an emphasis on peace had new significance to Josephus as he wrote after the destruction of the Second Temple. Though he did not share Chronicles' emphasis on the temple, he developed the emphasis on peace. According to Josephus' account, Solomon's first royal act is a defensive military strategy, rebuilding Jerusalem's walls. Only then could he direct the rest of the state affairs ἐπὶ πολλῆς εἰρήνης ("in perfect peace").

Josephus continues his general characterization of the peaceful nature of Solomon's rule with a lengthy set of participial clauses which establish Solomon's youthful competence during his peaceful rule. The emphasis on his youth comes at the beginning and end of this set of clauses:

> Neither *being prevented by youth* from both righteousness and preservation of the laws and, lastly, remembrance of those things which his father commanded,
> But completing all things like those *who have achieved advanced years* and attained great perfection.

As mentioned above, this extension of the description of Solomon's rule doubly indicates the leading theme of the entire introduction to Solomon's rule: Solomon's youthful competence during the best years of his rule. Having introduced this theme, Josephus is now prepared to begin his version of the Gibeon story.

---

[183] See 1 Chr 22:7-10.

Reward for Sacrifice: Antiquities VIII:22

3 Kgdms 3:4	2 Par 1:2-6	Josephus Antiquities (beginning of) VIII:22
	And Solomon spoke to all Israel, to the commanders of thousands and the commanders of hundreds and the judges and all the rulers in the presence of Israel to the hereditary rulers.	
And he arose and went to Gibeon to sacrifice there	And Solomon and the entire assembly went to the high place at Gibeon	Having arrived at Gibeon,[184] he then decided to sacrifice to God
for it was the highest and greatest	where the Tent of Witness which Moses, servant of the Lord, made in the desert, was.	on the bronze altar built by Moses,
	But David had brought up the ark of God out of the town of Kiryat-Yearim, for he had prepared a tent for it in Jerusalem. And the bronze altar which Bezalel, son of Uri, son of Hur, had made, was there before the tent of the Lord, and Solomon and the assembly sought the Lord,	
	and Solomon went up there on the bronze altar before the Lord who was in the tent,	
Solomon offered up a thousand burnt offerings on the altar in Gibeon.	and offered up on it a thousand burnt offerings.	and he offered a burnt offering of a thousand victims.

Once again Josephus appropriates elements from his precursors as they serve his ends. In this case he follows the Chronicler more closely. Like the Chronicler, Josephus is more interested in characterizing

---

[184] Here I follow Thackeray, *Jewish Antiquities, Books V-VIII*, p. 583 in taking Josephus' Γιβρῶνα ("Hebron") as a scribal error or slip for Γαβαῶνα ("Gibeon").

Solomon through his sacrifice than in characterizing Gibeon. In particular, Josephus portrays God's appearance to Solomon as a reward for his piety shown in his sacrifice at Gibeon. Therefore, Josephus follows the Chronicler in depicting Solomon's practices at Gibeon as a concrete act prior to God's appearance to him, an act for which God rewards him.

Since the emphasis is on reward, Josephus gives a new prominence to Solomon's *intent* to sacrifice. The structure of Josephus' first sentence highlights this intent. The sentence begins with the verb stating the fact of his decision (ἔγνω—"He decided") and ends with the content of his decision: to sacrifice to God on the bronze altar built by Moses. This two part description of Solomon's decision surrounds a brief participial clause locating Solomon's decision after his arrival at Gibeon: εἰς Γαβαῶνα παραγενόμενος ("having arrived at Gibeon").

Josephus' description of Solomon's decision to sacrifice follows 2 Chr 1:5-6 over against 1 Kgs 3:4b. 1 Kgs 3:4b merely mentions that Solomon sacrificed on ההוא המזבח ("that altar"), while 2 Chr 1:6 specifies that Solomon sacrificed on the *bronze* altar made by Bezalel. Like Chronicles, Josephus specifies that the altar on which Solomon sacrificed was the bronze altar from the wilderness period, but unlike Chronicles, Josephus claims that the altar was made by Moses, not Bezalel. Moreover, Josephus never mentions the tent of meeting or ark, thus confining this partial contact with Chronicles to a place where Chronicles merely seems to specify an item already in the Kings account.

Josephus' emphasis on the great number of sacrifices which Solomon offered at Gibeon resembles 1 Kgs 3:4b. Whereas 2 Chr 1:6 (in the Old Greek and Hebrew) begins with the verb describing Solomon's act, 1 Kgs 3:4b and Josephus' description of Solomon's sacrifice put the object of the sacrifice first. Placing the great number of Solomon's sacrifices at the beginning of the sentence (front-extra position) emphasizes his extravagance and implies that Solomon is not only worthy of reward for deciding to sacrifice on the bronze altar, but also for deciding to sacrifice such a large amount.

In sum, Josephus' introduction to the Gibeon story focuses on preparing for God's appearance to him. This means that, on the one hand, he appropriates and extends elements from 2 Chr 1:3-6 and 1 Kgs 3:4 which help explain God's favor: the picture of Solomon's sacrifice as a concrete act in 2 Chr 1:6 and the emphasis on the great number of sacrifices in 1 Kgs 3:4b. On the other hand, Josephus omits elements from 1 Kgs 3:4 and 2 Chr 1:3-6 which are not required to explain God's favor. 1 Kgs 3:4 and 2 Chr 1:3-6 both begin by describing Solomon's trip to Gibeon, and then turn to the narrator's explanation of why Solomon went there. Josephus, however, only briefly mentions Solomon's trip to Gibeon, and he does not explain it. Moreover, he does not emphasize wilderness implements as much as Chronicles, and he does not portray Solomon's trip to Gibeon as a corporate act, the inauguration of his reign. All such elements have been eliminated from Josephus' streamlined description of Solomon's worthy sacrifice at Gibeon.

3 Kgdms 3:5	2 Par 1:7	Josephus Antiquities VIII:22 continued
		Having done this he seemed to have greatly honored God, for God
And God appeared to Solomon at night in sleep, and the Lord said to Solomon, "Make a request for yourself."	On that night God appeared to Solomon and said to him, "Request what I may give you."	—appearing to him during sleep that night— called on him to choose what gifts God might grant him in return for his piety.

Josephus shares and extends the Chronicler's emphasis on a connection between Solomon's worship at Gibeon and his dream there. Chronicles had made the connection through describing Solomon's extravagant sacrifice as a concrete act prior to his dream and then emphasizing that God appeared to Solomon *that* night. Likewise, Josephus describes Solomon's sacrifice as a concrete act and then uses the far demonstrative to stress that God appeared to Solomon the night after he sacrificed, φανεὶς γὰρ αὐτῷ κατὰ τοὺς ὕπνους ἐκείνης τῆς νυκτὸς ("For appearing to him *that* night during his sleep..."). But Josephus goes beyond Chronicles by explicitly asserting in two ways that God's open ended offer to Solomon was in return for Solomon's great sacrifice:

1)　Josephus claims that "having done *this* [offered a burnt offering of a thousand victims] Solomon seemed "to have greatly honored God" (τοῦτο δὲ ποιήσας μεγάλως ἔδοξε τὸν θεὸν τετιμηκέναι), for God appeared to him and called on him to choose his reward. Again, the item which begins the sentence shows its primary emphasis. In this case, Josephus begins his epiphany introduction with a pronoun, τοῦτο ("this"), which refers back to Solomon's extravagant sacrifice.

2)　In his description of God's offer to Solomon, Josephus does not quote it, but instead states that God commanded Solomon to ask for gifts which God might grant him *in return for his piety* (ἀντὶ τῆς εὐσεβείας). This note occurs at the end of Josephus' description of God's response to Solomon.

Thus both the beginning and end of Josephus' description of God's offer to Solomon emphasize that it was in response to his sacrifice.

Whereas the Chronicles description of God's appearance still left it to the reader to deduce the connection between his sacrifice and God's appearance to him, Josephus makes this connection explicit. Moreover, through making the divine response so explicitly conditional on Solomon's sacrifice, Josephus has transformed the Gibeon story into an incubation story. Since incubation was widely known in the Hellenistic world, it would be easy to see Solomon's night revelation following a sacrifice as an incubation. Such a narrative transformation of the Gibeon story seemed as fitting to Josephus as it presently does to contemporary scholars who see an incubation account in 1 Kgs 3:2-15//2 Chr 1:1-13.

Reward for Request: Antiquities VIII:23-24

3 Kingdoms 3:6-9	2 Par 1:8-10	Josephus Antiquities VIII:23
And Solomon said, "You have done great mercy toward your slave, my father David when he prevailed before you in truth and in righteousness and in honesty of heart with you.	And Solomon said to God, "O one who has done great mercy with my father David	
And you preserved for him this great mercy, to put his son on his throne as this day	you have also made me king in his place.	
and now, Lord my God,	And now, Lord God, may your word to my father David be trustworthy for you have made me king	
you have set your slave in place of my father David and I am a small child and do not know my exit and entrance. But your slave is in the midst of your people whom you chose a great people who can not be counted	of a people great as the dust of the earth.	

		Then Solomon requested the best and greatest gifts, both most pleasant for God to grant and most profitable for humans to receive (for he did not request either gold or silver or other riches to which a person and a young one would have deemed worthy to attach himself (for these things are considered by most as almost the only things worthy of effort and of being gifts of God)),
And you will give your slave a heart	Now, give me wisdom and intelligence,	but "Give me," he said, "O Lord, a healthy mind and good understanding with which I might judge this people, having comprehended truth and righteousness."
to hear and judge your people in righteousness and then to distinguish between good and evil.	and I will go forth before this people and come in.	
For who will be able to judge this your troublesome people?	For who will judge this your great people?	

The other versions of Solomon's speech included long prologues where Solomon described his special need for ability to rule. Josephus' version moves directly to a description of Solomon's request, eliminating his skillful justification of his request. Letting the suspense build, Josephus says that Solomon asked for the "τὰ κάλλιστα καὶ μέγιστα καὶ θεῷ παρασχεῖν ἥδιστα καὶ λαβεῖν ἀνθρώπῳ συμφορώτατα (the best and greatest things, both most pleasant for God to grant and most profitable to humans to receive)," without specifying what these "great and beautiful things" are.

Once again Josephus is making explicit the connections between each event in the narrative. Previously he added an explanation of the divine appearance and open offer to Solomon. Now he is anticipating an explanation of God's extra promises to Solomon. As such, this explanation corresponds to God's own explanation of God's extra gifts in the divine speech prologues in 1 Kgs 3:11 and 2 Chr 1:11.

The parallels with 1 Kgs 3:11 and 2 Chr 1:11 are even more evident in the next clause. Here Josephus describes those things Solomon did not request. Unlike the lists of unrequested items in 1 Kgs 3:11 and 2 Chr 1:11, Josephus merely mentions one type of item: riches. Notably, this is the crucial point where he mentions Solomon's youth again. For Josephus emphasizes that Solomon is unlike most people, particularly youth, in not asking for riches. This is a democratization of the original point of the Deuteronomistic note in 1 Kgs 3:11. Whereas the Deuteronomistic note praised Solomon's difference from neighboring *kings*, Josephus praises his difference from humans in general and youth in particular.

Only after this long introduction does Josephus finally return to Solomon's request and specify the wonderful thing which he requested. According to Josephus' account, Solomon asked that God give him a νοῦν ὑγιῆ καὶ φρόνησιν ἀγαθήν (a healthy mind and good understanding (or prudence)) "with which I might judge this people, having comprehended truth and righteousness." This request resembles 1 Kgs 3:9 more than 2 Chr 1:10. The resemblance is particularly significant since Josephus describes God's promise of wisdom and honor in a way more similar to 2 Chr 1:12 (especially Old Greek), than to 1 Kgs 3:12.[185]

Josephus, however, does not describe Solomon's request in a way completely identical to that of 1 Kgs 3:9. First, the description of Solomon requesting φρόνησιν ("understanding") in Josephus' builds on the proto-"Lucianic" reading for 3 Kgdms 3:9 καρδίαν φρονίμην τοῦ ἀκούειν ("an understanding heart in order to hear").[186] Josephus' addition of the adjective ὑγιῆ ("healthy") conforms the passage to his summary of David's prayer for Solomon,[187] and thus continues a process of elucidation of 1 Kgs 3:9 through correlation with other texts in the Biblical narrative. Through adapting the difficult reference in 1 Kgs 3:9 to a "hearing heart," Josephus stands in continuity with 2 Chr 1:10. Moreover, his portrayal of Solomon as fulfilling the wishes of his father,

---

[185] Harry E. Faber van der Meulen, "Das Salomo-Bild im hellenistisch-jüdischen Schrifttum," (Ph.D. diss., Kampen, 1978), 84.

[186] This Lucianic reading is an assimilation to the Old Greek description of God's promise of wisdom to Solomon. For an argument for Josephus' dependence on a Greek text of Samuel close to that of the proto-"Lucianic" cf. Eugene Charles Ulrich, Jr., *The Qumran Text of Samuel and Josephus*, HSM 19 (Missoula, MT: Scholars Press, 1978), passim, but particularly the conclusion, 457-459.

[187] *Antiquities* 7 § 381 summary of 1 Chr 29:11-19. Van der Meulen, "Das Salomo Bild," 83.

David, is particularly close to the Chronicles picture of Solomon's continuation of David's legacy.[188] Specifically, just as the Chronicler's Solomon asks at Gibeon that God's word to David through Nathan be fulfilled, so Josephus' Solomon requests the very thing David requested from God for him.

3 Kingdoms 3:10-14	2 Par 1:11-12	Josephus Antiquities VIII:24
And it was pleasing before God that Solomon requested this thing And the Lord said to him, "On account of the fact that you requested this thing from me, and did not request for yourself many days, nor did you request riches nor did you request the life of your enemies, but you requested understanding to hear cases	And God said to Solomon, "On account of the fact that this was in your heart, and you did not request riches, possessions, neither glory nor the life of your enemies, and you did not request many days, and you requested for yourself wisdom and intelligence in order that you might judge my people over whom I have made you king.	God was pleased with these requests,

---

[188] Van der Meulen claims that Josephus' model for Solomon was Seneca's Lucilius ("Das Salomo-Bild," 85). Though this attempt to explain the appropriation of one tradition (1 Kgs 3:9), rather than another (2 Chr 1:10) is a praiseworthy advance over mere observation, van der Meulen goes farther than necessary for his explanation. As van der Meulen himself observes, Josephus' version of the request has clearer relationships with passages in Josephus himself. Moreover, his use of 1 Kgs 3:9 as a multivalent pivot point for further reflection is in continuity with the interpretation history of 1 Kgs 3:9.

Behold I have done your word, Behold I have given you an intelligent and wise heart so that one like you has not been born before you and after you none will arise like you.	Wisdom and intelligence I give to you	and promised to give him in addition to what he had chosen,
And that which you did not request I have given to you both riches and glory	and riches, possessions, and glory I will give to you	all the other things which he did not mention: wealth, honor, victory over enemies, and, above all, intelligence
so that no one like you has been born among the kings.	such as never has existed among the kings before you and after you will not exist.	and wisdom such as no one had ever had, neither king, nor commoner. Then he promised to guard the kingdom for his descendants a very long time if he remained righteous and obeyed God and imitated his father in those things he was best.
And if you go in my way guarding my commandments and statutes as your father David did, I will multiply your days.		

Josephus follows 1 Kgs 3:10 over against Chronicles in adding a brief note about God's reaction to Solomon's request. Josephus has already shown a tendency to explain the divine reaction to Solomon in his description of God's appearance and offer to Solomon. Moreover, he has already explained much of the divine response through his initial description of the virtues of Solomon's request. 1 Kgs 3:10 provides a convenient model for the continuation of this already existing tendency to explicate the narrative joints of the story. The structure of Josephus' explanation of God's extra promises resembles that of his explanation of God's initial appearance and open offer: both explanations begin with a near demonstrative pronoun, τοῦτο/τούτοις ("this thing/these things") which refers to a preceding action by which Solomon pleased God. Josephus then notes that the action pleased God and describes God's reward for the action.

In his description of God's promise to Solomon Josephus continues his tendency to paraphrase rather than quote. This allows him to emphasize that the noteworthy aspect of the divine response to Solomon was God's promise of items which Solomon did not request. Josephus only peripherally notes that God fulfilled Solomon's request. Instead he emphasizes that God promised him additional things: riches, honor, victory over enemies, and above all, incomparable wisdom. Not only does this list of additional gifts include military victory (not seen in either Kings or Chronicles), but *wisdom* is among the non-requested things which God grants. In contrast to Chronicles, Josephus preserves the distinction between the descriptions of Solomon's request present in the various layers of 1 Kgs 3:9, 11, and 12. Though Solomon asked for a "healthy mind and good understanding" (corresponds to "hearing heart" in 1 Kgs 3:9), God provided him with intelligence and wisdom (= 1 Kgs 3:12). Moreover, whereas in Chronicles everything *but* Solomon's wisdom was incomparable, in Josephus *only* Solomon's wisdom is incomparable.

Josephus draws heavily on 1 Kgs 3:14 for the end of his description of God's response: God promises to preserve the kingdom for Solomon's descendants if he continues to be righteous and imitate his father in those things in which he was best. Nevertheless, this promise differs from 1 Kgs 3:14 in its promise of a long dynasty rather than long life.[189] Since Solomon was not distinguished by a long life, but did have a long dynasty, this was Josephus' way of adapting the promise so that it came true. In addition, though modifying the divine promise so that it conforms to known history, Josephus preserves and strengthens the conditional element of 1 Kgs 3:14a, an element which agrees with his overall emphasis on divine reward and retribution.

Solomon's Response: Antiquities VIII:25

3 Kingdoms 3:15	2 Par 1:13	Josephus Antiquities VIII:25
And Solomon awoke, and behold a dream, and he got up and went to Jerusalem and stood before the ark of the covenant of the Lord in Zion and	And Solomon went from Maba which is in Gibeon which is in Jerusalem to before the Tent of Witness.	Having heard these things from God, Solomon immediately leaped from his bed. After doing obesience to God, he returned to Jerusalem,
and offered up burnt offerings and made peace offerings and held a great drinking party for himself and all his servants.	And ruled over Israel.	and after offering great sacrifices before the tabernacle, entertained his entire household.

---

189 This shift is not a reflection of messianism. Josephus takes care to specify that the dynasty will be preserved "ἐπὶ πλεῖστον χρόνον (for the longest time)," but not forever.

Finally, the conclusion to Josephus' account is very similar to 1 Kgs 3:15.[190] Once again Josephus initiates a new section with a near demonstrative, ταῦτα ("these things"), this time referring to God's preceding promises to Solomon. Solomon responds to these promises by worshiping God, returning to Jerusalem, and offering sacrifices and a banquet for his servants. As in his description of the divine promise, Josephus contradicts the Chronicles account. Whereas Chronicles specified that Solomon went *from* the Tent of Meeting, Josephus explicitly notes that Solomon returned to Jerusalem and to the great tent (σκηνῆς μεγάλας), the Tabernacle.

Concluding Reflections

Context, Themes and Theology

Josephus' work is not nearly as difficult to locate historically or institutionally as Chronicles. He explicitly states that the work was completed in 93-94CE (20:267). Standing just after the destruction of the Second Temple, though written by a Second Temple Jew, Josephus' version of the Gibeon story stands in the trajectory of previously discussed retellings of the Gibeon story. Like those versions, the Gibeon story is adapted for nationalistic and didactic purposes. After the disastrous war of independence, Josephus aims to demonstrate to gentile readers that Jewish history is characterized by high ideals, only lost when the nation attempted revolt against Rome. In the interests of nationalism Solomon is magnified as a culture hero. This must be understood within the context of his claim in Contra Apionem that famous Jews "are entitled to rank with the highest." Josephus makes this claim against Apion's arguments that the Jews have not produced any great thinkers, inventors, or sages. Feldman and van der Meulen painstakingly demonstrate a number of ways Josephus' picture of Solomon has been carefully tailored to present him as an Israelite figure who deserves rank with the greatest Greek thinkers. The Gibeon story is part of this nationalistic effort.[191]

---

[190] The difference is that Solomon jumps from his bed and does obeisance to God before returning to Jerusalem. Also, he sacrifices in front of the tabernacle instead of the ark.

[191] Louis H. Feldman, "Josephus as an Apologist to the Greco-Roman World: His Portrait of Solomon," in *Aspects of Religious Propaganda in Judaism and Early Christianity*, ed. Elizabeth Schussler-Fiorenza (Notre Dame, IN: University of Notre Dame Press, 1976), 69-98; van der Meulen, "Das Salomo-Bild," passim.

Solomon, however, is not just a nationalistic hero. Rather, his story occurs in a work designed on the model of the classical histories, such as that of Rome by Diodorus of Sicily. In the prologue to the *Antiquities*, Josephus indicates that, like the classical histories, his work is designed to not only inform, but morally instruct. Specifically, he tells the reader in his introduction that the main lesson to be learned is the following:

> I:14
>> That those who follow the will of God closely and do not attempt to transgress laws that have been well ordained, succeed in all things beyond belief, and happiness from God lies ahead as their prize;
>> Whereas insofar as they withdraw from carefully paying attention to these laws, the possible becomes impossible, and whatever thing they ever strive hard to do as good, is changed into an irretrievable disaster.

In order to illustrate the first half of this thesis, Josephus uses prominent Biblical figures as models of moral behavior and resulting divine reward.[192] Thus the young Solomon serves as an example of rewarded virtue, while the apostate Solomon is an example of how impiety turns incredible good fortune to disaster.

As part of his transformation of the Gibeon story into a didactic tale, Josephus' divides it into two sequences of virtue and reward. The divine speech prologues in 1 Kgs 3:11 and 2 Chr 1:11 already implied a distinction between the divine favor shown in promising non-requested items and the favor shown in God's initial open offer. Josephus, however, goes beyond his precursors in dividing the story into two parallel sequences, each of which contain the following elements:

1) An account of a virtuous act by Solomon. Here the description of the act is already tailored to show why God was pleased with it.

2) A note that God was honored/pleased by the action. Both notes begin with a near demonstrative referring to Solomon's action.

3) A description of God's reward for the action.

The first sequence begins with Josephus' streamlined description of Solomon's sacrifice on Moses' bronze altar. Following the model of 1 Kgs

---

192 Harold Attridge, *The Interpretation of Biblical History in the Antiquitates Judaicae of Flavius Josephus*, HDR 7 (Missoula, MT: Scholars Press, 1976); "Historiography," in *Jewish Writings of the Second Temple Period: Apocrypha, Pseudepigrapha, Qumran Sectarian Writings, Philo, Josephus*, ed. Michael Stone, vol. 2 of *The Literature of the Jewish People in the Period of the Second Temple and the Talmud*, CRINT, section 2 (Assen: Van Gorcum and Philadelphia: Fortress, 1984), 210-227.

3:10, Josephus then mentions that Solomon pleased God so much by this sacrifice that God appeared to him and commanded him to name his reward. The second sequence begins with Josephus' lengthy description of Solomon's request for a "sound mind and good understanding." Here Josephus moves the contents of God's positive description of Solomon's petition from the divine speech (as in 1 Kgs 3:11; 2 Chr 1:11) to his own description of Solomon's request. Then he inserts a comment that God was pleased by Solomon's action and concludes with a description of the divine reward. Through this narrative transformation Josephus produces two didactic sequences from one story. Both demonstrate his central thesis that God rewards those who follow God's will. Josephus' adaptation of God's conditional promise in 1 Kgs 3:14 is part of the same effort to show how God can be trusted to reward virtue.

In sum, Josephus applies a clear ethical orientation to the Gibeon story, making the Gibeon story into a lesson in being a good Jew through not assimilating to the drive for riches of the majority. Overall, he transforms the story into a double example of how God rewards virtue. This modification of the Gibeon story into an ethical lesson diminishes the royal and theocentric emphases of the Vorlage, Deuteronomistic edition, and 2 Chronicles. In contrast to both Kings and Chronicles, Josephus' Gibeon story does not have as one of its primary aims the legitimation of an existing or future socio-religious system. Its focus is almost exclusively on the correct moral priorities of the individual.

Stability and Adaptability in Use of Tradition

- *Adaptability*

Because of its genre as didactic history, Josephus' retelling of the Gibeon story is less closely connected to its sources than the versions of the 1 Kings and 2 Chronicles accounts or even the 2 Chronicles account in relation to 1 Kings. Josephus omits many items from the Kings and Chronicles accounts which do not contribute to his aim of instruction. Some of these items are minor, such as the mention of bringing Pharaoh's daughter into the city until the palace and temple were finished (1 Kgs 3:1b). Other omissions are more major: elimination of any note about Solomon's and the people's worship practices, lack of explanation of his trip to Gibeon, removal of both the prologue and epilogue from Solomon's petition, and the absence of an independent account of God granting Solomon's petition. Clearly, Josephus felt the freedom not to mention parts of the story which did not serve his purposes.

Though Josephus eliminates some significant parts of the Gibeon story, he takes steps not to contradict his precursors. Thus, when he quotes Solomon's request, he follows the Lucianic text fairly closely. In narrative, exact repetition is presumed to be possible with quotes of speech, while different words are expected with description of actions.[193] Josephus gives himself room to maneuver by turning most of the Gibeon story speeches into actions, paraphrasing rather than quoting them. In that way he highlights those items he considers most significant, while not conspicuously deviating from his Biblical precursors. As a result, the only elements of the Gibeon story speeches which remain are God's initial offer, Solomon's actual request (without the rationale), and God's promise of non-requested items. Everything else is superfluous for his purposes.

Josephus' description of Solomon's request is a good example of how his principle of didactic selectivity works. Whereas Solomon's speech in 1 Kgs 3:6-8, 9b and 2 Chr 1:8-10, 11b specified that he needed wisdom specifically to fulfill his royal duties, Josephus eliminates that rationale and adds a comment implying that though most people would not have requested such wisdom, they should have. Through such a maneuver Josephus widens the applicability of Solomon's example. Solomon is not just an example of a good king, but of a good person.

Another way Josephus intervenes in the story is through introducing explanations at each narrative juncture. His Biblical precursors had explanations of God's response inserted into the divine speech itself (1 Kgs 3:11/2 Chr 1:11) and immediately prior to it (1 Kgs 3:10). Josephus, however, goes beyond his precursors, in explaining each narrative transition and having the narrator (himself) do that explaining. Josephus leaves nothing to chance. Where 1 Kgs 3:2-15 and 2 Chr 1:1-13 allowed the reader to fill many of the narrative gaps, Josephus repeatedly intervenes, making sure that the reader makes the connection between Solomon's virtuous acts and God's rewards.

As in Auerbach's contrast between Genesis 22 and Homer's digression on Odysseus' scar, here we have a contrast between a Biblical narrative "fraught with background" and a Hellenistic version of it which foregrounds all the missing connections.[194] Specifically, it is the Hellenistic genre of didactic history which is operative here. Following

---

193 Sternberg, *The Poetics of Biblical Narrative*, 405-406.

194 Eric Auerbach, *Mimesis: The Representation of Reality in Western Literature* (Garden City, NY: Doubleday & Co., 1957), 1-20.

the norms of that genre, Josephus must make explicit the connections between virtue and reward for the Gibeon story to be an effective ethical lesson.

- *Stability*

Already while discussing "adaptability" we have mentioned ways Josephus preserved elements of his precursor's while adapting them. Thus many of his inserted explanations merely make previously implicit connections explicit. Moreover, in adding narrative explanations, Josephus merely followed and extended the model of the description of God's response in 1 Kgs 3:10. Josephus' parallel sequences of virtuous act - reward correspond to the implicit distinction in 1 Kgs 3:11/2 Chr 1:11 between God's initial favor of an open offer and God's promise of non-requested items. In some cases, such as his appropriation and adaptation of God's conditional promise of long life, Josephus preserves elements of 1 Kgs 3:2-15 that were not preserved in 2 Chr 1:1-13. Overall, however, Josephus' version is more ruthless than Chronicles in its elimination of many elements from the Gibeon story which did not serve his aims.

As we turn to examine those items which Josephus does preserve, we find that he relies more on the 1 Kgs 3:2-15 version than on 2 Chr 1:1-13. Unlike Chronicles, he includes mention of Pharaoh's daughter, building the city wall, the distinction between Solomon's request and God's promise of wisdom, and—most of all—the conditional character of God's favor for Solomon. Clearly the ethical emphasis of the Deuteronomistic Gibeon story was more amenable to Josephus' didactic aims than the cultic interests of the Chronicles account.

The one area where Josephus most draws on Chronicles is the separate Chronistic account of Solomon's sacrifice. This part of the Chronicles account is the cornerstone of Josephus' double sequence of virtue - reward. In Josephus, however, Solomon's sacrifice is a virtuous act by him alone, not an assembly and inauguration of his reign parallel to the inauguration of David's reign. As elsewhere, Josephus eliminates all elements of 2 Chr 1:2-6 which are superfluous to his purposes, including the presence of the Tent of Meeting and assembly of "all Israel."

Inter-textuality and Counter-textuality

Two factors make Josephus' intertextual situation decisively different from that of the Deuteronomist and Chronicler. First, Josephus combines two narrative precursors. Already in combining these narratives Josephus is making intertextual moves. Specifically, he draws primarily on the ethically focused 1 Kgs account, while using the 1 Chr 1:2-6 description of Solomon's sacrifice to complete his two part scheme of virtue-reward.

Second, Josephus does not limit himself to making connections to inner-Israelite literature. For example, Josephus makes the Gibeon story into a Greek incubation account through making God's night appearance an explicit reward for Solomon's sacrifice. In addition, he explicitly appropriates the Greek genre of didactic history to tell the Biblical story. The Gibeon story now functions in that history as an example of rewarded virtue.

In telling the Gibeon story as an example of rewarded virtue, Josephus focuses more on making the inner connections of the story clear than on making new connections between the story as a whole and an overarching narrative. On the one hand, he intervenes at narrative junctures inside the Gibeon story in order to make explicit the move from Solomon's virtue to God's reward. This is essential for his didactic aims. On the other hand, his single significant inner-Biblical intertextual innovation is modeling Solomon's request to agree with (Josephus' version of) David's prayer for him.

Finally, Josephus' treatment of Solomon's youth is so creative as to be almost counter-textual. His precursors treated Solomon's youth as a weakness. In the Vorlage and Deuteronomistic account, Solomon justified his request by contrasting his youthful inability with the great royal duties God had imposed on him. The Chronicler moved references to Solomon's youth to an explanation of why David made preparations to build the temple (1 Chr 22:5; 29:1). Mention of Solomon's youthful inability in 2 Chr 1:1-13 would have detracted from the Chronicler's attempt to magnify him as the chosen temple builder. In contrast, Josephus transforms Solomon's youth into an occasion to magnify praise of Solomon's competence. According to Josephus, Solomon was not only extremely competent, but he was competent *despite his youth*. As described above, this theme of youthful competence then becomes a major theme of Josephus' entire introduction to Solomon's reign.[195]

---

[195] See above, p. 115.

Chapter Six

INTERPRETATIONS IN INSTRUCTIONS

The narrative interpretations of the Gibeon story discussed in the previous chapter all retell the story within the context of histories of Israel. In the pilgrimage of the story from the Vorlage to Josephus, almost every interpretation on the one hand theocentrically emphasizes the divine initiative and on the other hand enhances Solomon's reputation as a culture hero. Moreover, there is a trend, from the Adonai editor onward, to emphasize aspects of the story which can make it serve as a moral example to individuals (not just kings). In other words, the story gradually changes from a document about royal ideology to a didactic piece about the technology of wisdom, how an individual gets what the rest of the world values by seeking divine wisdom (however wisdom is defined by the interpreter in question).

THE INSTRUCTION GENRE

To a large extent, genre limits the extent to which such interpretations adapt or downplay aspects of the story which do not promote such theological, nationalistic and didactic aims. Each of the successive additions to the Vorlage seem to be inserted between progressively larger structural units in the forming story, until things are merely tacked on the beginning. Chronicles rewrites and reconceptualizes the Gibeon story, making it into a paired account of Solomon's cultic inauguration of his reign and God's epiphanic endowment of the items needed to build the temple. Josephus' version maintains Chronicles' two part structure, but transforms the Gibeon story into a two-part didactic lesson for individuals about virtue and reward, in particular the benefits of youthful competence.

The instruction was another generic context for the retelling of the Gibeon story. Whereas histories are formulated in third person and have the implicit claim to authority of such a narrative style, instructions are formulated in first person and claim the authority of the ancient sage. Most of the exemplars of this genre are Egyptian, but a significant number of examples occur elsewhere as well.[196] Almost all begin with titles identifying the following text as an instruction and ascribing the text to an ancient king, bureaucrat or sage.[197] The title adds legitimacy and authority to the following instruction by presenting it as a product of a respected sage. Though some instructions were probably written by the sage to whom they were ascribed, many others probably claim this authority pseudo-epigraphically.[198]

---

[196] John Kloppenborg, *The Formation of Q: Trajectories in Ancient Wisdom Collections*, Studies in Antiquity and Christianity 1 (Philadelphia: Fortress, 1987), 276, lists Shuruppak (Sumerian/Akkadian), the Counsels of Wisdom, Shube-awilum, Advice to a Prince, and the Counsels of a Pessimist (Babylonian), Ahiqar (Aramaic - Syriac), and Proverbs 1-9; 22:17-24:22, 23-34; and 31:1-9.

Advice to a Prince does not appear to be an instruction. It has no title and its sections are not formulated in the second person.

[197] Egyptian instructions with titles include: Hardjedef, Ptah-Hotep, Merikare, Amen-em-het, Khety (Title includes setting), Ani, and Amen-em-opet. Two Ptolemaic Egyptian instructions have multiple titles indicating a system of subsections, Anksheshonq and Papyrus Insinger. The Instruction of Kagemeni lacks a title.

Non-Egyptian instructions with titles include: Ahiqar, Proverbs 1-9, Instruction of "The Sages" (Prov 24:23-34), and Instruction of Lemuel (Prov 31:1-9). The Israelite adaptation of the Amen-em-opet instruction (Prov 22:17-24:22) does not have a title. The Mesopotamian exemplars—The Instruction of Shuruppak, Counsels of Wisdom and Counsels of a Pessimist—do not have such a title. The Instruction of Shuruppak describes the text and attributes it in the quote introduction (Lines 1-3 of the Sumerian; 1-2 of the Akkadian version). If K13770 is the beginning of the Counsels of Wisdom, it includes a narrative description of the instruction process and admonition to pay attention to the instructor. Otherwise, Counsels of Wisdom lacks its beginning and any counterpart to a title. The beginning of Counsels of a Pessimist is not preserved.

[198] Hellmut Brunner, "Die Weisheitsliteratur," in *Handbuch der Orientalistik*, vol. 1, *Ägyptologie*, part 2, *Literatur*, (Leiden: E. J. Brill, 1952), 92-93; Kloppenborg, *The Formation of Q*, 275; Hans Heinrich Schmid, *Wesen und Geschichte der Weisheit: Eine Untersuchung zur alteorientalische und israelistischen Weisheitsliteratur*, BZAW 101 (Berlin: Töpelmann, 1966), 9-13.

In the simplest instructions, a quote of the instruction from the sage follows the title.[199] In several texts, however, this instruction begins with narrative descriptions (with the sage spoken of in the third person) of the setting of the instruction[200] or its aftermath.[201] Egyptian instructions often conclude with a colophon and a blessing or indication of the intended effect of the instruction. Non-Egyptian instructions, however, do not seem to have had such a typical conclusion.[202]

Judging from the content of the admonitions, instructions were created in a variety of institutional situations. Though some instructions seem intended for the royal schools or high levels of the scribal administration,[203] the form seems to have been democratized to instruct lower

---

[199] Hardjedef, Merikare, Amen-em-het, Khety, Amen-em-opet, Papyrus Insinger, Proverbs 1-9, Instruction of the Sages (Prov 24:23-34), Instruction of Lemuel (Prov 31:1-9).

[200] Ptah-Hotep, Amen-em-het, Anksheshonq, and Aḥiqar. The title of the Instruction of Khety includes such a description of setting. The Instruction of Kagemeni concludes with a setting description. In Anksheshonq, the narrative setting precedes the two instructions, both of which have their own title.

Though the title and narrative description of setting are formally distinct, they have often been treated together as the instruction "prologue." On prologues see Helmut Brunner, "Die Weisheitsliteratur," 90-92; Kayatz, *Studien zu Proverbien* 1-9, 24-26; and Kloppenborg, *The Formation of Q*, 265-267 and 276-280.

Kloppenborg, *The Formation of Q*, 278-279, argues that many prologues emphasize the "testing" of the sage, but his only examples of *prologues* which do this are Anksheshonq and Aḥiqar. Though he also mentions the Sentences of Secundus and the Wisdom of Solomon as examples of this, he does not designate these texts as instructions, and their "testing" sections do not occur in narrative prologues. Kloppenborg's argument seems designed to portray the temptation story as an integral part of the Q instruction. Overall, his focus on Q seems to have led him to overestimate the role of narrative setting in the instruction genre.

[201] The Instruction of Ani.

[202] Kagemeni, Ptah-Hotep, Merikare, Amen-em-opet, and Anksheshonq have colophons. Ptah-Hotep and Merikare have concluding blessings, while Khety includes a note on the intended effect of the instruction. Amen-em-het concludes with a description of the succession, the major theme and purported occasion for the instruction.

[203] Following McKane's analysis of the Sitz im Leben of Instructions, the following are among the instructions intended for royalty: Ptah-hotep, Kagemeni, and Merikare. Djedefhor and Amen-em-het are framed as advice to the crown prince, but distribution of copies suggests that at least Amen-em-het functioned in other contexts, since it was popular in New Kingdom scribal schools. Extra-Egyptian instructions with similar governmental connections include the Counsels of Wisdom, Prov 31:1-9, along with parts of Aḥiqar and Prov 22:17-24:22. William McKane *Proverbs: A New Approach*, OTL (Philadelphia: Westminster, 1970), 52-53, 65, 67, 154-155, 157, 169, and 407.

level scribes or even the young men of the community at large.[204] With few exceptions, the instructions share conservative intentions, urging their audience to act in accordance with the cosmic order (Maat or Wisdom) reflected in established social and political institutions.[205] The admonitions in instructions usually work together toward this overall end: producing prudent statesmen, scribes, and/or citizens in general who can "fit in" with the dominant socio-political ethos.[206] This conservative emphasis of most instructions is also reflected in their widespread portrayal of the relationship between the speaker and audience as that of a father to a son. This father-son scheme lays claim to the audience's obligations to the traditional order.[207]

QOHELET 1:12-2:26

Form-Critical Considerations

Genre and Structure of the Book of Qohelet

Though unconventional in many respects, Qohelet is an instruction. Like other instructions, the book begins with a title ascribing the text to the ancient sage, Solomon (1:1). Through such ascription, the book lays claim to Solomon's increasingly positive reputation in the post-exilic

---

204 McKane, *Proverbs*, 9; Kloppenborg, *The Formation of Q*, 283. Examples of instructions intended for lower levels of the scribal hierarchy include: Khety, Nebmarenakht, Pentaweret, Ani (McKane, 98-99), Amenemope (McKane, 105), Amunnakhte and Sirach. Instructions for a more general public include the Instruction of a Man, P. Insinger, P. Louvre D. 2414, and Ankhsheshonq in Egypt (cf. McKane, 118), along with Proverbs 1-9 outside Egypt.

This process of democratization is visible in two ways. First, even the royal instructions mentioned in the previous note came to be part of the more general scribal curriculum. Second, instructions such as Aḥiqar and the Counsels of Wisdom seem to witness to the process of conversion of an instruction from a royal manual to a general instruction (Kloppenborg, *The Formation of Q*, 283). They contain a mix of a group of admonitions relevant for a king, and a larger group of admonitions relevant for a larger audience.

205 McKane, *Proverbs*, 55-59, 67-72; Kloppenborg, *The Formation of Q*, 273.

206 This contrasts with collections of proverbs, which often contain contradictory sentences which require specific application by the reader. Kloppenborg, *The Formation of Q*, 285.

207 J. G. Williams, *Those Who Ponder Proverbs: Aphoristic Thinking and Biblical Literature*, Bible and Literature Series 2 (Sheffield: Almond, 1981), 27, 42; Kloppenborg, *The Formation of Q*, 274-275, 284; McKane, *Proverbs*, 151. Obedience to parents is a prominent theme in collections of proverbs (Prov 1:8-9; 13:1; 29:17).

period as the pre-eminent sage.[208] After a poetic piece incorporating many of the book's themes (1:2-11), Qohelet legitimates the thesis of the following instruction (2:12-26*) through reference to the sage's experience (1:12-2:11). Many general reflections and proverbs follow in 3:1ff.[209]

Qohelet uses the instruction form to undermine many of the very values which the form is typically used to promote. For example, many other wisdom texts, including instructions, juxtapose the way of wisdom and the way of folly.[210] Qohelet 1:12-2:23, however, claims that the ways of wisdom and folly are both essentially unproductive in light of the death which overtakes both the fool and sage. Instead, the speaker gives a qualified endorsement of eating, drinking, and enjoyment of work (2:24a). Though these things too are "vanity and striving after wind," they are the only limited values available to a sage accommodating himself to living under the shadow of death.

This leads to another important difference between Qohelet and other wisdom instructions. Other instructions urge accommodation to a created order infused with beneficent Maat/Wisdom. Qohelet, however, urges the individuals in the audience to accommodate themselves to a world order dominated by the final limit of death. These shifts from traditional wisdom in Qohelet highlight the way Qohelet is an "anti-

---

208 In addition to Qoh 1:16, the most specific indicators of attribution to Solomon occur in Qoh 2:8. The "personal property of kings and the provinces" mentioned in 2:8a probably refers to the gifts from foreign lands (1 Kgs 9:27-28; 10:10, 25) and tribute (1 Kgs 5:1; 10:14) which Solomon is described as receiving. Moreover, the reference to concubines in 2:8b unmistakably refers to Solomon. In addition, the references to the narrator's building projects (2:4-6), slaves (2:7a), livestock (2:7b), and riches (2:8a) all correspond to ancient traditions about Solomon.

On this question compare the opposing views of Aarre Lauha, *Kohelet*, BKAT 19 (Neukirchen: Neukirchener Verlag, 1978), 7, 29, 44, 51; and Kurt Galling, *Der Prediger*, HAT 18 (Tübingen: J. C. B. Mohr (Paul Siebeck), 1969), 88. For further arguments and survey on this question, see O. Loretz, *Qohelet und der alte Orient: Untersuchungen zu Stil und theologischer Thematik des Buches Qohelet* (Freiburg: Herder, 1964), 154, 161.

209 Other scholars identifying Qohelet as an instruction and/or recognizing Egyptian parallels as primary include: Rudi Kroeber, *Der Prediger*, SQAW 13 (Berlin: Akademie, 1963), 10; Georg Fohrer, *Introduction to the Old Testament*, trans. David Green (Nashville: Abingdon, 1968), 336; Gerhard von Rad, *Weisheit in Israel* (Neukirchen: Neukirchener Verlag, 1970), 292-293; J. A. Loader, *Polar Structures in the Book of Qohelet*, BZAW 152 (New York: de Gruyter, 1979), 19-20; Hengel, *Judaism and Hellenism*, 1:119 and 2:77-79; and Otto Kaiser, *Einleitung in das Alte Testament: Eine Einführung in ihre Ergebnisse und Probleme*, 5th revised ed. (Gütersloh: Gütersloher Verlagshaus Gerd Mohn, 1984), 394-395. For more discussion cf. Loretz, *Qohelet und der alte Orient*, 57-65.

210 Kroeber, *Der Prediger*, 11.

instruction," taking on the forms of traditional wisdom in order to subvert it. The anti-conservative character of Qohelet explains why the typical instruction father-son theme does not appear in it.[211]

Structure of Qohelet 1:12-2:26

Qoh 1:12 - 2:26 is the part of Qohelet which shows the closest connections to the Gibeon story.[212] It is a clearly identifiable subunit, bounded on both sides by poetic material and showing clear lines of connection within itself.[213] In 1:12-15 Solomon introduces himself as a Jerusalemite king who has planned and executed a comprehensive search of all which is done and found it useless. The introductory formulae in 1:16 and 2:1 (דברתי אני עם־לבי/אמרתי אני בלבי; "I thought to myself.") both refer back to this initial description of intent (1:13, ונתתי את־לבי; "I resolved to . . ."), but introduce more specific descriptions of Solomon's investigation. 1:16 introduces Solomon's investigation of wisdom (1:16-18), while 2:1 begins his description of a search for fulfillment in folly (2:1-11, see especially 2:3). After specifically describing his exploration of both wisdom (1:16-18) and folly (2:1-11), Solomon turns in 2:12-23 to a comparison of the two (2:12-17), concluding with despair (2:18-23).[214] Thus ends Solomon's argument against conventional wisdom. Qoh 2:24a, 26bβ is a qualified endorsement of the only alternative remaining after this relentless search for knowledge. This alternative is to eat, drink and enjoy work, though all this too is vanity.

By emphasizing God's reward of the righteous and punishment of the wicked, a later addition in Qoh 2:24b-26ba modifies Qohelet's original universal and pessimistic message toward the mainstream of Jewish theology. The introduction (2:24b) is clearly modeled on the original

---

[211] For discussion of the anti-(conventional) wisdom character of Qohelet, cf. Williams, *Those Who Ponder Proverbs*, 47-63.

[212] Since the structure of the book of Qohelet as whole is notoriously difficult to diagram, I limit myself here to the part of Qohelet which seems to build on the Gibeon story.

[213] Most commentators have recognized the unit extending from 1:12-2:26. For survey of the various positions on this see Addison Wright in "The Riddle of the Sphinx: the Structure of the Book of Qohelet," *CBQ* 30 (1968): 315-316.

[214] This set of divisions agrees with the subdivisions of the majority of commentators: 1:12-15, 16-18; 2:1-11; 12-17, 18-26. Qohelet has a way of concluding such subsections with proverbs, 1:15, 18; 2:11b, 17b, 23b. Moreover, as observed above, the beginnings of 1:12-15, 16-18 and 2:1-11 are analogous. The shift from the shared style of reflective introduction indicates the transition from the undertaking of the wisdom enterprise to the questioning of its worth.

conclusion in 2:26bβ. In contrast to the original conclusion that all "vanity and striving after wind," the addition in 24b claims that "this is from the hand of God." The two following elements of the scribal addition are subordinated to the introduction in 24b through the conjunction כִּי ("for"). According to the latter of these two elements (26abα) God gives wisdom, knowledge and joy to the one who is good before God, while sinners labor only to give to those who are good. This part of the scribal addition exempts the righteous from the overall futility described by Qohelet and applies this futility to the wicked. The scribal addition uses Qohelet to contrast the fates of the righteous and ungodly. This intent contrasts radically with Qohelet's argument that the righteous and ungodly suffer similar fates (Qoh 3:16; 7:15; 9:1-6).[215]

These considerations lead to the following tentative diagram of the structure of Qohelet 1:12-2:24a, 26bβ:[216]

---

[215] Moreover, the approving description of the righteous enjoying the fruits of the sinner's labor (2:26bα) contrasts with Qohelet's description of enjoyment of others' wealth as evil (6:1-2).

3:17 is probably another scribal addition modeled on 1:14, 16; 2:1 and the poem in 3:1-9. In any case, 3:17 emphasizes a future distinction between the fates of the righteous and wicked, while 2:26abα describes a distinction in the present.

[216] For text-linguistic arguments supporting the delimitation (though not the hierarchicalization) of the following units see Eberhard Bons, "Zur Gliederung und Kohärenz von Koh 1,12-2,11," *BN* 24 (1984): 80-87. He differs from the following diagram in considering Qoh 2:1-2 as a unit separate from 3-11. Bons confines himself exclusively to formal structural indicators, whereas the following diagram reflects the similarity in content between Qoh 2:1-2 and 2:3-11, suggesting that 3-11 is an expanded description of the search described in 1-2.

The whole argument builds on the speaker's claim to be a king who has achieved unparalleled wisdom and riches. Only on the basis of this experience can the speaker assert the equal unproductivity of both and urge the alternative presented in 2:24a, 26bβ. The addition in 24b-26ba is modeled on this original conclusion and strategically placed so as to harness the original description of universal futility toward more orthodox ends.

Qoh 1:12-2:26 as a Response to the Gibeon Story

The connections to the Gibeon story were obvious in 1 Kgs 3:2-15; 2 Chr 1:1-13 and Josephus VIII:22-25. The epiphany scene and petition scene aspects of the 1 Kings, 2 Chronicles, and Josephus' renderings of the Gibeon story are integral parts of their narrative structure, emphasizing the idea that *God* is the source of Solomon's wisdom, wealth, (possessions) and honor. Not only did each of these narrative accounts follow a similar plot, but they all used that story line to show the unexpected additional benefits of seeking knowledge from God.

Like its narrative precursors (1 Kgs 3:2-15; 2 Chr 1:1-13), Qohelet discusses Solomon, specifically his search for wisdom. As in the narrative versions of the Gibeon story, the wisdom of Qohelet's Solomon is incomparable. The incomparability formula in Qoh 1:16 resembles that used in 1 Chr 29:25bβ to describe the incomparable majesty of Solomon's reign:[217]

1 Chr 29:25bβ
[God gave Solomon] a royal majesty which had not been bestowed on any king over Israel before him [Solomon].

Qohelet 1:16aβγ
[I made myself great and increased] in wisdom over all who had been before me over Jerusalem.

Though the Qohelet 1:16aβγ incomparability formula assumes the first person perspective of its context, it is otherwise very close to that in 1 Chr 29:25. The main difference is that the Chronicles formula describes

---

[217] Galling, *Der Prediger*, 88; and Loretz, *Qohelet und der alte Orient*, p. 149, note 66, recognize this similarity. Because Galling takes 1:12-2:26 not to relate to Solomon, he claims that only the past reference (i. e. not a reference to Solomon) of the formula is appropriated here.

the incomparability of the splendor of Solomon's kingdom, while Qohelet is discussing his wisdom. According to Qohelet, the majesty of Solomon's kingdom was inextricably bound up in his possession of incomparable wisdom. Hence the book as a whole takes the form of a pseudo-epigraphic wisdom instruction in the name of Solomon, the incomparably wise sage. Qohelet supports Solomon's claim to knowledge by appropriating the 1 Chr 29:25bβ incomparability formula but applying it to Solomon's wisdom. This formula shares the distinctive temporal emphasis of the incomparability formula used in 1 Kgs 3:12 to describe Solomon's wisdom.[218]

Qohelet 1:12-2:23 as a whole is dominated by the very opposition which dominates its narrative precursors, namely Solomon's wisdom versus his riches and honor. In the Vorlage this opposition is presented as the opposition between petitioned gift and extra gifts. The Deuteronomistic version of the Gibeon story (1 Kgs 3:11 in particular), portrays this opposition as that between the pious search for wisdom and foolish pagan priorities. Chronicles appropriates this contrast between wisdom and other things, but emphasizes Solomon's "riches, possessions, and honor" more than his wisdom. Qohelet's Solomon first investigates wisdom (Qoh 1:16-18), only then going on to investigate riches and honor (Qoh 2:1-11). Moreover, Qohelet's characterization of his first search as a search for wisdom and the second as an investigation of folly (Qoh 1:17; 2:12) corresponds to the two part account of Solomon's reign in 1 Kgs 3-11. In 1 Kgs 3-11 (and Josephus) Solomon's reign has two main periods: the early portion where he was wise and successful and the later portion where he foolishly fell from God.

In addition to these general connections to the Gibeon story, there are two more subtle connections between Qohelet and the Chronicles version of the story. The latter version has God describe Solomon's virtuous request in the following terms: היתה זאת עם־לבבך (1:11, "this [intent] was in your heart"). Qohelet's description of his search for wisdom emphasizes Solomon's interior reflections by repeating the idiom with לב ("heart," 1:12, 16).[219] Also, the Chronicles version of the Gibeon story consistently describes Solomon's request in terms of the pair חכמה ("wisdom") and מדע ("knowledge"). Likewise, Qohelet 1:16

---

[218] See above, pp. 67-68. for a comparison of this formula with ones outside the Gibeon story which are used to describe Solomon.

[219] His reflection on that search in 1:16 resembles 2 Chr 1:11 yet more through having both לב ("heart") and the preposition עם ("with, in").

looks back on Solomon's search as one for חכמה ("wisdom") and דעת ("knowledge").[220]

Despite these elements shared with its narrative precursors, Qoh 1:12-2:26* is so different from them that its relationship to them is almost unrecognizable. Whereas the narrative versions of the Gibeon story described God's reward of Solomon's request for wisdom, in Qoh 1:12-2:26* Solomon discovers that wisdom is no more productive than folly. While Qohelet accepts the essential assertions of 1 Kgs 3:2-15 and 2 Chr 1:1-13 that Solomon was incomparably wise and rich, he uses the instruction form to undercut their message, presenting the "inside story" of Solomon's real lesson. Solomon himself now describes in the first person how he discovered that both wisdom (1:16-18) and greatness-folly (2:1-11) were futile. Moreover, Qohelet's instruction form allowed him to discard elements of the story which did not promote his overall argument against (conventional) wisdom. Unlike 1 Kgs 3:2-15 and 2 Chr 1:1-13, the wisdom of Qohelet's Solomon hardly led to unexpected benefits. Instead, his deeper wisdom about futility led him to despair (2:18-23) and a qualified endorsement of food, drink and labor (2:24a).

Qoh 1:12-2:26* is especially hard to recognize as a reflection on the Gibeon story because God has disappeared from Qohelet's account. Whereas the epiphany accounts in 1 Kings 3:2-15, 2 Chronicles 1:1-13 and Josephus VIII:22-25 emphasized God's role in rewarding Solomon's wise choice of wisdom, Qoh 1:12-2:26 is built around a structure which emphasizes *Solomon's* plan to acquire wisdom and wealth and his execution of that plan. The main point of the whole is not identification of the source of wisdom, wealth, and honor, but demonstration of the essential unproductivity of each. Perhaps this was the most disturbing shift for the one who added the theocentric and moralizing scribal addition in Qoh 2:24b-26ba.

Like Qohelet's appropriation of the instruction genre, Qohelet's response to the Gibeon story in 1:12-2:26* is another example of Qohelet's appropriation of wisdom *topoi* in order to undermine the themes of conventional wisdom.[221] Qoh 1:12-2:26* is an "anti-Gibeon story." Therefore,

---

[220] Elsewhere 1:12-18 alternates between using חכמה or דעת without the other to characterize Solomon's search.

[221] I am not the first to see relationships between Qohelet and the Gibeon story. Peterca, *L'immagine di Salomone*, 82-83, previously proposed that Qoh 1:16 is a reflection of the Gibeon story along with 1 Kgs 5:10-11. Loretz recognized how statements in Qoh 1:12-2:26 correspond to the picture of Solomon in the Gibeon story. Loretz, *Qohelet und der alte Orient*, 149-150.

it is better characterized as a "response" to the Gibeon story than as an "interpretation" of it.

Concluding Reflections

Setting and Connections to Hellenistic Popular Philosophy

Qohelet was probably composed in Palestine in the span of decades between 270 and 220.[222] Though previous efforts to establish Qohelet as the member of a particular Greek school have proven to be exaggerated, the contacts with popular Greek philosophy are unmistakable. In particular, Qohelet's critique of the traditional wisdom belief in divine retribution and reward grows out of the earlier widespread Greek doubt in the gods' justice. Moreover, he shares a hermeneutical position with the Greeks, i. e. an individuality of authorship, one which grounds an investigation almost exclusively based on experience, rather than received tradition.[223] This relentless search of experience leads to a limitation of the aims of both wisdom and life.

Since all events are now traced to the inscrutable and now somewhat arbitrary work of God, wisdom can only discern provisional rules for the securing of life within the narrow limits of human circumstances. Like the Greeks, Qohelet invites the audience to a limited form of *carpe diem*, enjoyment of food, drink and the rewards of toil, for this is their portion (חלק) in face of the common fate (מקרה) of death. Though not necessarily derived from Greek concepts of τύχη ("fortune") and μοῖρα ("portion, fate"), Qohelet's concepts of חלק ("portion") and מקרה ("fate, fortune") correspond to them. Their central position in Qohelet's thought witness to a shared tendency to impose impersonal concepts between the individual and a God perceived as increasingly distant. This twin emphasis on one's portion and on accommodation are typical of Hellenistic aristocratic rationalism. Formulated in the context of land owning classes supported by their holdings yet powerless in relation to the imperial bureau-

---

[222] The corrected second century copies of the book from Qumran and Ben Sira's familiarity with Qohelet exclude datings of it after 220 BCE. On the other hand, the language of the book is quite late, and it presupposes a long period of peace, not characteristic of Palestine between 350 and 300 BCE. Moreover, the oppressive system of administration and picture of the arbitrary power of the king seem to presuppose the Ptolemaic system of administration, and this is consistent with the numerous Egyptian contacts of the book.

[223] Tradition does emerge in the form of proverbs at summary and transition points, but these traditions are appropriated merely to articulate Qohelet's train of thought. Otherwise the role of tradition is purely negative, i. e. as object of critique.

cracy, this rationalism employed a fundamentally conservative hermeneutic in the drive for security and pleasure.[224]

Adaptability, Inter- and Counter-textuality

As discussed above, Qohelet shares most with Greek popular philosophy. It is Greek popular philosophical themes which lie behind
Qohelet's subversion of Israelite forms and texts through appropriation
of them. In Qohelet's hands, Solomon the pre-eminent wise man,
becomes an anti-sage. Qohelet's reflection on the story of Solomon's
triumph at Gibeon is an account of Solomon's failure to find fulfillment
in his incomparable wisdom, riches and honor. The conventional
wisdom form, "instruction," is appropriated to undermine a wisdom
story, providing a first person inside account of the essential futility of
wisdom as well as folly. Such massive adaptation minimizes Qohelet's
specific links with the Gibeon story in particular and Biblical tradition in
general. Only the minimum of "stability" in the tradition is maintained
in the process of undermining it.

Nevertheless, despite his Hellenistically inspired subversion of the
Israelite wisdom tradition, Qohelet did not take the final step of dismiss-
ing the integrity of God. As Hengel puts it:

> The main difference, however, remains that Koheleth could maintain the real-
> ity and omnipresence of God, whereas the polytheistic Greek pantheon had
> been fundamentally destroyed by criticism, and a very general, impersonal
> conception of God was maintained only with difficulty.[225]

To be sure, God for Qohelet is now almost exclusively האלהים, the dena-
tionalized, universalized God at home in the Greek world. Moreover,
Qohelet's חלק ("portion") and מקרה ("fate, fortune") do not have the
same autonomy independent of God, as the Greek concepts $\tau\acute{\upsilon}\chi\eta$
("fortune") and $\mu o\hat{\imath}\rho\alpha$ ("portion, fate") came to have in other parts of the
Hellenistic world.

Instead, Qohelet steers a middle path between two poles, on the one
side the wisdom tradition emphasis on the transparency of creation and
reliability of the act-consequence system, on the other side the Greek
gradual distancing from "the gods" and subsequent functional replace-
ment of them with fate. Though maintaining much of the Greek individ-

---

[224] The above reflections throughout this section on "Setting and Connections to
Hellenistic Popular Philosophy" are based on Hengel's masterful synthesis in *Judaism
and Hellenism*, 1:115-128.

[225] Ibid., 124.

ualist, rationalist hermeneutic, along with its results, Qohelet draws the line at denying the essential integrity of reality. One part of this is the refusal to emphasize God in describing Solomon's fruitless search for happiness in wisdom and folly. God no longer receives the credit for Solomon's greatness, but neither does God receive the blame for the failure of his attempts to find happiness. Though Qohelet radically adapts the Gibeon story scheme only to undermine it (counter-textuality), he does not completely sever his relationship with the God of Israel.

In contrast to the original Qohelet's lack of focus on God (1:12-2:24a, 26bβ), two out of three parts of the addition in Qoh 2:24b-26bα focus on God's role in providing any reward life has to offer. The enjoyment of food, drink and labor is from God (2:24b) because all enjoyment is from God (2:25). Furthermore, only the sinners suffer the futility described by Qohelet, laboring only to give the fruits of their labors to those who are good before God (2:26abα). In sum, this addition adds a theocentric focus to the original Qohelet's message and harnesses that message to contrast the fate of the wicked and righteous. Rather than responding to the Gibeon story, the addition responds to those aspects of Qohelet which undermined the Gibeon story. If Qohelet is a premier example of counter-textuality, this addition is an example of counter- counter-textuality.

THE WISDOM OF SOLOMON

Genre

Like Qohelet, the Wisdom of Solomon is an instruction pseudo-epigraphically ascribed to Solomon, and like several non-Egyptian instructions, the book begins with an exhortation to hear the following message (Chapters 1-6).[226] In addition, like several of the Egyptian instructions, Wisdom of Solomon includes an autobiographical account of the setting of the instruction (Wis 7-9).[227] Unlike most instructions, however, the first person style is only explicit in the middle chapters (6-9), and 2nd person imperatives only occur in the introductory exhortation (1-6). Nevertheless, the book as a whole presumes a first person form, and other late instructions are similarly characterized by a shift

---

[226] The relevant non-Egyptian instructions are: Prov 1-9; 22:17-24:22; Instruction of Shuruppak, Counsels of Wisdom.

[227] The relevant Egyptian instructions include Ptah-Hotep, Kagemeni, Khety, Amen-em-het, Anksheshonq, and Aḥiqar.

from predominant imperatives to wisdom sentences and other third person material.[228] Most importantly, the Wisdom of Solomon claims legitimacy through its ascription to an ancient authority, Solomon, the preeminent sage.

Structure

The first six chapters function to motivate the audience to listen to the entire following message. Two exhortations frame this section: one in 1:1-16 exhorting the audience to be righteous and one in 6:1-25 exhorting the audience to seek wisdom in order to be righteous. The intervening chapters indicate that the author of the Wisdom of Solomon sees the audience as in the midst of a crisis. In 2:1-5:23 the author describes a social situation with two major groups, the righteous and the ungodly. The audience has apparently witnessed the death of one termed "the righteous one" at the hand of the group described as "the ungodly." In the face of this crisis, the author argues that this apparent defeat is not the final chapter in the conflict between the righteous and ungodly. Instead, at some unspecified future point the righteous will triumph and ungodly will be punished. In other words, chapters 1-6 claim that the present social conflict must be viewed within the wider context of a future reversal in the fortunes of the righteous and ungodly.

The beginning of chapter six makes clear (6:1-11) that the author's audience is presently sympathizing with the wrong group, the ungodly. In order to respond to the call to be righteous in chapter 1:1-16, they must have wisdom. In other words, in order for the audience to join the group which will survive this present crisis—the righteous ones—they must know the wider dimensions of their social reality. They must see past the apparent defeat of the righteous, and have confidence in the hope of an afterlife and in their future triumph. This is the "wisdom" which they require, and the rest of the book focuses on persuasively presenting such wisdom.

This exhortation in Wisdom of Solomon 6 introduces the following explicitly autobiographical section by Solomon about how he acquired Wisdom, chapters seven through nineteen. These chapters are characterized by an ever increasing narrowing of the semantic focus. Like a zoom lens, the book moves from a general description of Solomon's quest for

---

[228] Late Egyptian (Anksheshonq and Papyrus Insinger) and non-Egyptian exemplars (Aḥiqar; Prov 1-9; 24:23-34) include much third person material which is not subordinated to 2nd person admonitions.

Wisdom (Wis 7-8), to a narrower focus on his prayer for Wisdom (Wis 9), then to a series of illustrations from the Torah (Wis 10) of the thesis mentioned in that prayer (Wis 9:18), and finally to a theocentric reexamination of one of those illustrations without reference to Wisdom (Wis 11-19). Each major unit (except the first) is nested in a unit begun by the subsection immediately preceding it. A diagram of the macro-structure follows:

Instruction 1:1-19:22

I. Introductory Exhortation 1:1-6:25

II. Instruction Proper 7:1-19:22

    A. Placement of Prayer in Context 7:1-8:21

    B. Prayer 9:1-19:22

        1. Wisdom's Power Versus Solomon's Weakness 9:1-6

        2. Link of Solomon's Task with Wisdom's Help 7-12

        3. Humans = Solomon in Need for Wisdom 9:13-19:22

            a. General Argument 9:13-18

            b. Support: Examples from the Torah 10:1-19:22

                1) Adam 10:1-3

                2) Noah 4

                3) Abraham 5

                4) Lot 6-9

                5) Jacob 10-12

                6) Joseph 13-14

                7) The People Israel 10:15-19:22

                    a) Narration with Wisdom 10:15-21

                    b) Narration without Wisdom 11:1-19:22

The overall effect of the structure is to direct ever increasing attention to the dynamics of Israel's history, encouraging the audience to seek a knowledge of such dynamics in order to insure their survival.

In addition to this structure of increasing focus on the Torah narrative, each major unit in the macrostructure of the Wisdom of Solomon is balanced by another. Both the first six and last nine chapters (11-19) contrast the destinies of the righteous and ungodly without reference to Wisdom. Chapters seven to eight and chapter ten both focus more particularly on the benefits which the righteous have enjoyed from Wisdom. Chapter nine, Solomon's petition for Wisdom, is the center of this concentric structure and exemplifies the aim of the book as a whole.

As the center of the book, chapter nine plays an important role in the movement from the first half of the concentric structure to the second. The units following chapter nine shift from being introductory to being retrospective and supportive. Both 1-6 and 7-8 are sections which introduce the following material. Both are concentrically structured, with five sub-units. And although the sections as a whole are both introductory in function, this function is particularly explicit in the last subsection of both 1-6 and 7-8.

Following chapter nine, however, each successive unit explicates and supports the last unit of the preceding section. Thus, chapter ten provides examples for the last part of chapter nine. Chapters eleven through nineteen renarrate from a non-wisdom perspective the events covered in the last example of chapter ten. In other words, after chapter nine, the last sub-unit of each major section shifts from making explicit the preparatory nature of the whole section, to being the focus of later sections which aim at reexamining it.

This shift from introduction to retrospection is part of the concentric pattern which characterizes both the larger and smaller units of the Wisdom of Solomon. Everything builds toward and away from Solomon's prayer for Wisdom in chapter nine. This chapter is the Wisdom of Solomon's version of 1 Kgs 3:6-9//2 Chr 1:8-10. Moreover, the Wisdom of Solomon appropriates elements from the Gibeon story as a whole in the introduction to this prayer in chapters seven to eight.

The following diagram is proposed in light of the above reflections. It focuses particularly on the Wisdom of Solomon's presentation of the Gibeon story in chapters seven to nine:

II. Instruction Proper 7:1-19:22

    A. Placement of Prayer in Context 7:1-8:21

        1. Autobiographical Background to Teaching 7:1-12

           a. Solomon = Audience in Resources 1-6

           b. Solomon's Achievement 7-12

        2. Teaching Regarding Wisdom 7:13-8:1

           a. Introduction 7:13-22a

           b. Speech Proper 7:22b-8:1

        3. Return to Audience's Point of Decision 8:2-21

           a. Solomon's Reasoning and Decision 2-16

           b. Prayer Introduction Proper 17-21

    B. Prayer 9:1-19:22

Interpretation of the Gibeon Story

Proverbs 8 in the Wisdom of Solomon

One of the most prominent innovations in the Wisdom of Solomon's interpretation of the Gibeon story is its integration of the Gibeon story with the substance of Wisdom's speech in Proverbs 8.[229] This is the call of the personified Wisdom figure from the gates of the city to its men to listen to her. After a narrative introduction describing the speech's setting (Prov 8:1-3), Wisdom's speech is quoted (Prov 8:4-36). This quote consists of an initial indication of the intended recipients (4-5) and a series of imperatives, with and without attached motive clauses (6-31). The greatest space in the call is devoted to the exhortation to prefer instruction in verses 10-31. This call has an extensive motivation section. One half of this section is a series of sayings which assert Wisdom's benefits (Verses 11-21). The other half argues for her power to provide those benefits through asserting her presence at and role in creation (22-31). The following is a summary of Proverbs 8, one which follows the relatively loose hierarchical organization of the text's structure:

---

229 For one list of passages where parts of the Wisdom of Solomon verbally resemble parts of Proverbs 1-9 cf. Chrysostrome Larcher, *Études le livre de la Sagesse*, Études Bibliques (Paris: J. Gabalda et Cie Éditeurs, 1969), 98, and notes on 332-333. As he observes (p. 349), Sirach and the Wisdom of Solomon share dependence on Proverbs 1-9, especially Proverbs 8, but represent different developments from this common body of tradition.

The section most central to this speech focuses on the need for preference for Wisdom over other valued items, a point quite close to that of the Gibeon story. Moreover, like the Gibeon story, Proverbs 8:10-31 claims that a preference for Wisdom can result in the reception of other valued goods in addition to her. The reason for such correspondences is that the Vorlage to the Gibeon story was originally built around a theocentric interpretation of the Wisdom tradition appearing in Proverbs 3:16

and 8:18. This tradition claims that Wisdom brings riches and honor with her. With the integration of Proverbs 8 and the Gibeon story in the Wisdom of Solomon, this background to the story becomes one of its essential elements.

An Exhortation to Seek Wisdom: Wis 6

Though the interpretation of the Gibeon story does not begin until chapter seven, chapter six plays a crucial role in introducing that interpretation. Specifically, the chapter as a whole converts the arguments in chapters two through five into an introduction to the message in chapters seven-nine. Verses 1-11 place the audience in the picture described in chapters two through five. Through indicating the importance of the following message to their situation, they introduce the hymn to Wisdom in 12-20. This section, particularly 6:9a, corresponds to the "Indication of Intended Recipients" section of Wisdom's call in Proverbs 8:4.

The hymn which follows is the place where the book introduces Wisdom as a personified female figure.[230] From this point onward, the Σοφιά ("Wisdom") described in the Wisdom of Solomon must be referred to with a capital S. The author begins with an almost exact citation of Proverbs 8:17 in 6:12. Proverbs 8:17 is a motive clause in Wisdom's speech which emphasizes her accessibility to those who love her. The verses in Wis 6:14-16 are less closely connected to particular texts of Proverbs eight, but develop the accessibility theme by appropriating the image in Proverbs 1-9 of Wisdom roaming the streets, looking for followers (6:14, 16)[231] and the image of the reliability of her reward for those who diligently seek her (6:15; Proverbs 8:34-35).

The accessibility of Wisdom thus asserted, the speaker turns to a *sorites* in verses 17-19. As the summary of the *sorites* in verse 20 indicates, the argument is intended to establish the connection between desire for Wisdom and political power. The content of Wis 6:17-19 is an elaboration of Proverbs 8:15-16, but the text is a beautifully constructed example of a Greek form, and its claims for Wisdom parallel Isis' promises of immortality to the king in enthronement hymns.[232] By the end of the hymn to

---

[230] σοφία is mentioned once in 6:9b, and spirits of wisdom 1:6 and of the lord 1:7 appear in chapter one.

[231] Proverbs 1:20-21; 8:2-3; 9:1-6.

[232] John S. Kloppenborg, "Isis and Sophia in the Book of Wisdom," *HTR* 75 (1982): 75-76. For an earlier treatment see Burton Mack, *Logos und Sophia: Untersuchungen zur Weisheitstheologie im hellenistischen Judentum*, SUNT 10 (Göttingen: Vandenhoeck & Ruprecht, 1973), 90-95. James M. Reese, *Hellenistic Influence on the Book of Wisdom and*

Wisdom in verse 20, the speaker has combined Biblical and Hellenistic motifs to make two points relevant to persuading the audience to seek Wisdom: 1) that Wisdom is accessible; 2) that Wisdom is important for political power.

In verses 21-25 the author applies the preceding reflections to the task of introducing the instruction in chapters seven and following. The speaker outlines the subject of the following message and asserts the veracity of his testimony in a way similar to that of Wisdom in Proverbs 8:6-9. Though these verses are the only explicit introduction to the following message, they are integrally linked with the preceding argument. In sum, 6:21-25 makes clear the introductory function of the preceding arguments.

Solomon's and the Audience's Resources: Wis 7:1-6

The message begins with a section emphasizing Solomon's mortal birth like all others. This emphasis on the mortality of royalty is held more in common with Hellenistic kingship tracts than with the Gibeon story.[233] Whereas the reference in 1 Kgs 3:7b is part of Solomon's contrast between his youthful incompetence and his great task, Wis 7:1-6 establishes the relevance of Solomon's instruction for the general public. The audience might suppose that Solomon was distinguished by his royal privilege. His speech in 1 Kgs 3:6aα, 7, 9, even suggests the important role his succession plays in his petition. But by emphasizing Solomon's mortality, specifically as manifest in his birth like others, the Wisdom of Solomon stresses the things Solomon shares with the audience and his lack of inherited privilege.

Solomon's Achievement: Wis 7:7-12

The emphasis on Solomon's lack of inherited privilege in 7:1-6 helps highlight the way he actually did receive all his fabled wisdom, riches, fame, etc. The next section, 7:7-12, begins by describing Solomon's prayer for and reception of Wisdom, with Wis 7:7 parallel to 1 Kgs 3:6-9 and 2 Chr 1:8-10.[234] Whereas 1 Kgs 3:6-9 and 2 Chr 1:8-10 in addition to Wis 9 all quote Solomon's prayer at this point in the text, the Wisdom of Solomon 7:7 merely describes the prayer in parallel lines. Moreover,

---

Its Consequences, AnBib 41 (Rome: Pontifical Biblical Institute, 1970), 40-48, also has a discussion. Cf. Kloppenborg's critique.

[233] Winston, *The Wisdom of Solomon*, AB 43 (Garden City: Doubleday, 1979), 162-163.

[234] Since Josephus postdates Wisdom of Solomon, parallels from him will not be cited.

unlike 1 Kings and 2 Chronicles, the Wisdom of Solomon links the description of his prayer for Wisdom directly to the description of his reception of her.

The Wisdom of Solomon also includes a description of Solomon's preference for Wisdom over other valued items, 7:8-10. Though the riches and power mentioned in 7:8 resemble the riches and military victory found in the lists of things Solomon did not request (1 Kgs 3:11; 2 Chr 1:11), the jewels, gold and silver mentioned in 7:9 derive from Proverbs 8:10-11.[235] 7:10 lists yet additional things commonly valued in the Hellenistic world over which Solomon preferred Wisdom. In sum, the description of things which Solomon did not request in Wis 7:8-10 integrates the Proverbs text with a democratized version of 1 Kgs 3:11/ 2 Chr 1:11 and adds yet more items which might be valued by his Hellenistic audience. This is part of the trend also seen in Chronicles and Josephus, to democratize the Gibeon story and make it relate to the lives of those who are not royalty. Notably, military victory is not even mentioned.

Wis 7:11-12 describes Solomon's reception of all these good things along with Wisdom. The placement of this description after the list of things he did not request resembles the arrangement of 1 Kgs 3:12-14 and 2 Chr 1:12. As in Qohelet, the focus now is on Solomon's wealth (11b). Any other additional benefits of his request are encompassed with such general descriptions as τὰ ἀγαθὰ ("the good things") or πᾶς ("all"). Like Chronicles, Josephus, and Qohelet, there is no mention in this context of long life.

In other respects, however, this description is distinct from the other interpretations of the Gibeon story. Though the Wisdom of Solomon elsewhere emphasizes the divine origins of *Wisdom*, 7:11-12 emphasize the Wisdom rather than the *divine* origins of Solomon's greatness. In order to articulate the connection between Wisdom and Solomon's great riches, etc., the speaker again draws on Proverbs 1-9, appropriating the Proverbs 8:18 image of wealth and honor accompanying Wisdom (7:11a) and the Proverbs 3:16b image of the same gifts in Wisdom's "hands."[236] In contrast, the narrative accounts of the Gibeon story portray the divine grant of these gifts as a reward for the virtue of Solomon's request for wisdom and rejection of other items. Both 1 Kgs 3 and 2 Chr 1 place a

---

235 7:9a (jewels), 9b (gold), 9c (silver) correspond to Prov 8:11a, 10b, 10a respectively.

236 The description of Wisdom "leading" these things and being their mother in 7:12 seems to be the author's own elaboration of the same theme.

note describing God's approval of Solomon's request (1 Kgs 3:10//2 Chr 1:11) between his request for Wisdom and God's gift of wisdom along with other things. No such notice occurs in the Wisdom of Solomon.

Despite these differences, there are important commonalities between the narrative stance of 7:7-12 and other interpretations of the Gibeon story. In particular, the past focus and time sequence of the narration in 7:1-12 correspond most with the traditional narrative versions of the Gibeon story. By building on such previous versions to describe his past success, "Solomon" validates his following claims about Wisdom in 7:15-8:1. Since he has actually experienced Wisdom and her benefits, we can trust what he has to say about her in 7:15-8:1. Such an argument from experience is typical in instructions. Then, once the teaching has been given, we will see Solomon in 8:2-21 look again at the Gibeon story, this time working from a different point in the story than that adopted in 7:7-12.

Teaching Regarding Wisdom: Wis 7:13-8:1

The first two verses of this section, 7:13-14, are a transitional piece which shows how the preceding account of Solomon's achievement (7:1-12) led him to the teaching about Wisdom which follows (7:15-8:1). Then, just like the hymn in 6:12-20, the teaching in 7:15-8:1 artfully combines Biblical and popular Hellenistic philosophical motifs to portray Wisdom's desirability. The structure of the argument is similar to the move made in Proverbs 8 between claim of benefits (8:11-21) and argument for Wisdom's ability to provide such benefits (8:22-31). The first half of the speech 7:13-21 ends on the note which dominates Proverbs 8:22-31, Wisdom's role in creation. But even at that point, the language to describe Wisdom's role, τεχνῖτις ("artist, craftsperson"), is Stoic and the surrounding forms and images used to describe her are likewise thoroughly Hellenistic. The twenty-one epithets for Wisdom, fivefold description of her relationship with God (7:25-26), Pythagorean transmigration imagery (7:27cd), and Stoic nomos conceptuality (7:22, 26; 8:1) all testify to the author's familiarity with popular Hellenistic philosophy and ability to harness it to his didactic ends.[237] Just like Proverbs 8:22-31, the whole aims to persuasively argue that Wisdom is capable of providing other goods in addition to herself.

---

[237] For the Hellenistic aspects of this section see Winston, *The Wisdom of Solomon*, 173-190, and Reese, *Hellenistic Influence*.

Return to the Audience's Point of Decision: Wis 8:2-21

8:2-21 returns back along the path traced by 7:1-12. Thus 7:1-12 and 8:2-21 are parallel sections, standing on either side of the teaching about Wisdom in 7:13-8:1. There are important differences, however, between these two sections. First, the speaker shifts from describing his reception of riches, etc. in the past (7:1-12) to anticipating their reception in the future (8:2-21).[238] Here his position resembles that seen in Chronicles and Josephus, where Solomon has already proven his reception of wisdom but looks forward to the fulfillment of the divine promises of riches and honor. But there is also a didactic program involved here. In this retracing of the Gibeon narrative in the second half of the concentric structure, the narrator assumes the position of the reader, who looks forward to a reversal of the fates of the righteous and ungodly and is considering Wisdom's prospective benefits. Solomon's perspective has shifted from validating his message by describing his success (7:1-12) to redescribing his situation so that it resembles the point of decision where his audience is located (8:2-21). As a result, by the end of chapter eight the audience is put directly in an early part of that story. Like Solomon, they too must consider petitioning God for Wisdom.

Second, Wis 8:2-21 further develops the metaphor of Wisdom imaged as female. From Proverbs (4:5-9; 7:4-5) through Sirach (15:2) and to the original version of the conclusion to Sirach (51:13-19*),[239] teachers exploited the erotic potentialities in the female Wisdom metaphor. Through such poetry, they could graphically articulate Wisdom's attraction. Such metaphors would be potent vehicles for such a message, particularly one directed at adolescent males!

More than any previous text, however, Wis 7:28; 8:2, 9, 16-18; 9:11-12) develops the metaphor of cohabitation with Wisdom as a partner. Though beautiful (8:2), she is desirable primarily because of her divine connections (8:3), companionship (8:16-18) and good counsel (8:9; 9:11-12).[240] The latter metaphor has connections with Wisdom's claim in

---

[238] Maurice Gilbert, "La figure de Salomon en Sg 7-9," in *Études sur le Judaisme Hellénistique*, eds. R. Kuntzmann and J. Schlosser, LD 119 (Paris: Les Éditions du Cerf, 1984), 229, brings attention to the correspondence between the judgment theme in Wis 8:11 and that in 1 Kgs 3.

[239] On this see James Sanders, *The Psalms Scroll of Qumrân Cave 11*, DJD 4 (Oxford: Clarendon, 1965), 79-85; idem. *The Dead Sea Psalms Scroll* (Ithaca, NY: Cornell Un. Press, 1967), 112-117.

[240] Thus the Wisdom of Solomon shows appreciation of the multi-dimensional character of feminine imagery in the Proverbs 1-9 Wisdom figure. On this see particu-

Proverbs 8:14a to have עצה ("counsel") in addition to salvation, understanding and strength, but the primary model for the picture of Wisdom in Wis 8:2-21 (as in Wis 6:17-19) is the Hellenistic Isis. Like Wisdom (8:3, 9), Isis is both the spouse of Osiris and of the king. She is the "lady of the house" and "royal spouse." Her intimate knowledge of both God and king make her a uniquely qualified intermediary between them. Through such knowledge she is all powerful to regulate the physical, social, and moral orders.[241]

Such a picture of a female deity able to provide for the king through her knowledge is uniquely suited to articulating the way Wisdom can provide benefits to those who love her. Whereas in Proverbs 8:22-31 Wisdom *was* involved in creation and an intimate of God, Isis *is* God's partner, and moreover, she can be the intimate partner of the king as well. In this way the Hellenistic Isis image resonates with the plot of the Gibeon story: royal preference for wisdom leads to additional benefits. Through appropriating motifs from the popular Isis cult, the author of the Wisdom of Solomon presents a version of the Gibeon story which would appeal to a population of Greek-speaking Jews with tenuous relations to the Greek culture in which they longed to have their own place, a population receptive to articulations of Biblical tradition in ways which emphasize commonalties with Greek tradition.[242]

Finally, several elements from the Gibeon story emerge which were not previously emphasized. First, Solomon's youth is mentioned twice (8:10, 19), thus continuing the theme first seen in 1 Kgs 3:7. Second, 8:10 describes the δόξα ("honor") which Solomon will command among the multitudes and in the presence of elders, though young. This corresponds to the emphasis on כבוד ("honor") in the Kings and Chronicles versions of the Gibeon story. Third, for the first time since the *sorites* in 6:18, Solomon describes how Wisdom brings immortality (8:13a, 17c) and

---

larly, Claudia V. Camp, *Wisdom and the Feminine in the Book of Proverbs,* Bible and Literature Series 11 (Decatur, GA: Almond, 1985), 69-147.

[241] Kloppenborg, "Isis and Sophia," 76-78.

[242] Ibid., 79-84. Another intriguing combination of Biblical and Hellenistic motifs occurs in Solomon's argument that Wisdom provides virtues, 8:7. This argument at least partially builds from the emphasis in Proverbs 8:10-21 on Wisdom's provision of knowledge of prudence, righteousness, strength, counsel, etc. Cf. Prov 8:20 (Wisdom in the ways of righteousness), 8:12 (Wisdom provides cunning and knowledge of prudence), and 8:14 (Wisdom brings counsel, salvation, insight, strength). But Wis 8:7 describes how Wisdom teaches the four cardinal virtues, a Platonic division continued by the Stoics, Zeno, and Philo among others. Winston, *The Wisdom of Solomon,* 194.

(contra Qohelet 2:16) a lasting remembrance (8:13b). This corresponds to the problematic promise of long life in 1 Kgs 3:14. Since Solomon was not unusually characterized by long life, the promise proved a point of commentary for the first Deuteronomistic editor, while the Chronicler omitted it and Josephus modified it into a promise of a long dynasty. As has already become evident in the extensive list of Wisdom's benefits, the Wisdom of Solomon does not share those narratives' concern for conforming the Gibeon story to Solomon's life. Moreover, immortality has already emerged as a major theme in chapters one to six as the unseen factor which guarantees future victory for the righteous. Thus the Wisdom of Solomon naturally includes its equivalent of a long life promise to Solomon. In this case, the long life promise takes the form of an assurance through Wisdom of a lasting remembrance and immortality.

The final section of chapter eight, 8:17-21, is a summary reflection which introduces the following prayer. Like the concluding section of chapter six, this unit indicates how the preceding arguments function to introduce the following message. The specifically introductory summary in these verses makes transparent the introductory character of the entire unit (chapters 1-8). The emphasis in these verses on Solomon's interiority corresponds to Chronicles and especially Qohelet 1:12, 16; 2:1, and 15, but Solomon comes to decisively different results than Qohelet. On the one hand Qohelet's emphasis on mortality has its counterpart here in the mention of Solomon's mortality (7:1-6; 8:19-21). On the other hand this is accompanied by a the mass of arguments for Wisdom's benefits (7:7-8:16). Seeing that his only way as a mortal to get Wisdom was by prayer, he petitioned God for Wisdom: chapter nine.

Wisdom's Power versus Solomon's Weakness: Wis 9:1-6

Like the next two sections, this one is built around a request for/reference to God's gift of Wisdom to Solomon.[243] The contrast presented here builds upon 1 Kgs 3:7b, but unlike that verse, Wis 9:1-6 emphasizes Solomon's common lot with humanity. Moreover, the invocation emphasizing Wisdom's pivotal role in creation once again corresponds more with Proverbs 8:22-31 than with anything in the Gibeon story. In contrast to the Gibeon story, Solomon justifies his first request for Wisdom after he makes it. Moreover, this justification begins with Solomon's emphasis on his lack of knowledge, thus preserving elements

---

243 Gilbert, "La structure de la prière de Salomon (Sg 9)." *Bib* 51 (1970): 305-320.

from 1 Kgs 3:6-9 in particular. Through its emphasis on Solomon's inability, this section helps establish the two poles: all humanity (even Solomon's) versus powerful Wisdom. God is the only one who can bring the two together, and the prayer aims to remove the distance between the two in the case of Solomon.

Link of Solomon's Task with Wisdom's Help: Wis 9:7-12

The text here is more specific about Solomon's vocation than the narrative versions of the Gibeon story, incorporating the legal/governmental emphasis of 1 Kgs 3:6-9/2 Chr 1:8-10 and the additional emphasis in the Chronicles version on Solomon as temple builder and even on the tabernacle (2 Chr 1:5). Like the narrative versions of the Gibeon story, Solomon mentions God's role in putting him in his present vocation. But unlike any previous version Solomon emphasizes that God has the solution, God's Wisdom, with whom God has worked so closely and who knows all God's works. The explicit emphasis in Wis 9:9cd, 10cd, and 11-13 on Wisdom's knowledge of God's will indicates that much of the Torah emphasis of the Deuteronomistic version of the story has survived with Wisdom taking on the role of Torah. In addition, the brief mention of Solomon being worthy of the throne of his father (9:12c) is an appropriation of the Deuteronomistic emphasis in 1 Kgs 3:3, 6aβb, 14a on "ethical succession" and Solomon's need to measure up to the high standards of his father David.

General Argument for Human Need for Wisdom: Wis 9:13-18

The rhetorical questions in this section correspond to 1 Kgs 3:9b[244] but the judicial emphasis of the 1 Kgs question is missing. Instead, in verses 13, 16-17, the discussion is widened from Solomon to humanity in general, and the speaker refers to the widespread wisdom *topos* of unanswerable questions to portray the universal human need for God given wisdom.[245] Once again, this more traditionally Biblical wisdom argument is elaborated with a concept from Hellenistic popular philosophy, the widespread emphasis on bodily obstruction of knowledge of heavenly matters.[246]

Perhaps the most important shift in this final section of Solomon's speech is that it expands into a Wisdom centered recital of the Torah

---

[244] Not 2 Chr 1:10b; cf. the previous chapter of this study on that half-verse.

[245] Examples of the topos include Prov 30:2-4; Job 37:14-24; 38:1-39:30; Sir 1:2-10.

[246] Winston, *The Wisdom of Solomon*, 208.

story (Wis 10) and then a theocentric retelling of the Exodus (Wis 11-19). Although on the surface level Solomon is making a case to God, in the author's communication situation he is making a case to the Jewish audience. He is attempting to persuade them to make a similar petition.

Concluding Reflections

The Context

* *Literary Context: Relationship to Qohelet*

The kind of appeal to tradition which the Wisdom of Solomon incorporates into Solomon's prayer for Wisdom could hardly be farther from the spirit of Qohelet. Already specific oppositions have appeared between Qohelet's and the Wisdom of Solomon's view of wisdom and remembrance (Qoh 2:16; Wis 8:13b). Similarly, though the books share an emphasis on interiority, they arrive at decisively different results (Qoh 1:13, 16; 2:1, 15 versus Wis 8:17-21).

These and other indicators suggest that though Qohelet and the Wisdom of Solomon are the only Second Temple Jewish instructions directly attributed to Solomon,[247] their messages are almost diametrically opposed. Whereas Qohelet's counter-wisdom describes a life conformed to the finality of death, the Wisdom of Solomon advocates a way of life built on a belief in afterlife and future reversal. Qohelet concludes a reflection on how retribution does not overtake the wicked, by claiming that all their deeds are in the "hand of God," and the same fate (death) overtakes them all (8:10-9:6). Wis 3:1-9 contradicts claims by the ungodly similar to those in Qohelet (2:1-20) by arguing that righteous ones only seem to die, but in fact they are in the "hand of God," preserved for the eschatological reversal. The Wisdom of Solomon then takes Qohelet's description of how all can expect to die and be quickly forgotten (Qoh 8:12-17; 9:5-6), and applies it exclusively to the ungodly who predict such a death (prediction Wis 2:1-5; death Wis 3:17-19).

In addition, Qohelet and the Wisdom of Solomon have opposing views of the role wisdom can play in securing life. Qohelet 9:11 claims that riches do not come to the intelligent, while Wis 7:11 claims the opposite. Qohelet 2:16 claims that the wise are forgotten after their deaths, while Solomon in Wis 8:13 claims that he will have immortality and a lasting remembrance thanks to Wisdom. Finally, Qohelet concludes his description of his search for Wisdom by quoting a proverb

---

247 Though later ascribed to Solomon, the contents of the instructions in Proverbs 1-9 and 22:17-24:22 do not build on this attribution.

which portrays wisdom in negative terms, as a multiplication of כַּעַס ("irritation") and מַכְאוֹב ("pain"; Qoh 1:18). The Wisdom of Solomon, however, portrays Wisdom in unequivocally positive terms, as a wife desirable to pursue and dwell with (Wis 8:2-18).

This opposition between Qohelet and the Wisdom of Solomon is also apparent from a comparison of the speech of the ungodly in Wis 2:1-20 with Qohelet. In this speech, the ungodly state that since they will die, they might as well passionately immerse themselves in pleasure seeking and feel free to oppress the "righteous one." To be sure, this picture of passionate hedonism could only be a parody of Qohelet's qualified endorsement of enjoyment of food, drink and toil. Nevertheless, the line of reasoning is quite similar.

Moreover, there are some more specific parallels between the speech of the ungodly and the book of Qohelet. Like Qohelet, the ungodly describe life as short and sorrowful (2:1b).[248] They know there is no remedy for death (2:1c), and no one returns from it (2:1d, 5b).[249] This discussion of the shortness of life concludes with the ungodly describing their expectation that they will be forgotten after their death (2:4),[250] their life having been no more than a passing shadow (2:5a).[251] From this they conclude that they must seek the pleasure which they can find in this life,[252] because this is their μερὶς ("portion").[253]

Many other items in the speech of the ungodly are closer in formulation to parts of Job or other books; the description of oppression in 2:10-20 is specific to the situation of the book;[254] and the signs of the influence of Hellenistic popular philosophy are clear.[255] Moreover, the Wisdom of Solomon itself goes far beyond critiquing the views of the ungodly. It is hardly just a work of opposition, but presents an powerful alternative program, involving a re-presentation of Wisdom and a rereading of

---

[248] For shortness of life in Qohelet, see Qoh 2:3; 6:12. For sorrow of life, see Qoh 2:22-23.

[249] Qoh 8:8. For the translation of 2:1d as referring to "returning" rather than "liberating," see David Winston, *The Wisdom of Solomon*, 115-116. See also Job 7:9-10 for Wis 2:1d and 5b. Patrick W. Skehan, "The Literary Relationship of the Book of Wisdom to Earlier Wisdom Writings," in *Studies in Israelite Poetry and Wisdom*, CBQMS 1 (Washington, D. C.: Catholic Biblical Association of America, 1971), 192.

[250] Qoh 1:11; 2:16; 4:16; 9:5, 15.

[251] Qoh 6:12; 8:13.

[252] Qoh 2:24-25; 3:12-13, 22; 5:17-18; 8:15; 9:7-10; 11:8-10.

[253] חלק in Qohelet: 2:10; 3:22; 5:17-18; 9:9.

[254] The ungodly here contrast with Qoh 3:16-17 and elsewhere.

[255] See Winston, *The Wisdom of Solomon*, 113-123.

Israel's traditions. Nevertheless, the opposition in the Wisdom of Solomon to a position quite close to Qohelet is unmistakable. Not only are the messages and methods of the books opposed, but Qohelet is the one Biblical book which presents the most corollaries in spirit and wording to the speech of the ungodly in 2:1-20.[256]

- *Historical and Institutional Context*

Scholars almost universally agree that the anti-Egyptian elements of the book indicate a probable Alexandrian origin for it. This would also help account for the book's conspicuous Hellenistic component. The probable reference to the *pax romana* in 14:22[257] and description of social crisis in chapters two through five correspond with a dating sometime after the Roman annexation of Egypt by Octavian in 30 BCE. The lack of any reflection on the destruction of the Second Temple rules out a dating after 70 CE. Several items make a dating later in that range most probable. The vocabulary of the book is late,[258] and its thought shows numerous points of affinity with Philo of Alexandria.[259] In addition, the struggles of the Alexandrian Jewish community were most intense during the reign of Caligula (37-41 CE).[260] Lacking suitable generic parallels or other indicators, the institutional context is difficult to determine.

---

[256] The above discussed connections between Qohelet and the Wisdom of Solomon are so obvious that scholars have recognized the special relationship between Qohelet and the Wisdom of Solomon since the middle of the nineteenth century. Nevertheless, this has not stopped some scholars from vigorously denying such a relationship. The most thorough recent attempt along these lines is Skehan's essay on the relationship between Qohelet and the Wisdom of Solomon: "The Literary Relationship of the Book of Wisdom to Earlier Wisdom Writings," particularly 192-193, 220-224.

There are serious deficiencies with Skehan's approach. Not only must he draw on diverse sources for often distant parallels to Wisdom of Solomon (outside Qohelet), but he fails to take into account the nature of the Wisdom of Solomon's critique. The Wisdom of Solomon is a portrayal of a contemporary group's appropriation of Qohelet's perspective, and hardly an accurate portrayal at that. Instead, the Wisdom of Solomon's polemical version of their speech in 2:1-20 plays a certain role in Wisdom's critique of their position. This is a parody of their position, and in it the ungodly condemn themselves. On this see Hengel, *Judaism and Hellenism*, 1:127-128.

[257] Maurice Gilbert, *La critique des dieux dans le Livre de la Sagesse*, AnBib 53 (Rome: Pontifical Institute, 1973), 172.

[258] Winston, *The Wisdom of Solomon*, 22-23.

[259] Ibid., 59-63.

[260] M. Stern, "The Jewish Diaspora," in *The Jewish People in the First Century*, vol 1., *The Jewish People in the First Century: Historical Geography, Political History, Social,*

The work is a highly integrated piece. It was written as a propagandistic piece, aimed to persuade the members of its embattled Jewish audience to maintain their Jewish identity in the face of forces encouraging them to deny it. Whereas they intensely desired a place in the Hellenistic world, they had to forsake their Jewish identity in order to obtain it. The Wisdom of Solomon articulates the heart of the Biblical tradition in a way which resonates with the ethos of popular Hellenism. In the context of the Alexandrian Jews' ambiguous position between the Greeks on the one hand and the native Egyptians on the other, such a unification of Greek and Biblical tradition would have been particularly attractive. As such it could serve as one component in an overall effort to establish the essential unity of the best in Judaism with the Greeks and the opposition of Judaism to anything Egyptian.

Hermeneutics

• *Adaptability, Inter- and Counter-Textuality*

Overall, in the Wisdom of Solomon we see an appropriation of those elements of various versions of the Gibeon story which can play a role in the author's persuasive and didactic program. In particular, the author omits or downplays elements which limit the story to royalty or Solomon, elements such as references to David and Solomon's royal tasks. The setting is radically different. The Gibeon story is no longer the third person narrative of the dream epiphany petition scene of a particular monarch, in this case Solomon. Rather than justifying the unique legitimacy of a monarch, the story has become a type case of a petition which all Jews can and should imitate.

These massive shifts in narrative setting and didactic aims have already been seen in more radical form in Qohelet. As in Qohelet, the instruction form alters the way the Gibeon story is presented. The narrative standpoint shifts from third person to first person. Rather than relying on the impersonal authority of an unseen narrator, "Solomon's" representation of his experience is heard. In addition, the focus on instructing a search for Wisdom means that other aspects of Solomon's reign fade into the background. Both Kings and Chronicles used the Gibeon story to introduce larger narratives about his temple building, wealth, riches, and power. The Wisdom of Solomon, however, briefly refers to those stories only to highlight Wisdom's gifts. Both 1 Kgs 3:2-15

Cultural, and Religious Life and Institutions, CRINT, section one (Assen and Philadelphia: Van Gorcum and Fortress, 1974), 125-131.

and 2 Chr 1:1-13 build to a climax in God's promise of both wisdom and other things to Solomon. Although chapters seven and eight of the Wisdom of Solomon refer to those gifts, these chapters merely introduce Solomon's requests for Wisdom in chapter nine. Finally, the instruction form allows extra flexibility in the telling of the Gibeon story. Wis 7:15-8:1 is an extended, almost hymnic teaching which breaks the flow of the narrative. Moreover, the anticipatory character of 8:2-21 breaks in an even more striking way from the past tense scheme which characterizes both 7:1-12 and the retellings of the Gibeon story in the context of histories of Israel.

As argued above, the Wisdom of Solomon is in part a critique of the Qohelet's instruction, an instruction which appropriates parts of the Gibeon story. As would be expected, their hermeneutics are diametrically opposed, though both remain in the tension between the Biblical (Wisdom) tradition and Hellenism. Appropriating the more individualistic Hellenistic hermeneutic, Qohelet takes on the Solomon persona for a pure argument from experience. Solomon is reputed to have enjoyed unrivaled wealth and wisdom, so he is the natural one to say that all is "vanity and striving after wind." If he says that wisdom and riches are relatively worthless, so must everyone else (Qoh 2:12).

The Wisdom of Solomon, however, appropriates specific Biblical and popular Hellenistic traditions in order to provide an alternative to Qohelet. Often reformulating Biblical traditions using Hellenistic concepts and forms, the author builds on Solomon's post-exilic reputation for wisdom, along with traditions from Proverbs 1-9 and the Torah story. This Solomon begins by describing his own search for Wisdom through prayer, but this description only leads into a rereading of Israel's sacred traditions (Wis 10-19). These traditions confirm Solomon's own "experience," that Wisdom teaches people what pleases God and saves them (9:18).[261] In sum, Qohelet appropriates the *Hellenistic method* for a critique of Biblical tradition on the basis of experience. In contrast, the Wisdom of Solomon opposes that critique by arguing on the basis of Biblical traditions refracted through *Hellenistic idioms*.

- *Theology*

With regard to theological perspective, the Wisdom of Solomon displays contradictory tendencies. On the one hand, the book reinte-

---

[261] This description in 9:18 once again builds on Isis imagery. See Kloppenborg, "Isis and Sophia," 67-73.

grates the Proverbs 1-9 personified Wisdom figure back into the plot of how Solomon got extra benefits in addition to Wisdom. The rhetoric of chapters six to ten constantly emphasizes Wisdom's role in granting benefits rather than God's. On the other hand, this prominent Wisdom figure disappears in the subsequent theocentric retelling of parts of the Haggada story, chapters 11-19. This may indicate the limited didactic aims of the Wisdom metaphor, a metaphor designed to attract the audience to learn God's ways (9:10-13, 17-18) much as they are discussed in chapters 11-19.

Apart from the reintegration of Wisdom into the story, the Wisdom of Solomon implies God's initiative more than the other versions. Rather than arguing that good works lead to divine gifts, the Wisdom of Solomon claims that Wisdom leads to good works, a Wisdom only obtainable through the gift of a good soul or body (8:19-20) and the subsequent petition to God for her. Moreover, the doctrine of immortality is the author's attempt to find a way out of Qohelet's bleak universe, a way which preserves a place for faithfulness in the face of adversity. Such an emphasis on righteousness beyond prudence is not typical in the Jewish wisdom tradition, but neither are immortality or a host of other new *topoi* introduced by this late Second Temple period diaspora teacher.

Finally, given the fairly harsh descriptions of the audience in 6:4 and 9, the author seems to see his message as critical of their present behavior. In this respect the Wisdom of Solomon shares more with Qohelet than the various narrative versions of the Gibeon story. These narrative versions supported either a current socio-political program (1 Kgs 3:2-15; 2 Chr 1:1-13) or the reputation of a people with no political power (Josephus). Qohelet, however, breaks out of the narrative constraints of the story, and uses the instruction form to turn certain elements in the story against themselves. The result, in both Qohelet and the Wisdom of Solomon, is a highly original statement. Neither Qohelet nor the Wisdom of Solomon, however, departs as far from the Solomon-Wisdom-Riches topos as the following example of a Second Temple reflection on the Gibeon story within the context of an instruction.

Q 12:22-31

The last Second Temple Jewish interpretation of the Gibeon story to be treated is that in Q 12:22-31.[262] The following discussion is limited to

---

[262] As mentioned above, references to Q in this study follow Luke's versification.

Q 12:22-31 for several reasons. First, this is an integrated unit, showing clear lines of interconnection in itself. Second, 12:22-31, and not its immediate context, is kept together by the author/redactors of Matthew and Luke. Though some have proposed that parts of Luke 12:32ff. or even Luke 12:13-21 were originally part of the context of Q 12:22-31, the methodological control of Matthew and Luke's double witness does not exist for these proposed reconstructions of the literary context of Q 12:22-31. Third, as a Christian document produced before the destruction of the Second Temple, Q pre-dates the decisive split of Christianity from Judaism. Already with Matthew and Luke, Christianity is beginning to take its own course.

Reconstruction

Though reconstruction of Q can often be a very difficult job, Q 12:22-31 is a section with unusually large amounts shared between Matt (6:25-34) and Luke (12:22-31). Moreover, many of the remaining differences between them are the clear products of redaction on "Matthew" or "Luke's" part. The following is a presentation of a reconstructed text of Q (the variants are discussed in an appendix to this study):

Reconstructed Text

Reconstructed Text of Q 12:22-31

22a)	On account of this I say to you
22bα)	Do not be anxious
22bβ)	about your life, what you will eat,
22bγ)	nor about your body, what you will wear.
23)	Is not life more than food
	and the body more than clothing?
24a)	Look to the ravens, they neither sow
24b)	nor reap, nor gather into storehouses
24c)	and God feeds them.
24d)	are you not of more value than they?
25)	And which of you by being anxious can add
	a cubit onto the span of life?
26)	And about clothing do not be anxious.
27a)	Consider the lilies, how they grow.
27b)	They neither toil nor spin.
27c)	But I say to you that
27d)	Not even Solomon in all his glory

	was arrayed like one of these.
28a)	If God so clothes the grass which is alive in the field today and tomorrow is thrown into the oven,
28b)	how much more will God thus clothe you, O ones of little faith!
29)	Therefore, do not be anxious, saying, "What will we eat?" or "What will we drink?" or "What will we wear?"
30a)	For all these things are what the nations seek.
30b)	But as for you, the Father knows that you need these things.
31a)	Rather, seek his kingdom,
31b)	and these things will be added to you.

Structure

Q 12:22-31 consists almost exclusively of forms typical of wisdom literature. The text begins with a first person teaching introduction, 22a, and another appears in 27c. 22b and 29 are admonitions, the latter in debate form. 23, 24, 25 (a "who" saying), and 28 are all rhetorical questions. 24 and 27-28 are two visual instructions (*Anschaung Unterricht*), built around the principle of קל וחמר (qal vaḥomer). The complex as a whole is a "double-illustration-word," common throughout the synoptic Gospels.[263] For lack of a better term, 30 can be termed a contrast. 31 is a concluding injunction.

The following is a diagram of the structure of Q 12:22-31:

```
Wisdom Instruction ................................................. Q 12:22-31
    I.   First-person Teaching Introduction .................................... 22a
    II.  Teaching Proper ................................................................. 22b-31
         A. Admonition ................................................................. 22b-30
            1. Initial Statement ........................................................ 22b
               a.  Restricted Behavior: Worry ............................... 22bα
               b.  Restricted Objects: ......................................... 22bβ-γ
                   1)  Life: Eating .................................................. 22bβ
```

---

[263] This is an English calque from the German *Doppelbildwort*. On this form cf. Michael Steinhauser, *Doppelbildworte in den synoptischen Evangelien*, FB 44 (Würzburg: Echter, 1981), passim.

Tradition History

The only clearly secondary verse in Q 12:22-31 is the insertion in Q 12:25. Q 12:25 is not well integrated into its context. Its comment about adding to one's life[264] neither fits with the emphasis of its immediate context on food and clothing, nor is this theme resumed later in the saying. These structural irregularities indicate that 12:25 was not part of the original saying. Instead, it was inserted between the two visual instructions in 24 and 26-28 in accordance with the principle of catchword asso-

---

[264] See Joseph Fitzmeyer, *The Gospel According to Luke, X-XXIV. Introduction, Translation and Notes,* AB 28B (Garden City: Doubleday, 1985), 978-979, for discussion of this translation and references.

ciation. Its verb, μεριμνάω, agreed with that of the preceding and following admonitions. This would agree with rules which govern the development and organization of instructions in general.[265] The addition and adaptation of the insertion happened well before the saying reached Matthew or Luke.[266]

With the exception of verse 25, the passage is highly integrated, and there is not sufficient evidence to further subdivide the text into originally independent sayings.[267] The ascription to an authority, first person teaching style, and predominance of imperatives indicate that Q 12:22-24, 26-31 is a multi-segmented unit of a wisdom instruction.[268] The segments of the unit are all forms predominant in wisdom literature,[269] and the style is highly interactive, requiring the audience to concede points in the argument through intensive use of rhetorical questions. The arguments in 23 and 24-28* are built around the bipartite structure of the admonition in 22a, and the whole builds to a crescendo in the sudden appearance of an alternative mode of behavior in verse 31.

Response to the Gibeon Story

Nothing on the surface of Q 12:22-31 suggests that this teaching is a reflection on the Gibeon story. Nevertheless, just as in the case of Qohelet

---

[265] Kloppenborg, *The Formation of Q*, 268, 280-281.

[266] My reconstructed Q 12:26, however, is not a secondary adaptation of 12:25 to its context. Unlike Luke 12:26, Q 12:26 does not relate to the content of the 12:25 insertion, nor does it adapt that insertion to its context. Instead, it resumes the "clothes" half of the admonition after the interruption of the "food" illustration in 12:24. The insertion of 12:25 merely added to this preexisting interruption.

[267] Scholars who have divided the passage yet more include: Rudolph Bultmann, *Die Geschichte der synoptischen Tradition*, 2nd revised ed. (Göttingen: Vandenhoeck & Ruprecht, 1931), 82, 84, 107 (on 25-26), 92 (on the history of the rest of the unit); Erich Klostermann, *Das Matthäusevangelium*, HNT 4 (Tübingen: J. C. B. Mohr, 1927), 62; Dieter Zeller, *Die weisheitlichen Mahnsprüche bei den Synoptikern*, FB 17 (Würzburg: Echter, 1977), 86-87, 92-93; and Kloppenborg, *The Formation of Q*, 218. Cf. also Siegfried Schulz, *Q: Spruchquelle der Evangelisten* (Zürich: Theologischer Verlag, 1972), 194 and D. Catchpole, "The ravens, the lilies and the Q hypothesis: A form-critical perspective on the source-critical problem," *SUNT* 6-7 (1981-1982): 78-83.

[268] By "multi-segmented" is meant an integrated teaching consisting of a variety of smaller form-critically distinct units functioning together toward one overall point. See Kloppenborg, *The Formation of Q*, 280.

[269] Contra Schulz's attempt to establish the prophetic-apocalyptic character of this passage (*Q: Spruchquelle der Evangelisten*, 153-155). Cf. Zeller, *Die weisheitlichen Mahnsprüche*, 84-85 and Kloppenborg, *The Formation of Q*, 218-219.

1:12-2:26, further investigation shows probable connections.[270] First and foremost, the climax to which the entire text builds, verse 31, shares the germ of the plot of the Gibeon story. Just as Solomon requested wisdom and received other items, so the audience is told to seek the kingdom and their other needs will be met.[271] Like the Gibeon story (1 Kgs 3:11), Q 12:22-31 puts a high value on both the search for the right thing (now the kingdom) and the lack of a search for the wrong thing (now food, drink and clothing). Finally, Q 12:29-31 claims that search for the wrong things is characteristic of "the nations," while search for the right thing is the requirement for the faithful. As seen previously, the Deuteronomistic version of the Gibeon story shares this contrast. There Solomon was portrayed as the model Israelite king in rejecting the values of Israel's neighbors and preferring the gift of judicial wisdom (= Torah knowledge). Now the disciples' kingdom priorities are contrasted to those of the "nations."[272]

Such parallels show the similar dynamics of the Gibeon story and Q 12:22-31.[273] If such were all there were, there would not be sufficient indicators to show that Q 12:22-31 reflects specifically on the Gibeon story. But there is also the reference to Solomon in 27d. Q 12:22-31 puts considerable emphasis on this reference. Not only is it the only conclusion in the argument (23-28) which is stated positively, but the first-

---

270 Williams, *Those Who Ponder Proverbs*, 47-63 argues persuasively that Qohelet and Jesus stand together as examples of the aphoristic wisdom of counter-order, a type of wisdom which is built more on personal experience than tradition, which tends to use paradoxical metaphors, and which encourages deviation from traditional beliefs or values rather than accommodation to them. Along the lines of the latter characteristic of counter-order wisdom, Williams (p. 50) uses Q 12:22-31 as an example of Jesus' deviation from traditional wisdom *topoi* (cf. Prov 6:6-8).

271 I am indebted to my friend and colleague Kenneth Pomykala (Calvin College) for first pointing out the correspondence between the theme of Q 12:31 and the Gibeon story. This was my first clue that Q 12:22-31 might be a reflection on the Gibeon story.

272 Thus, contra Catchpole's attempt to establish the awkward and thus secondary character of Q 12:30a ("The Ravens and the Lilies," 81), this verse makes sense as a transformation of an opposition originating in the Deuteronomistic Gibeon story.

273 Heretofore, the closest anyone has come to recognizing the relation between the Gibeon story and Q 12:22-31 is Zeller, *Die weisheitlichen Mahnsprüche*, 91, who recognizes some of the parallel dynamics described above. Kloppenborg, *The Formation of Q*, 219, argues that the most striking parallel to this saying occurs in Wis 7:7-14. Obviously the approach adopted in this study does not take these references as mutually exclusive alternatives.

person teaching introduction which immediately precedes it also highlights the importance of the comparison with Solomon.

Outside the genealogies, mention of Solomon's portico, and one other Q text (Q 11:29-32), Q 12:27 is the only place where Solomon is mentioned in the New Testament. Both Q 11:31 and 12:27 undermine traditional positive evaluations of Solomon. Q 11:31 builds on the traditions regarding people flocking to Solomon for Wisdom (1 Kgs 5:14; 10:24//2 Chr 9:22-24), specifically the Queen of Sheba (10:1-10/2 Chr 9:1-9), and claims a still greater wisdom for Jesus. Q 12:27 refers to the traditions of Solomon's wealth, and claims that God takes better care of the lilies, and yet better care of those who seek the kingdom (Q 12:28b, 31).

Concluding Reflections

The Context

Because of the theoretical nature of the Q text as a whole, locating it historically and institutionally is even more difficult than for already problematic texts previously discussed in this study. Scholars who agree on its existence share a consensus that it was written sometime between Jesus' death and the destruction of the Second Temple. Whether 25 or 22b-24 along with 26-31 originated with Jesus is difficult to say. The above investigations, however, indicate that the passage was formulated with pedagogical purposes in mind, and probably functioned in some kind of didactic context in later Christian tradition. Moreover, the overall emphasis of the passage on renunciation of worldly security conforms with some descriptions of Jesus and his followers as traveling teachers.[274]

Adaptability, Inter- and Counter-Textuality

Q 12:22-31 (like Q 11:29-32) is a wisdom text in dialogue with traditions about the pre-eminent Israelite sage, Solomon. The Gibeon story portrays Solomon as having the correct priorities, and receiving his unparalleled wisdom, riches and honor for making the right choice. In the Deuteronomistic version in particular, God rewards Solomon with riches and honor for choosing wisdom and rejecting those things which pagan kings value (1 Kgs 3:11). Very little of this scheme is recognizable in Q 12:22-31. Solomon in Q 12:27d is only an example of riches fallen

---

[274] Luke (Q) 9:58 (//Matt 8:20); 10:2-12 (//Matt 10:5-15); Mark 10:29-30 (//Matt 19:28-29//Luke 18:29-30). For additional arguments for this context for Q 12:22-31, see Zeller, *Die weisheitlichen Mahnsprüche*, 93; Schulz, *Q: Spruchquelle der Evangelisten*, 155-157; Kloppenborg, *The Formation of Q*, p. 220 and note 202.

short of the gifts God can provide those who seek the kingdom. Rather than seeking Solomon's wisdom, one must now seek the kingdom (Q 12:31). Instead of rejecting pagan royal values, one must not be anxious about food, drink or clothes—for these are what "the nations" seek.

Though Q, like Qohelet, undermines Solomonic traditions while building past them, the document is too ambivalent about Solomon for this to develop into a critique. Both Q 11:29-32 and 12:22-31 build on *and beyond* the example of Solomon. Specifically, Q 12:22-31 shares the dynamics of the Gibeon story while replacing Solomon with Jesus as the pre-eminent sage, and wisdom with the kingdom as the ultimate priority. Each of these substitutions have their antecedents in Q's Wisdom theology.

When the Q Jesus speaks the wisdom saying in Q 12:22-31*, he does so as Wisdom's spokesperson. Second Temple Jewish Wisdom traditions emerge in early Christian Christological hymns as a mythic resource for talking about Jesus,[275] and the importance of Wisdom Christology in Matthew is now securely established.[276] The Q community reflects an even earlier stage in this type of reflection. Just as *Sophia* in the Wisdom of Solomon passed into holy souls, making them prophets and friends of God, so the Q Jesus is one of *Sophia's* messengers. In Q, Jesus (along with John) is among the children who justify *Sophia* (Lk/Q 7:33-35/Matt 11:18-19). This is the same *Sophia* who sends prophets and apostles, only to have them killed and persecuted (Lk/Q 11:49-51/Matt 23:34-37a) and will require their blood of this generation.[277]

But though Jesus is now the pre-eminent sage (Q 11:29-32), he is not a member of the traditionally "wise." Instead, he thanks God for hiding these things from the wise, and revealing them instead to babes (Lk/Q

---

[275] For a methodologically sophisticated approach to these hymns and review of literature, see Elizabeth Schüssler Fiorenza, "Wisdom Mythology and the Christological Hymns of the New Testament," in *Aspects of Wisdom in Judaism and Early Christianity*, ed. Robert L. Wilken, Judaism and Christianity in Antiquity 1 (Notre Dame: University of Notre Dame Press, 1975), 17-41.

[276] M. Jack Suggs, *Wisdom, Christology and Law in Matthew's Gospel* (Cambridge, MA: Harvard University Press, 1970).

[277] This picture of Jesus' as Σοφία's (Wisdom's) messenger is the probable context of Q 12:10 (/Matt 12:32), where Jesus says that blasphemy against the Holy Spirit (feminine) can not be forgiven, whereas blasphemy against him can. Schulz, *Q: Spruchquelle der Evangelisten*, 249-250; James Robinson, "Jesus as Sophos and Sophia: Wisdom Tradition and the Gospels," in *Aspects of Wisdom in Judaism and Early Christianity*, 5-6; Elizabeth Schüssler Fiorenza, *In Memory of Her: A Feminist Theological Reconstruction of Christian Origins* (New York: Crossroad, 1985), 134.

10:21/Matt 11:25-26). This saying is immediately followed by one where now Jesus, not *Sophia*, is the exclusive mediator of hidden divine knowledge.[278]

Similarly, Jesus' kingdom wisdom is counter-wisdom. For example, Q 12:22-31 draws in multiple ways on wisdom traditions while subverting their substance. The saying is set in an instruction and includes admonitions, rhetorical questions, and vivid illustrations typical of such didactic literature. In his illustrations he focuses his audience's attention on *Sophia'a* handiwork in creation. As we have already seen in Proverbs 8 and the Wisdom of Solomon, wisdom was personified in the Second Temple period as a female figure able to care for those who love her because of her presence at and role in creation.[279] Finally, Q 12:22-31 turns the Gibeon story reward scheme toward the kingdom goal. Now the truly "wise" will seek the kingdom first and let God take care of them. The conventional wisdom concern for security and quality of life is contradicted by this deeper wisdom of the itinerant teacher.

The radicality of the innovation emerges in a comparison with the Wisdom of Solomon, a document written at almost the same time as Q. In the Wisdom of Solomon, Solomon concludes the 6:17-19 *sorites* by claiming that desire for this Wisdom "leads to a kingdom." ($\dot{\alpha}\nu\dot{\alpha}\gamma\epsilon\iota$ $\dot{\epsilon}\pi\dot{\iota}$ $\beta\alpha\sigma\iota\lambda\epsilon\dot{\iota}\alpha\nu$).[280] Q 12:22-31, however, does not share the Wisdom of Solomon's fiction of Solomon speaking to other rulers. Nor does Q 12:22-31 share the Wisdom of Solomon's connections to traditional wisdom and the valuing of wealth, riches, and power. Now in Q 12:22-31, Wisdom's messenger instructs a different wisdom. Now Jesus, the itinerant teacher, is speaking, the $\beta\alpha\sigma\iota\lambda\epsilon\dot{\iota}\alpha$ ("kingdom") being discussed is God's, and *God* takes care of those who seek it. The didactic adaptation of the Gibeon story has been pushed to the limit.

---

[278] Robinson, "Jesus as Sophos and Sophia," 8-9. Note the contrast with Wis 6-9.

[279] During the Second Temple period wisdom was personified as a figure able to care for those who love her because of her presence at and role in creation. See the discussion of the Wisdom of Solomon in this study, above and Proverbs 8:22-31; Wisdom of Solomon 7-9; Job 28:23-27 and Sirach 1:1-10 among other texts.

[280] Wis 6:20.

Chapter Seven

SUMMARY AND CONCLUDING REFLECTIONS

In this chapter, the history of early Jewish interpretation of the Gibeon story is considered from the following three perspectives: adaptability, stability and inter-textuality/counter-textuality. Though these perspectives have already played an important role in the summaries of individual interpretations, the comprehensive focus of this review adds new insights. At the end of each section, I will consider some of its implications for modern interpretation of canonical texts.

But before I proceed, I should briefly discuss the tentative nature of many of the arguments summarized here. This study is an example of relatively confident historical criticism. Throughout the preceding chapters I have made a number of delicate exegetical judgments upon which the following summary is based. Thus, I have worked from reconstructed texts of the Vorlage, redactional layers of 1 Kgs 3:2-15 and Q 12:22-31. I opt for a minority position on the existence of a seventh century redaction of the Deuteronomistic history, and my identification of Qohelet and the Wisdom of Solomon as instructions (along with my description of instructions) is open to debate. Perhaps most importantly, I may not be followed by all in arguing that Qohelet 1:12-2:26 and Q 12:22-31 stand in a trajectory of instructional reflections on the Gibeon story.

It is because all these and other exegetical judgments required argument that the previous chapters have been necessary. Nevertheless, the impact of most of these judgments on the following summary and application is non-cumulative. That is, though I am probably not right about every one of my exegetical decisions, the survey as a whole still provides a basis for dialogue with contemporary interpretation. In the following, I presuppose the above cautionary comments, but note some additional places where a particular conclusion is especially dependent on a preceding analysis.

ADAPTABILITY

Summary

As in previous summaries of individual interpretations, I begin by looking at how the Gibeon story was adapted to speak new messages to new situations. Each of the following subsections discusses an interpretation of the Gibeon story in its attempt to answer the following questions:

1)   What context did it speak to?
2)   What was its primary message?
3)   What genre was the vehicle for that message?
4)   What parts of the Gibeon story were particularly emphasized or reacted to?
5)   What theological perspective informed this message?
6)   How did a given interpretation prepare for later ones?

It will not always be possible to answer each of these questions. Nevertheless, an overview which answers those questions which can be answered will illuminate the dynamics of adaptation.

The Vorlage

The Vorlage was written in the context of a local sanctuary. The text's main focus is on promoting Solomon as divinely favored, and allowing the sanctuary at Gibeon to partake of his prestige. The vehicle for this message is a dream epiphany report enclosing a petition scene initiated by the petitioned. Such a petition scene is a narrative elaboration of the royal ideological presupposition that the pious, legitimate king enjoys unlimited favor from god(s).

In order to enhance this picture of divine favor, the Vorlage theocentrically appropriates the originally Egyptian traditions which claim that a personified female Wisdom figure brings riches and honor. Now *God* (not Maat or Wisdom) shows overflowing generosity to Solomon by giving him riches and honor in addition to what he requested. Moreover, if our reconstruction of the Vorlage is correct, this plot is developed in an artful way to promote the cultic emphases of the story as a whole. Working through the (reconstructed) Vorlage, the reader awaits Solomon's request after God's initial offer, only to be given Solomon's long speech leading up to his unusual request for a "hearing heart." Then, this gap is resolved through God's assertion that God is acting "according to [Solomon's] words" in God's subsequent promise of a "wise and intelligent heart." Yet with the resolution of this gap, God opens up yet another one: why God went on to give Solomon additional benefits ("and also that which you did not request I give to you.") Within the confines of the reconstructed Vorlage this gap is never explicitly resolved. Nevertheless, the genre of the story and its cultic focus subtly incline the reader to provide their own answer: king Solomon's piety, particularly his patronage of the Gibeon sanctuary, made God favor him.

The First Deuteronomistic Edition

As argued previously, the first Deuteronomistic edition is part of an overall history designed to legitimate a seventh century Judaen nationalistic, anti-pagan program of cultic centralization and reunification of the Northern and Southern kingdoms. The main message of this edition is that God favors Solomon insofar as he proves to be the legitimate successor to David by following the Deuteronomistic law. Thus Solomon becomes an image of the success which can come to a Davidic king who is part of the Deuteronomistic program. Later, in 1 Kgs 11, the Deuteronomist describes the dissolution of Solomon's empire as an example of what happens when the Davidic king allows himself to be corrupted by foreign influences.

The generic vehicle for this message is the dream epiphany form of the Vorlage, but this Vorlage is thoroughly reworked through insertions on the microstructural level. These insertions neutralize the royal ideological elements of the Vorlage and assert God's sovereignty over against and in judgment of royal sovereignty. Now rather than accusing God of placing him in an impossible situation, Solomon introduces his request by praising God for God's faithfulness to God's promises.

In addition, the Deuteronomist fills the gaps in the Vorlage, subtly reconstruing both the nature of Solomon's request and the reason for God's provision of extra benefits. Through recontextualizing Solomon's request, the Deuteronomist reconceptualizes it as a petition for legal wisdom. Then the Deuteronomist adds a prologue to the divine speech which explains God's additional gifts (1 Kgs 3:11aα4-βγb). According to this prologue, God responds favorably to Solomon's petition not only because he requested an item consistent with the Deuteronomist's ideal for kingship (now conceived as legal wisdom), but also because he rejected items seen as valued by non-Israelite kings. In this way the Deuteronomist exploits the narrative junctures of his Vorlage to speak a new message to his audience, a people just emerging from Assyrian domination and recovering their ancient indigenous traditions.

Later Deuteronomistic Additions

Not much can be said about the historical background of the final redaction of the Gibeon story. In general, the context of these later additions is the post-exilic lack of restoration of the monarchy and concomitant increased emphasis on Solomon as culture hero, one of Israel's great kings. Both the Adonai editor's insertion in 1 Kgs 3:15bα1-6 and the Deuteronomistic supplement at 1 Kgs 3:2 build on the cultic centralization presuppositions of the first Deuteronomist, but contradict the first Deuteronomist's mild critique of Solomon in 1 Kgs 3:3b. In the addition at 1 Kgs 3:15bα1-6, the Adonai editor portrays Solomon as learning from his epiphany experience by going to Jerusalem to offer his thanksgiving sacrifices. Moreover, by adding God's affectional response to Solomon's request in 1 Kgs 3:10, the Adonai editor stresses the virtue of that request for wisdom. The generic vehicle for both these additions by the Adonai editor are insertions between major structural junctures of the story.

The generic vehicle for the Deuteronomistic supplement (1 Kgs 3:2) was originally a marginal gloss. Only later was it inserted at the very beginning of the story. The intent of the gloss is to excuse Solomon's practice of sacrificing outside Jerusalem through reference to the prevailing pre-temple sacrificial customs. In order to support its argument, the gloss uses a Deuteronomistic regnal formula to describe the pre-temple sacrificial customs of the people. Through using the formula, the glossator claims that Solomon was exempt from the centralization rule even on the Deuteronomistic tradition's own terms.

The Chronicler

Chronicles was written during the Persian period to support the Second Temple cult. The main message of the Chronicler's Gibeon story is that God responded at Gibeon to Solomon's inaugural sacrifice by equipping him to build the temple. Thus the original description of Solomon's practices at Gibeon (1 Kgs 3:4b), becomes an independent narrative, one which places wilderness cultic items at Gibeon and describes

Solomon as sacrificing there. Whereas the Vorlage merely implied that Solomon's patronage of Gibeon played a role in God's favor to him, the Chronicler makes the connection between sacrifice and epiphany more explicit: God appeared to Solomon *that* night. Thus through making an implicit narrative connection explicit, the Chronicler continues a trend of narrative explication begun by the Deuteronomist's insertion of the divine speech prologue.

In Chronicles, Solomon is a flawless temple builder. In order to present this picture of Solomon, the Chronicler omits or adapts any element detracting from Solomon's perfection. As a result, this picture of a flawless Solomon resonates with the emphasis on God accomplishing God's purposes through him. The narrative is thoroughly theocentric. Through such emphasis on divine provision, the story encourages hope in God's ability to provide what is required to provide for the Second Temple.

Josephus

Josephus' version of the Gibeon story was written in the context of post-70 CE Jewish demoralization and gentile vilification of Jews. He adopts the Greek model of apologetic and didactic history to portray Solomon as a cultural hero and moral example, as one of those Jews who are "entitled to rank among the highest." In retelling the Gibeon story, he uses aspects from both the Chronicles and Kings versions as they suit his didactic and apologetic ends. On the one hand, he appropriates the Chronicles emphasis on Solomon's pious sacrifices, but on the other hand, he shares the Kings version's focus on the ethical aspects of the story.

Also, Josephus' version more liberally adapts the story than Chronicles. He describes rather than quotes most of the speeches, rearranges Solomon's request to add suspense, reduces the things Solomon rejects to one item (riches), and consistently clarifies the narrative junctures of the story, showing two ways in which Solomon's virtue was rewarded by divine favor. In these ways Josephus radically rewrites the story in order to assure his readers, even in the shadow of a destroyed Second Temple, that virtue is rewarded and evil punished.

Qohelet 1:12–2:26

The interpretations discussed above all stay close to the story's narrative framework. The Vorlage, Deuteronomistic edition, Chronicles, and Josephus show the tendency of such narrations to be constitutive and promote concrete socio-political projects (Vorlage, Deuteronomistic edition, Chronicles) or groups (Josephus). Towards this end, they portray Solomon's request in terms of their own priorities, and build on his increasing reputation. Moreover, beginning with the Deuteronomistic prologue to God's response to Solomon, these narrative interpretations show a tendency to fill gaps in the Vorlage and clarify narrative junctures of the story. Finally, beginning with Chronicles, these narrations also have a didactic element, adapting the story and its moral to speak to the individual members of an increasingly powerless audience.

Such a didactic focus on individuals is dominant in instructions which reflect upon the Gibeon story. Qohelet is written to the members of the landed aristocracy of Ptolemaic Israel, people supported by their holdings, but powerless against an autocratic and ruthlessly efficient Hellenistic monarchy. He appropriates the genre of instruction to argue on Greek terms against conventional Biblical wisdom and for a limited form of *carpe diem*, accepting one's portion (food, drink, and work) in the face of one's fate (death).

In order to argue that even incomparable riches and wisdom are essentially unsatisfactory, Qohelet uses the instruction form and Solomonic fiction to redescribe *from the inside* Solomon's search for fulfillment in wisdom and riches. As Qoh 2:12 asserts, "Why should a person who follows after the king [i.e. Solomon], do what he already did?" In such terms Qohelet builds on Solomon's reputation to form an anti-Gibeon story, one which leads not to success, but to knowledge through failure. The original story and subsequent retellings of it (Deuteronomistic, Chronicles, Josephus) were built around the claim that wisdom leads to additional benefits. Qohelet, however, applies the Greek focus on individual experience to the story's theme of Solomon's search for wisdom, only to argue for the essential *unproductivity* of wisdom. Rather than merely reconstruing the Gibeon story plot about wisdom's extra benefits, Qohelet denies its truth. According to his argument from experience, wisdom is ultimately as unproductive as folly. Through such a critique of the claims of traditional wisdom, Qohelet makes room for a Hellenistic focus on limited enjoyment in the face of individual destiny.

In notable contrast to any other reaction to the Gibeon story, Qohelet does not mention God in the description of Solomon's search for fulfillment in wisdom and folly. Solomon, not God, receives the blame for this fruitless endeavor. Nevertheless, in contrast to many Greeks, Qohelet maintains the reality of God despite his critique of the wisdom tradition. Though God's will is unpredictable and inscrutable, God is still the power behind reality.

The Wisdom of Solomon

The Wisdom of Solomon was written to an Alexandrian community of Jews in crisis, probably at some point after the Roman annexation of Egypt in 30 CE. This audience is hesitating to be righteous because of the threats and Qohelet-like arguments of a group described as the "ungodly." In order to counter this group's claims, the Wisdom of Solomon is framed as a Solomonic instruction with a different message. Whereas Qohelet argues for acceptance of limited fulfillment in the face of death, the Wisdom of Solomon argues for faithfulness to tradition supported by belief in immortality and a future reversal of the positions of the "ungodly" and "righteous ones." Whereas Qohelet used the instruction form and Solomonic fiction to undermine traditional wisdom, the Wisdom of Solomon uses the same elements to undermine a position similar to Qohelet's.

This argument is undergirded by a new construal of the link between wisdom and its extra benefits. The narrative interpreters portrayed this link as divine reward for virtuous priorities, while Qohelet questioned the connection between wisdom and extra benefits. In contrast, the author of the Wisdom of Solomon draws on Isis traditions along with Wisdom traditions from Proverbs 1-9 to describe a female Wisdom figure. This figure could be seen by his Hellenistic audience as a dependable provider of riches, honor, power, and other items valued by them. Whereas Qohelet's Solomon merely gave an *inside* account of his search for knowledge, now (the Wisdom of Solomon's) Solomon provides an *intimate* account of his special relationship with a female Wisdom figure.

Q 12:22-31

The wisdom saying in Q 12:22-31 seems to be intended for a community of traveling teachers. It encourages those teachers not to concentrate on securing the basic necessities of life, arguing that if they exclusively focus on God's kingdom, God will provide life's basic necessities. Unlike the Wisdom of Solomon, this Q saying replaces the description of Wisdom's benefits with an argument for the advantages of seeking God's kingdom. Now, Jesus, not Solomon, is the instructor, and Jesus' appeal to creation rather than Solomon's experience is the basis for the wisdom teaching. In this saying, Jesus uses the Creator God's care for nature as an image of God's care for Jesus' followers. As in Qohelet, Q's Solomon is great, but his wisdom and riches are not the ultimate in human experience. Rather, Q's Solomon is surpassed by Jesus in wisdom, and his riches are surpassed by nature.

Conclusions

Trends in Adaptability

Thus in its early interpretation the Gibeon story was transformed from a royal ideological text into a resource for early Jewish identity and morality. If the story had remained exclusively oriented to its original royal-cultic Sitz im Leben and intention, it never would have functioned as powerfully as it did for later communities. But later communities found a variety of ways to adapt the story to speak messages to their contemporary situations. Some interpreters (the Deuteronomist, Adonai editor, Deuteronomistic Glossator, Chronicler and Josephus) exploited the narrative junctures of the story, redescribed Solomon's request, and reconstrued the connection between divinely given wisdom and additional benefits. Other interpreters (Qohelet, Wisdom of Solomon) yet more radically adapted the story through reflecting on it in the context of instructions. These interpreters went beyond the third person perspective of the narratives to provide a first person, inside account of Solomon's search for wisdom. Finally, the Q Jesus undermines previous accounts of *Solomon's* experience through using rhetorical questions to appeal to the *audience's* experience of nature. In this way Q subtly subverts the wisdom search for secure happiness.

This is only a partial listing of the ways interpreters creatively reconstrued the Gibeon story to articulate perspectives with lasting meaning, perspectives on what really matters in human existence and what does not, on the divine context of an empire or of life in general, and on the relationship between the knowledge which comes with faith and the goods which the world values. Though the Gibeon story began as an example of royal ideology, by the end of its journey through the Second Temple period it has become "adaptable for life." No longer focusing on Solomon's privileges with God, it now speaks to everyone about how the knowledge which faith provides is the key to finding everything truly valuable in human existence.

Adaptability and the Truth of the Biblical Witness

Frei's history of eighteenth and nineteenth century hermeneutics shows how the rise of the historical-critical method and the enlightenment understanding of meaning as reference led to a fragmentation of the typologically constructed unity of the Testaments and split Biblical Hermeneutics into two basic approaches to discerning the truth in the scriptures: either establishing the independently verifiable truth of the events to which the texts refer or using the texts as indicators of the perspective of the authors, an enterprise which developed into the modern philosophical discipline of hermeneutics. As Frei puts it:

> Let us recall the hermeneutical polarity concerning biblical narratives, corresponding to, and largely occasioned by, the issue of the positivity of revelation. The mediating positions tended to be pushed either toward a specific, ostensive, or referential interpretation, i. e. the affirmation of biblical literalism and the factual reliability of the accounts, or toward a completely historical, nonostensive understanding of the narratives...The choice of subject matter finally came to be between the two extremes of literally intended accounts which are reliable factual reports, and historically understood mythical accounts which have no essential connection with fact reporting.[281]

As Frei points out, both approaches suffer from serious deficiencies. On the one hand, the independently verifiable truth of many of the events to which the text refers has proven increasingly difficult to establish using the critical disciplines customarily employed to evaluate such claims. On the other hand, the attempts of theologians to reconstruct the truth of Biblical texts in terms of the intention of the Biblical authors, have had difficulty incorporating the realistic, history-like character of the Biblical narrative and claims implicit in that character. Instead, the meaningfulness of Biblical statements is construed in relation to modern accounts of general human experience. The transcultural kernel of insight is extracted from the culture bound idioms and mythology of the author, but the Biblical witness appears increasingly superfluous in comparison with the modern philosophical systems used to lend it meaning.

The early Jewish texts surveyed in this study long predate this eighteenth century crisis in Western hermeneutics and even the literal-figural style of interpretation which it undermined. Nevertheless, since this study concerns a text which Frei would claim has a realistic, history-like character, a study of the approaches to this character of the Gibeon story's earliest interpretations can shed new light on this modern problem.

---

[281] Hans W. Frei, *The Eclipse of Biblical Narrative: A Study in Eighteenth and Nineteenth Century Hermeneutics* (New Haven and London: Yale University Press, 1974), 255.

At the beginning of the stream of tradition stands the Vorlage, with no traceable precursors. This text makes certain claims about Solomon in particular. As a royal ideological text, it describes God as particularly favorable to him, and it portrays this favor as undergirding his judicial wisdom, riches and honor. As a cultic text, it claims that he acquired his wisdom at Gibeon, a sanctuary at which he frequently offered God huge sacrifices. To the extent that this text opposes the claims of social groups opposing Solomon and/or the claims of other sanctuaries, the Vorlage's intent is identical with its history-like, realistic character. Its attempt to buttress Solomon and Gibeon can be considered an example of mystification, i. e. a language utterance designed to accomplish certain social aims over against another social group, an utterance which at the same time depends for its success on that other social group's lack of awareness of the real aims of the text in question.

Several important factors, however, distinguish the Vorlage from later interpretations in this respect. As is typical in many early societies, these interpretations begin with a prima facie acceptance of the historical truth of this (by their time) ancient text. But they also demonstrate considerable freedom in modifying it in accordance with their own theological understandings of God's relationship to those in power and to humans in general. On the basis of such considerations the Deuteronomist inserts very specific words in Solomon's and God's mouths. It is possible that he may have claimed some special tradition or particular social authority to do this, but such is not indicated in the text. Since the story is placed in a history beginning with Deuteronomy and written from its perspective, its placement and agreement with that Law suggest that the insertions are grounded in the theological and legal truth of the Deuteronomistic Law. Such a grounding in theological presuppositions is not identical with the historical reference of the insertions, though the author of the insertions obviously makes certain historical claims on the basis of such presuppositions.

The same can be said for the other narrative and instructional reflections on the Gibeon story. Though beginning with a prima-facie acceptance of at least some of its historical truth, each interpretation adapts central elements of the story to articulate or reflect on certain beliefs brought to it. In particular, the instructions seem ambivalent about specific claims of authority on the basis of the historicity of the events described in the Gibeon story. Though Qohelet, like many other instructions, assumes the fiction of being written by an ancient authority (Solomon), this fiction is so vague as to lead some modern scholars to deny it, and it is discarded in chapters three and following. Rather than relying on Solomonic authority, Qohelet makes a number of arguments from experience, using Solomon, the incomparably wise and rich king, as his mouthpiece. Similarly, the Wisdom of Solomon never refers directly to Solomon himself, and the fiction of his authorship appears most prominently in chapters 7-9 to critique Qohelet's contrary presentation of him. Moreover, the speaker supports his claims through the use of certain arguments and through the thoroughgoing integration of Biblical wisdom with Hellenistic idioms and forms.[282] In summary, both Qohelet and the Wisdom of Solomon seem to assume a certain distance from their fiction of Solomonic authorship, and this distance must have been recognized in the circles responsible for their early transmission.[283]

This study of the early interpretations of one historical narrative from the Bible suggests that the problems of historical reference and theological appropriation go back into the very period where the text was becoming scripture. These interpreters solved the problem by retelling the story in a way which integrated their theological perspective, or, yet more radical, shifted the generic context (and in Q the speaker) so as to have a fictional Solomon speak from his "experience." Such an approach partially preserved the history-like character of the Biblical narrative, but it certainly did not take any particular history-like version of the story as absolute.

This suggests that Frei's description of the options explored by modern interpreters is much narrower than the potentialities explored by the early Jews who formed the Biblical text and established it as part of our canonical tradition. The early Jewish interpretations of the Gibeon story suggest other generic possibilities for modern interpretation. For example, one option building directly on the model of the Josephus and Chronicles is interpretation through conscious retelling. The instructions suggest yet more radical recontexualization of the story. A modern didactic analogy to them would be dramatization of the story or classroom experiential re-creation of its dynamics.[284]

---

[282] Likewise, Q 12:22-31 is certainly attributed to Jesus, but the heart of the passage is an argument on the basis of natural examples. The attribution to Jesus is more problematic to evaluate than Qohelet's and the Wisdom of Solomon's ascriptions to Solomon.

[283] Note the clear concept of the author as a teacher in the first appendix to Qohelet, Qoh 12:9-11.

[284] Examples of such actualization of the Biblical text can be seen in Adrienne and John Carr's *Experiment in Practical Christianity*, 2nd revised ed. (Nashville:

STABILITY

Summary

However much early Jewish interpreters adapted the story, they did not just do anything at all with it. Instead, they consistently preserved certain elements of the story, even while radically adapting these elements to serve their own purposes. In this section I survey these elements and look at how they were preserved while being adapted. Whereas previous summary sections focused on this process in individual interpretations, here I focus on the stability of the Gibeon story *across* interpretations. In addition, I briefly discuss some elements of the story which were preserved in some interpretations and not in others.

Solomon's Reputation

One of the most consistent elements of the interpretations is an emphasis on Solomon's reputation. Almost every interpretation builds upon or reacts to the promotion of Solomon's reputation originally seen in the Vorlage. Nevertheless, each reconceptualizes the grounds for this reputation. Through its formulation of Solomon's speech and petition scene, the Vorlage emphasizes God's unlimited favor to Solomon as the pious king and David's legitimate successor. The Deuteronomist adds an ethical component, presenting Solomon as divinely favored and a legitimate successor only if he follows his father's example in being faithful. The addition by the Adonai editor in 1 Kgs 3:15ba1-6 protects Solomon's reputation by bringing him back to Jerusalem for his thanksgiving sacrifice. Finally, the marginal comment by the Deuteronomistic glossator in 1 Kgs 3:2 enhances Solomon's reputation by neutralizing the Deuteronomist's critique of Solomon's sacrificial practices (1 Kgs 3:3b).

This trend of shared focus on Solomon's reputation, along with redescription of its grounds, continues in the later interpretations of the story. 2 Chr 1:1-13 focuses almost exclusively on Solomon, tailoring every element of the story to present him as God's chosen temple builder. In Josephus' *Antiquities*, Solomon is portrayed as one of the Jewish people's great sages and as a didactic example of pious sacrifice and wise preferences.

This emphasis on Solomon's reputation is also a central component in the three interpretations of the Gibeon story which appear in instruc-

---

Discipleship Resources, 1985) and *The Pilgrimage Project: Renewing Our Sense of God's Presence and Purpose* (Nashville: Upper Room, 1987).

tions. Like many instructions, Qohelet's ascription to an authority (Solomon) and autobiographical prologue legitimate its message. In this case, however, Qohelet appropriates the Solomonic fiction to argue for the unproductivity of incomparable wisdom and riches, thus undercutting conventional values for which Solomon stood. The Wisdom of Solomon then uses the Solomonic fiction to critique Qohelet's message. Now the autobiographical component of the wisdom instruction legitimates the argument against Qohelet that a personified Wisdom figure *can* provide bountiful benefits, just as a counselor provides success to a king whom she advises. Finally, in Q 12:27 Solomon's incomparable riches are an example which is surpassed by nature.

The Promise of Long Life

The interpretation of the long life promise begins with the Deuteronomistic edition of the Gibeon story. As mentioned in the redaction analysis, Solomon was not unusually gifted with long life. This presented a problem to early interpreters of the Gibeon story. Even in the Vorlage, the promise of long life was subordinated to the promises of wisdom, riches and honor. This promise is probably included at this early stage as a traditional part of a cultic inscription. The Deuteronomist, who presupposes long life in the land as a reward for obedience, takes this promise as an opportunity to emphasize the ethical context of Solomon's reign. Specifically, he adds a condition to it specifying that Solomon must walk in God's ways as his father did if he wants to live a long time.

This struggle with the long life promise continues in the later interpretations of the story. Chronicles eliminates the promise, and no reflection of it appears in Qohelet or Q 12:22-31.[285] Josephus assimilates the promise to the Nathan oracle, having God promise Solomon a very long dynasty rather than long life. The Wisdom of Solomon replaces the promise of long life with emphasis on how the personified Wisdom figure is immortal and bestows immortality.

This theme of immortality is important for the Wisdom of Solomon, much as long life is important to the Deuteronomist. Because each have such components as major parts of their systems, the Deuteronomist and Wisdom of Solomon are able to integrate the anomalous promise of long

---

285 Interestingly, the addition in Q 12:25 does concern long life, but it was probably added merely because of its common focus on μέριμνα ("anxiety") with Q 12:22, 26, and 29. It does not constitute an additional reflection on the Gibeon story.

life into their retellings of the story. In this way, similarity of thought facilitates integration of certain motifs from Biblical passages.

Plot of the Gibeon Story:

As argued in a previous chapter, the plot—preference for wisdom leads to additional benefits—originates in ancient wisdom traditions. The Gibeon story Vorlage theocentrically appropriates Egyptian wisdom traditions which argue that a personified female Wisdom brings riches and honor. In the Vorlage, wisdom is no longer personified, but instead *God* responds to Solomon's request for wisdom by providing riches and honor as well, along with a long life to enjoy them (an aspect of cultic inscriptions in general). As described above, the (reconstructed) Vorlage develops this plot in an artful way. First there is a temporary gap regarding the exact character of Solomon's request. Upon the resolution of this gap, another gap is opened up: why God not only gave Solomon what he requested, but also favored him with additional gifts. This latter gap is only implicitly resolved: God favored Solomon because of his regular and extravagant patronage of Gibeon.

Most subsequent interpretations share the thesis that additional benefits follow a search for wisdom, but each develops this thesis in a different way. Thus, the Deuteronomist exploits his Vorlage's own gaps regarding both the nature of Solomon's request and the reason for God's extra gifts to him. According to the Deuteronomistic recontextualized version of Solomon's request and insertion into the divine speech, God gave Solomon extra gifts because he rejected pagan royal priorities and chose legal wisdom instead. These modifications then serve as the basis for later interpretations, which redescribe what Solomon requested, what he rejected, and the relative importance of each. The first example of an interpretation which builds on 1 Kgs 3:11 is the addition of the Adonai editor in 1 Kgs 3:10. Like many subsequent interpretations, this addition focuses on the virtue of Solomon's preference for wisdom, rather than highlighting his rejection of other items.

Like his precursors, the Chronicler preserves but modifies the Gibeon story plot. In particular he presents Solomon's wisdom as temple building knowledge and Solomon's "riches, possessions, and honor" as temple building supplies. These gifts are now God's fulfillment of God's promise to David that Solomon would build the temple. The Chronicler also redescribes Solomon's request and the list of things he rejected so that they correspond more to the interests of the non-royal public. Now Solomon requests wisdom and knowledge, not the more specifically governmental judicial wisdom. In addition, the military victory mentioned in the 1 Kgs 3:11 list of things Solomon rejects (an item specific to the Mesopotamian royal dedicatory and blessing traditions against which the Deuteronomist argues) is made to refer more specifically to "haters," again an item more relevant to the general public and unconnected to royalty.

Josephus modifies both Solomon's request, the list of what he rejects, and the list of God's extra gifts to him. Now Solomon requests that which his father wished for him: νοῦν ὑγιῆ καὶ φρόνησιν ἀγαθήν ("a sound mind and good understanding"). Moreover, the list of things Solomon did not request is reduced to one item: riches, the item exclusively valuable to τοῖς πλείστοις ("most people"), clearly a non-royal public. Finally, Josephus includes military victory in the list of extra divine gifts to Solomon, rather than in the list of things Solomon rejected.

The instructions even more radically reconstrue Solomon's request, rejection of items, and divine gifts to him. Whereas all of the narrative interpretations of the story preserved the basic plot (God rewards Solomon for requesting wisdom), none of the instructions preserve this plot unchanged. Qohelet portrays Solomon as pursuing *both* wisdom and riches, only to discover the essential unproductivity of both. His only reward is the knowledge that the only things worthy of pursuit in life are food, drink and the rewards of toil. In contrast, Q 12:22-31 preserves part of the plot "preference for wisdom over other items leads to acquisition of them," now it is preference for *God's kingdom* over food and clothes which leads to God's provision of such basic necessities.

The Wisdom of Solomon preserves more of the plot than Qohelet or Q. It portrays Solomon as petitioning God to send a personified Wisdom to him as a counselor, thus preferring her to jewels, gold, silver, and other items mentioned in Proverbs 8 or otherwise valued in the Hellenistic world. Though this description contains a counterpart to Solomon's acquisition of other items through preferring Wisdom to them, now Wisdom herself is conceptualized as a counselor and thus provider of the additional benefits. No longer the direct giver of riches, honor, etc., God is the sole provider of Wisdom to individuals, and (on analogy with Proverbs 8) it is Wisdom's relationship to God which enables her to provide benefits to the individuals who receive her. The plot of the Gibeon story has come full circle. Whereas the Vorlage eliminated the feminine Wisdom figure from its picture of Solomon receiving riches and honor along with wisdom, the Wisdom of Solomon brings her back into the story in order to more persuasively establish the link between wisdom and extra benefits.

In summary, just as with Solomon's reputation, so with the plot, the various interpretations share an aspect of the story, but adapt this aspect in various ways. Nevertheless, (with the exception of the Deuteronomistic modifications) even these varied interpretive adaptations share an inclination to democratize the story. They no longer include either the Vorlage's conventional royal ideology or the Deuteronomist's reformist royal ideology. Instead, they emphasize the technology of faith, that is, the way preference for the knowledge provided by faith over things typically valued by individuals leads to acquisition of additional benefits (to the individual).

Other Interpretive Modifications

The three themes discussed above are shared by almost all of the interpretations of the Gibeon story, but there are a number of other interpretive modifications which are shared by a smaller group of texts. The following is a list of the most important examples:

1) Reconceptualization of Solomon's presence at Gibeon (1 Kgs 3:3b (Deut 1); 1 Kgs 15bα1-6 (Adonai editor); 1 Kgs 3:2 (Deut Glossator); 2 Chr 1:1-6)

2) (Related to 1) Emphasis on how Solomon's sacrifice prepared for his experience at Gibeon (2 Chronicles 1:1-6, 7; Josephus)

3) Adaptation of the original reference to Solomon's youth in his petition: Solomon's youth appears as the justification for David's temple preparations in Chronicles (1 Chr 22:5; 29:1), and it heightens the uniqueness of Solomon's request in Josephus and the Wisdom of Solomon (Josephus VIII:23; Wisdom of Solomon 8:19). Solomon's youth becomes a major unifying theme in the first part of Josephus' account of Solomon's reign. In the Wisdom of Solomon, Solomon's youth underlines the greatness of the honor which he anticipates as a result of his reception of wisdom (8:10).

4) Mention of Solomon's process of thought (2 Chr 1:11, Qohelet, Wisdom of Solomon)

The above list does not include the items omitted by more than one interpretation.[286] Thus 2 Chr 1:7-13, Josephus and all of the Instructions

---

[286] This is not to mention the many unique interpretive moves described in previous chapters.

eliminate references to the dream aspect of the Gibeon epiphany; David fades into the background in all the interpretations after the Deuteronomist; and all of the instructions drop most references to Gibeon or the events which preceded and followed the epiphany.

One thing shared in common, between all of these additions and omissions, is that Chronicles is a member of every single group of interpretations which share a particular addition or subtraction. From the outset it is clear that post-Biblical interpretations of the Gibeon story read the Kings account in conjunction with the Chronicles interpretation of it. Both 1 Kgs and 2 Chr are part of the larger body of sacred Scripture, and for this reason they both stood available to subsequent communities, who drew on the potentialities of both for their retellings of and reflections on the Gibeon story. Because of its accessibility to later readers through being a part of the Hebrew canon, the influence of Chronicles on later interpretations of the Gibeon story is unmistakable.

Conclusions

In the first part of his book on theological use of Scripture, David Kelsey investigates several different twentieth century theologies asking the following question: "What aspect(s) of scripture is (are) taken to be authoritative?"[287] The same can be done for any interpretive tradition, including those surrounding the Gibeon story. Just as Kelsey uncovers diversity in twentieth century answers to his question, so the interpretations of the Gibeon story show a broad range in their own answers. Indeed, the ancient picture of variety of foci in interpretation is even more pluralistic than the modern one provided by Kelsey. Whereas modern interpreters often focus on the meaning of a Biblical text (however construed), ancient interpreters worked within a wider range, appropriating a variety of narrative and/or thematic elements from the Gibeon story to make their points. The emphasis on Solomon's reputation and how faith leads to additional benefits proved particularly productive. More problematic elements of the story—such as the promise of long life—were adapted by those interpreters who had a place for such elements, while other interpreters dropped them.

Most of all, these early Jewish interpreters are consistently guided by their overall theological vision as it speaks to their particular social situation. The truth of their interpretation stands or falls on the success of

---

[287] *The Uses of Scripture in Recent Theology* (Philadelphia: Fortress, 1975), 15. The investigation is on pp. 14-119, "Construing the Text."

their articulation to their community of their theology and praxis using images, themes, and plot borrowed from a community tradition: the Gibeon story. Notably, articulation of this theology and praxis totally irrespective of the tradition is not an apparent option. Even Qohelet and the Q Jesus explicitly refer to Solomon, if only to use Solomonic traditions to undermine themselves. These early Jewish interpreters and their audiences stand in a certain line of tradition, and their arguments (even against the tradition) draw life from it by being articulated in terms of those stories and images which make it up.

In the third part of his book on modern theological use of Scripture, Kelsey presents a view of the relation of Scripture and theology which is broad enough to articulate the principles operative in such early Jewish interpretation. He argues that one test of theological use of scripture is the productivity of the interaction between the two in speaking to a community's situation.[288] Of course, if the use of scripture does not articulate the theology, then the enterprise is obviously doomed. A more common problem, however, is that the encounter with scripture is so superficial as to make its use superfluous, or even more serious, the theological perspective is so alien to anything found in scripture that no fruitful encounter is possible.

If applied to the early Jewish context, this principle would suggest that early Jewish interpreters needed to make connections to central elements of their interpreted tradition, in this case the Gibeon story. Indeed, an interpretation of the story which omitted reference to such central elements would hardly have cause to refer to the story at all. This does not mean that interpreters needed to stay true to the story's original intention. Rather, effective interpreters had to build (whether in a positive or negative way) on the traditions and texts which they wished to

---

288 *The Uses of Scripture in Recent Theology*, 173-175, 196-197. His major claim is that a theologian's choice of certain patterns in scripture as normative is dictated by that theologians prior imaginative construal of his or her community's theological *discrimen*, a vision of God's presence among them (pp. 167, 193, and 212 (among others)). Though this picture better accounts for the theologian's half of the dialogue with scripture, there are several problems with it. First, Kelsey's description of the *discrimen* is too narrowly focused. Different communities have a multiplicity of different categories which play important roles in their encounter with scripture. Second, the concept of one *discrimen* fails to reflect the diversity of approaches which (Kelsey himself recognizes) each theologian uses. Third, by describing the theologian's commitment to and construal of this *discrimen* as prior to doing theology, Kelsey does not account for the kind of interaction between theology and scripture which produces something new.

extend or subvert. In order to have an interpretive impact, these interpreters needed to make more than a superficial connection to the plots, characters, and/or themes of their interpreted text.

In the case of the Gibeon story, early interpretations consistently emphasized two things: Solomon's reputation and the story's plot: preferring X (wisdom) leads to X, Y, and Z (additional benefits). To be sure, even as we have reviewed this stability of the story in its interpretation, we have seen the many different ways interpreters made a connection to these common elements. Nevertheless, this survey has shown that the story enjoyed a continuity of interpretation in the midst of variety, a being over against its various adaptations.

The basis for this continuity lies not only in the structure and imagery of the story itself, but also in the common aspects of the interpreters' situations. Thus, the greatness of king Solomon's reign was an appealing image to Second Temple Jews who were increasingly powerless. The claim that wisdom led to riches and honor was attractive to a Jewish people whose members were generally neither rich nor honored in their Hellenistic world.[289] Moreover, as early Jews repeatedly re-interpreted the story and reflected on it, the story's interpretive trajectory developed a life of its own. Jews would counter the belief in Solomon's incomparable greatness or wisdom's benefits through subversive inversion of these elements of the story.

These attractive elements in the Gibeon story and the existence of this interpretive trajectory help explain why it was among the more frequently interpreted texts in early Judaism. Though early and later Jews creatively interpreted a vast array of Biblical texts, certain texts like the Gibeon story were interpreted particularly frequently. Such frequently interpreted texts had central elements which could interact particularly productively with their interpreters' concerns and aims. Thus individual interpreters often repeatedly referred to certain texts which were pivotal for them, and early Jewish interpreters as a group focused more on certain texts than others. Again, with regard to the latter phenomenon, not only did certain texts prove consistently adaptable to early Jewish interpretive ends, but early Jews often scored their most radical theological points by re-interpreting these pivotal texts.

Whereas some elements like Solomon's reputation and the plot of the story appear in all interpretations of the story, other elements like the

---

[289] Though individuals, particularly in the diaspora, did achieve riches and honor, this was often in spite of their Judaism rather than by virtue of it.

long life promise only appear in interpretations which have a place for it. In these cases, elements of the story are only central to the extent that they interact with its interpreters' aims. Sometimes the story elements present a particular problem to some interpreters. For example, Solomon's sacrifice outside Jerusalem at Gibeon was a particular problem to the Deuteronomist, later Deuteronomistic editors, and (possibly) the Chronicler. At other times, a certain element of the story corresponded to an aspect of an interpreter's theology. For example, since the Deuteronomist already saw long life as a primary reward for obedience, he was able to adapt the long life promise to his own purposes.

Whether an element was a problem or opportunity, the interpreter often adapted it to contribute to his aims. Thus, it is not clear how the Chronicler felt about the 1 Kgs 3:4b description of Solomon's patronage of Gibeon. He may have been disturbed by Solomon's apparent disregard for Jerusalem, or he may have seen this as an opportunity to connect Solomon with wilderness implements already placed at Gibeon earlier in the narrative. In any case, what is clear is that the Chronicler completely reconceptualized Solomon's sacrifice at Gibeon. Now this narrative describes Solomon's cultic inauguration of his reign. It is an initial presentation of Solomon acting like a chosen temple builder.

To be sure, in other cases elements of the story were simply omitted: whether deemed hopelessly contradictory to the interpreter's aims or simply unnecessary. For example, the Chronicler and later interpreters omit much of the Vorlage's and Deuteronomist's emphasis on David. Instead, later interpreters focused ever more exclusively on the great king Solomon: his wise choice and God's additional gifts to him. As interpretation of the story progressed, this process of omission seems to have had a cumulative effect. Later interpretations such as Josephus and Q pared the story down to focus almost exclusively on its central elements: Solomon's reputation and the story plot: preference for X leads to X, Y, and Z.

In sum, our look at stability and adaptability in early Jewish interpretation has revealed a suggestive contrast between the consistently textual orientation of early Jewish thought and its free use of tradition, between the frequent need to dialogue with tradition and the apparent freedom to subvert it. As early Jews continually articulated their visions and values in terms of their communities' traditions, they expanded their interpretive repertoire in order to speak textually to their situation. A limit in one area (need for inter-textuality with the Bible) prompted flexibility in another (range of interpretive latitude).[290]

Such emphasis on inter-(Biblical) textual theology and creative interpretation contrasts with the modern emphasis (in some quarters) on historical-critical exegesis as the only legitimate mediator to the Biblical text taken as canonical. As discussed in the introduction, much modern scholarship, particularly religious scholarship, still puts a special premium on those types of Biblical interpretation which discern and extend at least part of the original intention of the Biblical text. This relative rigidity in interpretation contributes to alienation from the Bible and a tendency toward types of theological discourse which do not refer to the Bible. In both early Judaism and modern Christianity, a limit in one area (emphasis on inter-textuality with the Bible, modern focus on original intention) corresponds to flexibility in another (interpretive creativity, tendency toward lack of relationship with the Bible). The comparison with early Judaism can lead us to more consciously choose how we limit and free ourselves.

INTER-TEXTUALITY ALONG THE CANONICAL CONTINUUM

Summary

As stated in the introduction, this study focuses on early Jewish interpretations partly because they can provide insights into early operative concepts of canon and canonical interpretation. Nevertheless, the interpretations we have examined have not presented an entirely unified picture. Not only do they differ in their choice of traditions to interpret and in their stance toward them, but there is a development in these differences: the earliest interpreters of community traditions seem to have had different interpretive options from those of later interpreters.

Sanders has proposed imaging this process in terms of a "canonical continuum," extending from stabilization of oral traditions into writing, through redaction, collection, textual stabilization, and development of hermeneutical rules to render adaptable what had become stable.[291] This

---

[290] Here and in the next paragraph I build on Jonathan Smith's fascinating cross-cultural study of lists, catalogues, and canons: "Sacred Persistence: Towards A Redescription of Canon," originally published in *Approaches to Ancient Judaism: Theory and Practice*, ed. William Scott Green, BJS 1 (Missoula, MT: Scholars Press, 1978), 11-28.

[291] *Canon and Community*, 28.

canonical continuum image is a useful way to recognize significant changes in the interpretive stance of earlier and later interpreters without drawing sharp dividing lines between them. In the following I examine two ways in which the intertextual connections of the Gibeon story changed as it moved along the "canonical continuum." I begin by considering the formal relationship of each interpretation to the Gibeon story itself, and then consider the way each interpretation integrated the story with other texts and traditions.

Stance Toward the Gibeon Story: the Move Out of the Text

If the sequence of the redactional analysis in chapter two is correct, there is a gradual movement out of the text in the successive additions to 1 Kgs 3:2-15. The redactional additions to 1 Kgs 3:2-15 are of different types, and moreover, are introduced at different levels of the hierarchy of the text's structure. The stages in this process are the following:

1) Extensive intervention in a written source and integration of it into a larger narrative (1 Kgs 3:3, 6aβb, 8-9, 11aα4-b, 12b$\beta\gamma$, 13b, 14a; 1st Deuteronomistic edition)

2) Introduction of transitions from one part of the source to another (1 Kgs 3:10, 15bα1-6; Adonai editor)

3) Marginal gloss standing outside the story, but included right before it (1 Kgs 3:2; Deuteronomistic glossator)

These three phases move from intervention throughout the text to intervention only outside progressively larger structural units. The Deuteronomist generally leaves the clauses of the Vorlage intact and only intervenes outside them. The Adonai editor intervenes inside the text, but only between major structural breaks. The Deuteronomistic glossator intervenes outside the text, in a margin. When this gloss is inserted in the text, it is only included outside the Gibeon story.

Such movement suggests that the contributors to the text had some awareness of the structural shape of the Gibeon story. Taking Sanders' image of a "canonical continuum," we see a progressive impermeability of the text as it proceeds along the early part of that continuum. The Vorlage was authoritative enough that the first Deuteronomistic editor left most of its clauses intact, but reinterpreted them with additions. After the Gibeon story had been modified and inserted by the Deuteronomist into the history, the history as a whole and the story within it began to grow in authoritativeness, but not enough to prevent the

Adonai editor (quite close in spirit to the original redactor) from intervening slightly between major structural seams.[292]

Subsequently, modifications occurred outside the bounds of the story. The gloss in 3:2 was probably written in the margin, only later being added onto the beginning of the story. The ultimate development of this process is the creation of free-standing reflections on 1 Kgs 3:2-15 which are separate from the text: 2 Chr 1:1-13; Josephus; Qohelet 1:12-2:26; Wisdom of Solomon 7-9; and Q 12:22-31.

As seen in the previous discussion of adaptability, such free-standing interpretations of the Gibeon story became progressively more creative in their reformulation of it. The gloss in 1 Kgs 3:2 merely appropriated a Deuteronomistic model to soften the critique of Solomon in 1 Kgs 3:3b. The Chronicler completely reshaped the story, freely dropping or adapting aspects of it which do not magnify Solomon. Moreover, he added elements to make the story promote the temple-centered political vision so important to the Chronicler. Josephus continued this trajectory of narrative reformulation of the story, but his modifications are more radical than those in Chronicles. In particular, he was able to be more flexible in reshaping the story's speeches through only indirectly describing rather than quoting them.

Finally, beginning with Qohelet, the reflections on the Gibeon story in the context of instructions yet more creatively reformulated its message. In particular, through using the first person instruction form, Qohelet and then the Wisdom of Solomon were able to provide the "inside story" of Solomon's true search for wisdom, thus subversively undermining their textual precursors. Indeed, the instructional reflections on the Gibeon story so radically invert their precursors (whether the Gibeon story itself or (in the Wisdom of Solomon) Qohelet), that their counter-textual relationships to those precursors are almost unrecognizable.

Other Texts: The Widening Scope of Inter-textuality

Though the Vorlage theocentrically appropriated Wisdom traditions to make its point, the Deuteronomist is the one to really introduce inter-textuality into the interpretation history of the Gibeon story. It is with the Deuteronomist's appropriation of the Gibeon story into an authoritative history of Israel that it is transformed from a Gibeonite to an all-Israelite

---

[292] As I argue in "Royal Ideology and the Technology of Faith," 81-85, 322, the textual fragment in 1 Kgs 3:1 is another example of this process. It was added at the very beginning of the story late enough in the story's tradition history that the Old Greek manuscript tradition does not place it here.

tradition. Moreover, the Deuteronomist initiates the process of correlating the Gibeon story with other parts of Israel's historical tradition. Now, the story plays a role in a larger narrative context, following the succession narrative and anticipating later texts describing Solomon's reign. Moreover, the Deuteronomist subtly builds on traditions elsewhere in the Deuteronomistic history. The introduction to the story (1 Kgs 3:3) now presupposes the Deuteronomic cultic centralization regulations (Deut 12), and the body of the story assumes the Deuteronomistic kingship ideal (Deut 17:14-20). Also, various Deuteronomistic insertions allude to the patriarchal promises, Moses figure, and Nathan oracle. Finally, the Deuteronomist counter-textually undermines originally anti-Solomonic traditions and critiques the perceived priorities of non-Israelite kings.

The Chronicler selectively adapts many of the Deuteronomist's inter-textual moves, but also adds some moves of his own. These new moves are concentrated in his expanded account of Solomon's inaugural sacrifice at Gibeon. The Chronicler relates Solomon's sacrifice to the cult of the wilderness period through mention of the Tent of Meeting, ark, tabernacle, and Bezalel's bronze altar. Moreover, the assembly of "all Israel" and mention of wilderness cultic implements makes Solomon's inauguration parallel to David's. Both these inter-textual moves *extend* the story so that it can better depict both Solomon's close relationship with David and Solomon's status as the one chosen by God to build the temple. The mention of the tent of meeting in the 2 Chr 1:6 gloss is a similar extension of the story.

As mentioned above, from Chronicles onward, almost all reflections on the Gibeon story except Q clearly draw on both 1 Kgs 3:2-15 and 2 Chr 1:1-13 for aspects which serve their purposes. Thus Qohelet appropriates aspects of 1 Kgs 3:12b and 1 Chr 29:25 to describe the incomparability of Solomon's wisdom. The Wisdom of Solomon transforms Solomon's description of his youth into a description of his common heritage with humanity in general (Wis 7:1-6). But, as in Chronicles, the Wisdom of Solomon emphasizes how God's gift of wisdom will help him build the temple (Wis 9). Similarly, Josephus adapts elements from both the Kings and Chronicles accounts, drawing primarily on the ethically focused Kings account, while appropriating parts of the Chronicles description of Solomon's sacrifice at Gibeon.

As the first Hellenistic reflection on the Gibeon story, Qohelet marks two important shifts in the shape of inter-textuality along the continuum. It is with Qohelet that we first see subversive appropriation of Israelite traditions and intense dialogue with aspects of Hellenistic culture. Though it is obvious how dialogue with Hellenism could be occasioned by Israel's encounter with Hellenistic rule, Qohelet's subversive hermeneutic was also connected to the massive cultural shifts involved in this encounter. In contrast with Qohelet, the Deuteronomist, later editors of the Gibeon story and Chronicler all stood in essential cultural continuity with each other and the early pre-Deuteronomistic Vorlage. All were formed in dialogue with inner-Israelite traditions, only rarely and polemically relating to non-Israelite traditions. But with the advent of Hellenism in Israel, interpreters confronted another body of cultural and textual tradition, one which they did not immediately see fit to reject completely. In this context, Qohelet adapted a stance toward tradition from Greek popular philosophy and radically critiqued the Israelite wisdom tradition from that perspective. Moreover he formulated this radical critique through inverting traditional wisdom forms, sayings, and themes. Thus, in the context of radically different cultural circumstances from his precursors, Qohelet writes an anti-instruction, transforming Solomon into the anti-sage, and reconceptualizing the dynamics of the Gibeon story so that traditional wisdom categories are undermined.

Like Qohelet, the Wisdom of Solomon is thoroughly infused with Hellenism, but unlike Qohelet, the Wisdom of Solomon uses Hellenistic categories to bring its Hellenistic Jewish readers to a positive encounter with their ancestral traditions. Whereas Qohelet subverted Israelite tradition from a Hellenistic perspective, the Wisdom of Solomon makes Israelite traditions attractive and persuasive through using Hellenistic categories to reconceptualize them. The reflection on the Gibeon story is part of this process. It melds Israelite and Hellenistic traditions to describe the benefits of a search for wisdom—with wisdom being conceived as special insight into God's work in history—thus setting the stage for a provision of such insight through a retelling of Israel's formative history.

In addition, the Wisdom of Solomon is distinguished from its precursors by a positive relationship with non-narrative Israelite traditions. In their inter-textual reformulations of the Gibeon story, the Deuteronomist and Chronicler limited themselves to other narrative traditions. For example, the Deuteronomist used the promise-fulfillment scheme to connect the story with the patriarchal promises and Nathan oracle, while the Chronicler focused on making the first part of the story parallel to David's inauguration of his reign. Qohelet merely used the structure of a narrative tradition—the Gibeon story—to undermine non-narrative

Israelite traditions—conventional wisdom. In contrast, the Wisdom of Solomon drew not only on its Kings and Chronicles precursors, but also on Proverbs 8, to reconceptualize traditional wisdom and critique Qohelet.

Since Q does not explicitly draw on other Biblical traditions, Josephus is the next and final example of explicit inter-textuality in early Jewish Gibeon story interpretations. His interpretation stands almost as a summary of the inter-textual innovations of his precursors. Like the Deuteronomistic redactional additions and Chronicles, Josephus integrates the story with its narrative context, modifying Solomon's request to agree with David's prayer for him. Like other post-Chronistic reflections on the Gibeon story, Josephus draws on both the Kings and Chronicles accounts. Finally, like Qohelet and the Wisdom of Solomon, Josephus is in dialogue with Hellenism, didactically transforming the story so that it can function well in the context of a Greek apologetic and didactic history.

Conclusions

The previous sections on adaptability and stability have shown how early Jewish interpreters of the Gibeon story consistently drew deeply on its imagery while freely adapting it to speak new messages to new situations. This section on inter-textuality/counter-textuality has more precisely investigated how such preservation and adaptation changed along the canonical continuum. Whereas early interpreters apparently felt free to rework community traditions through insertions on the microstructural level, later interpreters gradually moved out of the text, ultimately producing free-standing narrative retellings of the Gibeon story and instructional reflections on it. Moreover, this change in genre corresponds to a change in interpretive stance toward the Gibeon story, from extension to potential subversion.

As modern interpreters, we stand at the other end of the canonical continuum from the interpretations studied in this book. Our position late in the process means that we cannot do certain things. For example, unlike the Deuteronomist, we can not definitively re-edit our ancient tradition. Unlike the glossators, we can not insert our own brief comments and corrections. Instead, we are limited to free-standing interpretations.

As this study has shown, however, this limit can also mean an opening of interpretive possibilities. Particularly with the disjunction produced by the encounter with Hellenism, the later Gibeon story interpreters took advantage of the interpretive freedom of independent interpretations, radically reconstruing the story and its major emphases. Indeed, Qohelet and the Wisdom of Solomon's (along with Q) recontextualization of the Gibeon story enabled yet more radical adaptation of the story than was possible in narrative rewriting.

Like Qohelet, the Wisdom of Solomon, Q and Josephus, we too stand at major remove from the culture and times of the Biblical texts. It is in this context that the early Jewish example of interpretive flexibility is particularly attractive. As already argued in the introduction, such interpretive flexibility is as necessary now as it was when the Biblical texts were being recognized as canonical. Particularly in the present socio-theological situation, interpreters of the Bible are confronted with the necessity to exploit the Bible's potential to be adaptable for life.

There is another aspect of our position at the late end of the canonical continuum. Throughout the early part of the continuum, interpreters correlated the Gibeon story with an increasingly wide scope of material. By the point represented by the Wisdom of Solomon, the Gibeon story could be correlated to the entirety of Biblical tradition. Now, in so far as we focus on a text because of its participation in the larger canon, we too have the opportunity to correlate each individual text with the canon in which it participates. Though the text may never have been written in relation to other texts included in that canon, we can take advantage of its participation in the canon to see how its imagery, plot, and themes correspond to or contradict those of other canonical texts.

"Resonance" is a good image for this possibility of mutual reinforcement and influence. When brought into close relationship with each other, the imagery of these texts can "resonate," producing a result which none of the texts would have individually produced. Thus, the Wisdom of Solomon, for example, creatively combined the Proverbs 8 image of feminine Wisdom with the Gibeon story plot. Consider as an modern example, Phyllis Trible's powerful concluding reflections on the stories about Hagar's flight and expulsion (Gen 16:1-16; 21:9-21):

> . . . Hagar foreshadows Israel's pilgrimage of faith through contrast. As a maid in bondage, she flees from suffering. Yet she experiences exodus without liberation, revelation without salvation, wilderness without covenant, wanderings without land, promise without fulfillment, and unmerited exile without return. This Egyptian slave woman is stricken, smitten by God, and afflicted

for the transgressions of Israel. She is bruised for the iniquities of Sarah and
Abraham; upon her is the chastisement that makes them whole.[293]

In this way, Trible first memorializes Hagar's suffering through contrast
with the formative history of Israel, then uses imagery from Second
Isaiah (Isa 53:5) to depict Hagar's suffering as redemptive. Moreover, in
the latter move, Trible sets up an unexplicit resonance between Hagar's
redemptive suffering and Christ's. For it is Christ's suffering which
Christian theology has traditionally depicted in terms of Second Isaiah's
suffering servant imagery.[294] Through this creative linkage and juxtaposition of disparate texts in the canon, Trible actualizes the Bible's potential to be adaptable for life.

Finally, standing at the late end of the canonical continuum, we have
the opportunity to imitate the early Jewish examples of intense and
creative integration of contemporary culture and Biblical text. Just as
Qohelet, the author of the Wisdom of Solomon, and Josephus, radically
re-interpreted their community traditions in the context of a pluralistic
Hellenistic culture, so we stand immersed in a relatively homogeneous
media culture and have access to a variety of sub-cultures: Native
American, Afro-American, Eastern, etc. Moreover, just as early Jews
found truth through reconstruing their community texts through the
medium of their Hellenistic culture, so we can find truth through radical
reconstrual of our traditions in relation to the multitude of cultures
which we encounter. Consider as a modern example of this process,
Carter Heyward's integration of the Genesis 1 creation account and
Native American traditions:

> In the beginning was God
> in the beginning
> the source of all that is

---

[293] Phyllis Trible, *Texts of Terror: Literary-Feminist Readings of Biblical Narratives*, OBT
13 (Philadelphia: Fortress, 1984), 28.

[294] Though the above description does hold for the quoted paragraph, I should note
that in the next paragraph Trible returns to the memorializing theme of the book as a
whole. Drawing back from the soothing implications of her use of Second Isaiah,
Trible returns to her stark contrast between Hagar and Israel:

> Hagar is Israel, from exodus to exile, yet with differences. And these differ-
> ences yield terror. All we who are heirs of Sarah and Abraham, by flesh and
> spirit, must answer for the terror in Hagar's story. To neglect the theological
> challenge she presents is to falsify faith.

Texts of Terror, 28-29.

In the beginning
God yearning

God moaning
God laboring
God giving birth
God rejoicing
And God loved what she had made.
And God said,
"It is good."[295]

Not only does her poem offer feminine imagery of God, but it beautifully articulates God's passionate connection to God's creation. Much like the early Jewish interpreters studied in this book, Heyward makes her interpretation more effective by exploiting the narrative junctures of the Genesis 1 account, using Native American mother God imagery to explicate the connection between God's creation and God's concluding pronouncement, "it is good."

FINAL REFLECTIONS

In the introduction I suggested that the early Jewish interpreters studied here practiced neither exegesis, nor eisegesis, but an intensely creative interpretive mode which might be termed "sunegesis:" combining *and/or* doing battle with community traditions. Not only did this involve radically adapting traditions to speak to new situations, but it also meant drawing deeply on those traditions, exploiting the immense potential of their imagery, narrative junctures, contradictions, etc. Indeed, as we looked at interpretations which stood later on the canonical continuum, we saw how interpreters grew yet more radical in their reinterpretation of the story, and how they drew on earlier interpretive traditions, other canonical texts, and contemporary Hellenistic traditions to produce a combined result which mere correlation of ancient text and contemporary situation would never have achieved.

To be sure, we can not completely adopt early Jewish interpretive modes. For example, if we are clear about the distinction between the original purposes of the text and our contemporary use of it as canon, we must be more conscious than these early interpreters may have been, that

---

[295] Carter Heyward, "Blessing the Bread: A Litany," in *Our Passion for Justice: Images of Power, Sexuality, and Liberation* (New York: Pilgrim, 1984), 49.

our use of the text is just that, *our* use of the text. We can not honestly beat other people over the head with our interpretation, maintaining that they have to subscribe to our reading of this or that text in the Bible. The Bible has been used as a weapon long enough, whether for good or ill. Now recognizing our role in any use of the Bible as canon, we must beat that sword into a plowshare.

Further investigation of the exact criteria for modern Biblical interpretation would go beyond the scope of this study of early Jewish interpretation. Though early Jewish interpretations, like modern interpretations, depend to some extent for their viability on the depth of their interaction with Scripture, this is a necessary and not sufficient condition for good interpretation. Moreover, early Jewish interpreters merely offer potential models for modern interpretation in their interaction with a variety of aspects of Scripture, creative interpretive modes, connection of the Gibeon story with other parts of the canon, and thorough integration of their interpretations with Hellenistic conceptuality. Though I have presented preliminary arguments in the introduction for the contemporary need for such models, further consideration of issues raised there and in the body of the study must await another context. These exegetical arguments and interpretive proposals have reached the point where further discussion is required for them to be sharpened and extended. It is in this spirit that I offer all which precedes, looking forward to the dialogue which I hope this book will provoke.

APPENDIX

RECONSTRUCTION OF Q 12:22-31

DISCUSSION OF VARIANTS

The following discussion follows the notation for Q reconstruction developed by the Q project at the Institute for Antiquity and Christianity at Claremont, California. Since this discussion revolves around reconstruction of a Greek text and thus involves constant reference to Greek phraseology and vocabulary, I will not translate the Greek in this section. Greek knowledge is presupposed.

Sigla

In the following, each discussion begins with a Greek citation of the reconstructed Q verse. The relationship of these reconstructed verses to Luke and Matthew are indicated using sigla developed by the Institute for Antiquity and Christianity Q project (Claremont, California). The following is a key to these notations adapted from the unpublished "Formatting Conventions for the "Q" Database" worksheet.[296]

[ ]   Square brackets in the text enclose words or letters found in Luke, but not in Matthew.

( )   Parentheses enclose words or letters found in Matthew, but not in Luke.

---

[296] P. 2 of the January 22, 1988 version.

If there is an element in Luke which does not appear in Matthew, but also does not seem to have been part of Q, this is indicated by empty square brackets, separated by one space.

If there is an element in Matthew which does not appear in Luke, but also does not seem to have been part of Q, this is indicated by empty parentheses, separated by one space.

/ \   Slashes surround transpositions in the order of Matthew and Luke's shared material. The relative position where the other evangelist has placed the indicated material is shown by the siglum / \, enclosing no text.

Finally, raised numbers next to the sigla indicate the number of the variant. These variants are then investigated in the following discussion of Q reconstruction.

Discussion of Variants Proper

Q 12:22

[ ]¹Διὰ τοῦτο λέγω ὑμῖν
μὴ μεριμνᾶτε τῇ ψυχῇ (ὑμῶν)² τί φάγητε ()³
μηδὲ τῷ σώματι (ὑμῶν)² τί ἐνδύσησθε

1) Luke 12:22a, Εἶπεν δὲ πρὸς τοὺς μαθητὰς αὐτοῦ, is missing in Matt 6:25 and appears to be a transition added by Luke. With it, the passage has a double introduction, Luke's third person quote introduction (22a) and the shared first person teaching introduction, διὰ τοῦτο λέγω ὑμῖν. The use of εἶπεν πρὸς with the accusative is characteristic of Lukan redaction, and the sentence as a whole resembles the Lukan introduction to chapter twelve (12:1).²⁹⁷ Luke 12:22a and the clearly Lukan 12:32b (τὸ μικρὸν ποίμνιον, "little flock") share the idea that 12:22b-31 is spoken to the disciples, but 12:22b-31 does not have any internal indicators that it was somehow meant for the disciples. Luke 12:22a may have been intended

---

²⁹⁷ Those scholars who discuss Luke 12:22a almost universally agree on its redactional character. See in particular: Joseph Fitzmeyer, *The Gospel According to Luke, X-XXIV*, 976 and 978 and Joachim Jeremias, *Die Sprache des Lukasevangeliums: Redaktion und Tradition im Nicht-Markusstoff des dritten Evangeliums* (Göttingen: Vandenhoeck & Ruprecht, 1980), 33 and 216.

to indicate that in 12:22b-31 Jesus told the disciples in clear language that which he told the multitudes in a parable in 12:16-21.[298]

2) Matthew has second person plural possessives after both ψυχῇ and σώματι, while Luke does not. As Schulz argues, Luke probably omitted the possessives in order to universalize the saying. This would be particularly important, given the fact that Luke has limited the audience of the saying by adding the introduction in Luke 12:22a. Matthew lacks the introduction and thus lacks any need to expand the saying's applicability. The ὑμῶν in Matt 6:25 applies to a wider audience.[299]

3) Matthew adds ἢ τί πίητε at the end of this line. The secondary character of this addition is clear from the fact that even Matt 6:25b (//Luke 12:23) does not include an element corresponding to his earlier ἢ τί πίητε. Rather, the text of Q agreed with Luke 12:22 in this respect. In it Jesus admonishes the disciples to not worry about their lives, what they will eat (for life is more than food) or about their bodies, what they will wear (for bodies are more than clothing). Matthew's added ἢ τί πίητε matches the introductory saying in Matt 6:25a/Luke 12:22 with the imperative in Matt 6:31//Luke 12:29.[300]

Q 12:23

(οὐχὶ)¹ ἡ [ ]¹ ψυχὴ πλεῖόν ἐστιν
τῆς τροφῆς καὶ τὸ σῶμα τοῦ ἐνδύματος

1) Whereas Matthew (the above reading) has a rhetorical question here, Luke has a statement connected to the preceding by the sentential adverb γάρ. Both Matt 6:27 and Luke 12:25 preserve one of Q's rhetorical questions, but Matt 6:25b, 26b, and 30b have rhetorical questions expecting "yes" answers, while Luke 12:23 is no longer a rhetorical question, and Luke 12:24b and 28b are now softened to question-exclamations. Since the turn of the century, exegetes have agreed that in all three of these

---

298 So Bernard Weiss, *Die Quellen des Lukasevangeliums* (Stuttgart and Berlin: J. G. Cotta, 1907), 471.

299 Siegfried Schulz, *Q: Spruchquelle der Evangelisten*, 149. So also Michael Steinhauser, *Doppelbildworte in den synoptischen Evangelien*, 216; Fitzmeyer, *The Gospel According to Luke X-XXIV*, 976.

300 H. Schürmann, *Traditionsgeschichtliche Untersuchungen zu den synoptischen Evangelien* (Düsseldorf: Patmos, 1968), 119, considers Matthew's reading to be original.

cases Luke has smoothed the original interrogative character of this wisdom saying.[301]

Q 12:24

(ἐμβλέψ)¹ατε (εἰς)¹
τ[οὺς κόρακας]² ὅτι οὐ σπείρουσιν οὐδὲ θερίζουσιν
[ ]³ οὐδὲ (συνάγουσιν εἰς)³ ἀποθήκ(ας)³
καὶ ὁ [θε]⁴ὸς τρέφει αὐτ[οὺς]²
(ουχ)⁵ /ὑμεῖς\⁵ μᾶλλον /\⁵
διαφέρετε (αὐτ)⁶ῶν

1) κατανοεῖν is one of Luke's preferred verbs. In Luke 12:24 it is clearly a Lukan stylistic improvement.[302]

2) On the one hand, some argue that Luke's inserts a more specific bird here, ravens, so that this example will correspond to the more specific image in Luke 12:27.[303] This argument, however, would not explain why Luke inserts τῶν πετεινῶν at the end of the verse.[304] On the other hand, there are good reasons for taking Luke's reading as original and Matthew's as the modification. As Jeremias points out, ravens are portrayed in the Hebrew Bible as unclean birds (Lv 11:15; Deut 14:14) for which God nevertheless cares (Ps 147:9; Job 38:41).[305] In antiquity ravens were known as birds so careless that they did not even return to their nests.[306] This background adds to the significance of Luke's version of Q 12:24. Matthew accommodated this expression to the more frequent τ(ὰ πετεινὰ τοῦ οὐρανοῦ) in order to avoid the problem of having God care for

---

[301] Adolf von Harnack, *Sprüche und Reden Jesu: Die zweite Quelle des Matthäus und Lukas,* Beiträge zur Einleitung in das Neue Testament, no. 2 (Leipzig: ET, 1907), 9; Schulz, *Q: Spruchquelle der Evangelisten,* 149, 150, 151; Steinhauser, *Doppelbildworte in den synoptischen Evangelien,* 216, 218, 219.

[302] So Harnack, *Sprüche und Reden Jesu,* 9; Schulz, *Q: Spruchquelle der Evangelisten,* 149; Steinhauser, *Doppelbildworte in den synoptischen Evangelien,* 261-261; Jeremias, *Die Sprache des Lukas evangeliums,* 217; Fitzmeyer, *The Gospel According to Luke X-XXIV,* 978.

[303] So Harnack, *Sprüche und Reden Jesu,* 10; Schulz, *Q: Spruchquelle der Evangelisten,* 150; Steinhauser, *Doppelbildworte in den synoptischen Evangelien,* 217.

[304] This is variant (6). For argument that it is an insertion see below. The argument would still hold if τῶν πετεινῶν was in Q and preserved by Luke.

[305] Jeremias, *Die Sprache des Lukasevangeliums,* 217.

[306] Fitzmeyer, *The Gospel According to Luke X-XXIV,* 978. Note, however, that ravens are responsible for feeding Ezekiel in 1 Kgs 17.

unclean birds.[307] This modification also required him to change the pronoun following τρέφει.

3) Whereas Matthew's reading συνάγουσιν εἰς ἀποθήκας is the third sentence in a series which describes what the birds do not do, Luke's reading (οἷς οὐκ ἔστιν ταμεῖον) has this third element as a subordinate clause describing the birds and this subordinate clause includes an element, ταμεῖον, not included in Matthew's reading. Luke's subordinate clause appears to be a stylistic improvement on the Matthean series of three verbs separated by nothing more than οὐ and οὐδὲ.[308] ταμεῖον then serves as a parallel complement to ἀποθήκη in this subordinate clause.

4) ὁ πατὴρ ὑμῶν ὁ οὐράνιος in Matt 6:26 is a Mattheanism. Luke's shorter reading is to be preferred.[309]

5) This is the second place where Luke softens one of Q's rhetorical questions.[310] In addition, Matthew's reading preserves the front extra position of the second plural pronoun in this rhetorical question, a position which emphasizes the contrast between the subject of this clause and the subject of the previous one. Luke, however, switches the positions of ὑμεῖς and μᾶλλον as part of his substitution of πόσῳ for οὐχ.

(6) Luke's τῶν πετεινῶν appears to be a clarification of the antecedent of the pronoun seen in Matt (αὐτῶν). It is more difficult to see Matthew's reading as a simplification of Luke's.[311]

Q 12:25

τίς δὲ ἐξ ὑμῶν μεριμνῶν δύναται
/προσθεῖναι\\¹ ἐπὶ τὴν ἡλικίαν αὐτοῦ /\\¹
πῆχυν ()²

---

307 I. Howard Marshall, *The Gospel of Luke: A Commentary on the Greek Text*, The New International Greek Testament Commentary (Exeter: Paternoster, 1978 and Grand Rapids: Eerdmans, 1978), 527. τὰ πετεινὰ τοῦ οὐρανοῦ occurs in Matt 8:20//Luke 9:58; Matt 13:32//Luke 13:19 and Luke 8:5 (//Matt 13:4//Mark 4:4 have τὰ πετεινὰ); Acts 10:12; 11:6.

308 Harnack, *Sprüche und Reden Jesu*, 9; Schulz, *Q: Spruchquelle der Evangelisten*, 150; Steinhauser, *Doppelbildworte in den synoptischen Evangelien*, 150.

309 So Schulz, *Q: Spruchquelle der Evangelisten*, 150; Steinhauser, *Doppelbildworte in den synoptischen Evangelien*, 217.

310 For discussion, see the above discussion of Q 12:23.

311 Schulz, *Q: Spruchquelle der Evangelisten*, 150.

1) Matthew places προσθεῖναι before the prepositional phrase, while Luke places it after. Luke's version of Q 12:22-31 is more characterized by such switches in order than Matthew. Luke may have placed the verb between the prepositional phrase and object of the infinitive in order to improve the clarity of the verse, but Matthew's reading could almost as easily be the later one. In either case, the variation does not affect the meaning.[312]

2) ἕνα at the end of Matt 6:27 appears to be an interpretive addition. It would be more difficult to explain Luke's omission of the number.[313]

Q 12:26

(καὶ)[1] /\\[2] περὶ (ἐνδύματος)[3] /τὶ\\[2] μεριμνᾶτε

1) Though ἐνδύμα is a favorite word of Matthew's,[314] his reading is probably closer to the original text of Q 12:26. Matt 6:28a (=Q 12:26) is an admonition about clothes which introduces the following example of the lilies of the field. It preserves the harshness of the transition from Q 12:25 to 26, and this harshness could hardly be the product of a modification from Luke's reading. In contrast, Luke 12:26 talks not of clothes, but of τὸ ἐλάχιστον ("the rest"), a more general designation particularly typical of Luke.[315] By using such a general designation, Luke allows the verse to serve as a bridge between the comment on lengthening life in Q 12:25 and the example of God clothing nature in Q 12:27-28.

Q 12:27

Κατα(μάθε)[1]τε τὰ κρίνα ()[2] πῶς αὐξάν(ουσιν)[3]
ου κοπι(ῶσιν)[3] οὐδὲ νήθ(ουσιν)[3]
λέγω δέ ὑμῖν (ὅτι)[4]
οὐδὲ Σολομὼν ἐν πάσῃ τῇ δόξῃ αὐτοῦ
περιεβάλετο ὡς ἓν τούτων

---

312 Cf. Jeremias, *Die Sprache des Lukasevangeliums*, 217.

313 Schulz, *Q: Spruchquelle der Evangelisten*, 150.

314 Marshall, *The Gospel of Luke*, 528. Also, Jeremias, *Die Sprache des Lukasevangeliums*, 217 argues that Luke does not typically use substantive neuters (τὸ ἐλάχιστον).

315 Harnack, *Sprüche und Reden Jesu*, 9; Schulz, *Q: Spruchquelle der Evangelisten*, 150; Steinhauser, *Doppelbildworte in den synoptischen Evangelien*, 218.

1) Whereas κατανοεῖν is Lukan and has already been substituted for another verb in Q,[316] Matthew's καταμανθάνειν is a hapax legomena. Matthew's reading is clearly earlier.[317]

2) Matthew's reading of τοῦ ἀγροῦ is taken from Q 12:30 (Matt 6:30). There is no reason why Luke would have omitted an earlier fuller reading.[318]

3) Luke's singular verbs for neuter plural subjects are an improvement on the Greek of the earlier reading in Matthew.[319]

4) Matthew has ὅτι, while Luke does not. Either reading is possible.

Q 12:28

εἰ δὲ /\¹ [ἐν]¹ ἀγρ[ῷ]¹ /τὸν χόρτον\¹
/ὄντα\² σήμερον /\²
καὶ αὔριον εἰς κλίβανον βαλλόμενον
ὁ θεὸς οὕτως ἀμφιέ[ννυσιν]³
(οὐ)⁴ πο(λλ)⁴ ᾧ μᾶλλον ὑμᾶς ὀλιγόπιστοι

1) Luke's placement ἐν ἀγρῷ as an independent prepositional phrase at the beginning of 12:28, means that the verse develops a double contrast between the grass 1)in the field 2)today and the grass 1)in the oven 2)tomorrow.[320] Matthew's τὸν χόρτον τοῦ ἀγροῦ does not have this contrast, but instead seems to rearrange the elements of Luke's reading to conform to Biblical and liturgical usage.[321]

2) There is no compelling reason to prefer Matthew or Luke here, and their readings are semantically equivalent. Since Luke's reading right before this variant is preferable, his reading is given here.

3) Matthew's ἀμφιέννυμι and Luke's ἀμφιέζω are semantically equivalent. Since ἀμφιέννυμι occurs earlier in Q (7:25//Matt 11:8), it is slightly more probable here.[322]

---

[316] Q 12:24, see the above discussion of this verse.

[317] Schulz, *Q: Spruchquelle der Evangelisten*, 150-151; Steinhauser, *Doppelbildworte in den synoptischen Evangelien*, 218.

[318] Schulz, *Q: Spruchquelle der Evangelisten*, 151.

[319] Ibid., 151; Fitzmeyer, *The Gospel According to Luke X-XXIV*, 976.

[320] Marshall, *The Gospel of Luke*, 529. Jeremias, *Die Sprache des Lukasevangeliums*, 218 notes that the phraseology of Luke's reading here occurs exclusively in pre-Lukan non-Markan material.

[321] Harnack, *Sprüche und Reden Jesu*, 10.

[322] Steinhauser, *Doppelbildworte in den synoptischen Evangelien*, 219.

4) This is the third place where Luke softens one of Q's rhetorical questions.[323]

Q 12:29

μὴ (οὖν)[1] (μεριμνήση)[2]τε (λέγοντες)[3]
τί φάγ(ωμεν)[3] (ἤ)[4] τί πί(ωμεν)[3]
(ἤ)[4] (τί περιβαλώμεθα)[5]

2) Matthew's reading of the verb μεριμνάω is probably earlier than Luke's ζητέω. Q 12:29 concludes the previous sayings, and μεριμνάω is the verb which linked them together. Kloppenborg objects that Matthew may have added the verb precisely for that reason, assimilating the verse to the section which it concludes and forming "a bridge to his redactional verse 6:34."[324] The more likely possibility, however, is that Luke substituted ζητεῖτε for μεριμνήσητε in order to assimilate the verb to the much closer verbs ἐπιζητοῦσιν in Q 12:30 and ζητεῖτε in Q 12:31.

1) Just as Matthew's reading of μεριμνήσητε preserves the connection between Q 12:29 and the preceding verses which it concludes, so Matthew's οὖν looks back on the preceding. Luke's reading of καὶ ὑμεῖς is part of Luke's assimilation of Q 12:29 to the following verses. It emphasizes the contrast between the disciples and the nations (verse 30) and anticipates the focus on the disciples' behavior in verse 31.[325]

3) Matthew once again preserves the dialogical aspect of the Q saying, while Luke omits the plural participle and converts the following direct speech into part of the negative command.

4) Luke's reading of καὶ in these contexts would be impossible with Matthew's direct discourse. Once Luke converts this discourse into part of the negative command, however, he can also intensify that command to encompass all of the concerns mentioned in it.

5) At this point, Luke substitutes for Matthew's περιβαλώμεθα, a rare Greek verb μετεωρίζεσθε and uses it to summarize the preceding

---

[323] For discussion see the above discussion of Q 12:23.

[324] Kloppenborg, *The Formation of Q*, p. 218, note 189. He adds that both of these (proposed) Matthean additions would be distinguished from their context by their use of the aorist from the rest of Q 12:22-31, which uses the present tense. Jeremias, *Die Sprache des Lukasevangeliums*, 218 adds that antithetical parallelism is not Lukan, but Q 12:29-31 is not a clear example of antithetical parallelism.

message. But in the preceding verses of Q this message was formulated with the verb μεριμνάω. Here, just as at the beginning of the verse (ζητεῖτε for μεριμνήσητε), Luke substitutes more sophisticated language for that of the Q Vorlage. Moreover, as in Q 12:26, Luke radically transforms a section regarding dressing to serve his redactional purposes.[326]

Q 12:30

/ταῦτα\¹ /\¹ γὰρ /\¹ /πάντα\¹
τὰ ἔθνη [ ]² ἐπιζητοῦσιν
/ὑμῶν\³ /\³ δὲ⁴ ὁ πατὴρ /\³ /οἶδεν\³
()⁵ ὅτι χρῄζετε τούτων ()⁶

1) On the one hand, Matthew's order places ταῦτα after πάντα and the conjunction γὰρ, thus emphasizing that the nations seek *all* these things. Though Matthew's arrangement superficially seems to agree with the spirit of the preceding admonition not to be concerned about food, drink and clothes, the main point of that admonition is not to worry about *any* of these things. Thus Matthew's emphasis that the nations seek *all* these things misses the point.[327] He makes the same addition, without any Lukan parallel to πάντα at the end of his verse 33 (Lk/Q 12:31).[328]

On the other hand, Luke's placement of ταῦτα at the very beginning of the verse helps this near demonstrative function better to link the two verses; the very things which the audience should not seek are the same things which all the nations (of the world) seek. Moreover, Luke's arrangement has the following chiastic structure:

ταῦτα
   γὰρ
      πάντα τὰ ἔθνη (τοῦ κόσμου)
            ἐπιζητοῦσιν
      ὑμῶν
   δὲ
ὁ πατὴρ οἶδεν ὅτι χρῄζετε
τούτων

325 Harnack, *Sprüche und Reden Jesu*, 10; Steinhauser, *Doppelbildworte in den synoptischen Evangelien*, 220.
326 Schulz, *Q: Spruchquelle der Evangelisten*, 151; Steinhauser, *Doppelbildworte in den synoptischen Evangelien*, 220; Fitzmeyer, *The Gospel According to Luke X–XXIV*, 976.
327 So Marshall, *The Gospel of Luke*, 529.
328 Schulz, *Q: Spruchquelle der Evangelisten*, 152.

The one thing which does not fit into the structure is the very thing which should make the difference between the audience's behavior and "all the nations," i.e. knowledge from this saying (Q 12:24, 26-28) that God will take care of them. Matthew's reading destroys two parts of this concentric structure: 1) the balance between the ταῦτα at the beginning and τούτων at the end of the verse and 2) the contrast between the audience on the one hand and *all* the nations on the other. Luke could have rearranged the verse to provide a smoother transition and this chiastic structure. The more plausible alternative, however, is that Matthew moved the πάντα to the beginning of the verse under influence of the preceding three part list of things not to be worried about.

2) Luke reads τοῦ κόσμου after τὰ ἔθνη. Though this expression is undoubtedly pre-Lukan,[329] it is an expansion of Matthew's shorter reading. The latter reading is much less easy to explain as secondary.

3) The positions of ὑμῶν and οἶδεν are interchanged in Matthew and Luke. By having ὑμῶν in front extra position, right before the disjunction (but *you*), Luke's reading preserves the contrast between all the nations and the audience.[330] Moreover, the placement of a possessive pronoun (ὑμῶν) before the noun it modifies is highly uncharacteristic of Lukan redaction.[331] Therefore, Luke's reading is almost certainly earlier than Matthew's.

4) Similar considerations make Luke's reading of a disjunction, δὲ, preferable to Matthew's reading of γὰρ. Once again, Matthew's reading softens the contrast between the nations and the audience. It implies that the nations seek all these things because God knows that the audience needs them. Such a reading makes little sense. It is probably an assimilation to the γὰρ which opens the verse and/or a reaction to the problem of two successive adversatives, here and at the beginning of Matt 6:33 (Lk/Q 12:31).

---

[329] Marshall, *The Gospel of Luke,* 529; Jeremias, *Die Sprache des Lukasevangeliums,* 209-210, 218.

[330] See above for a diagram of the chiastic structure, which shows the importance of this contrast.

[331] Jeremias, *Die Sprache des Lukasevangeliums,* 142-143, 218. Marshall, *The Gospel of Luke,* 529-530 also notes that the use of the possessive with a God name is not characteristic of Lukan redaction.

5) As in Matthew 6:26 (Lk/Q 12:24), ὁ οὐράνιος is a Matthean expansion.[332]

6) Matthew's longer reading conforms the τούτων at the end of the verse to his rearrangement of its beginning, πάντα (γὰρ) ταῦτα. Luke's reading is not as explainable as a modification of Matthew's.

Q 12:31

¹/()¹ π[λὴ]¹ν \¹
ζητεῖτε /\¹ τὴν βασιλείαν ()² αὐτοῦ
κὰι ταῦτα ()³ προστεθήσεται ὑμῖν

1) Luke reads the adverbial conjunction πλὴν at the beginning of the verse, while Matthew reads the conjunction δὲ and the adverb πρῶτον. Jeremias argues persuasively that the πλὴν in Luke is pre-Lukan.[333] The same, however, can not be said for Matthew's reading. Not only is it longer, but it softens the injunction by allowing the audience to seek food, drink and clothing second.

2) Matthew's modifying phrase, τοῦ θεοῦ καὶ τὴν δικαιοσύνην, is distinguished as secondary by both its extra length and its Matthean character. δικαιοσύνη is a term particularly favored by Matthew.[334]

3) Once again Matthew's reading is more expansive. Unlike at the beginning of Matt 6:32 (Lk/Q 12:30), the πάντα modifying ταῦτα in Matthew has no corresponding πάντα anywhere in Luke's text.[335]

---

[332] See the above discussion of Q 12:24.
[333] Jeremias, *Die Sprache des Lukasevangeliums*, 139-140.
[334] Harnack, *Sprüche und Reden Jesu*, 10; Schulz, *Q: Spruchquelle der Evangelisten*, 152.
[335] Schulz, *Q: Spruchquelle der Evangelisten*, 152.

RECONSTRUCTED GREEK TEXT OF Q 12:22-31

22a) [ ] Διὰ τοῦτο λέγω ὑμῖν

22bα) μὴ μεριμνᾶτε

22bβ) τῇ ψυχῇ (ὑμῶν) τί φάγητε ()

22bγ) μηδὲ τῷ σώματι (ὑμῶν) τί ἐνδύσησθε

23) (οὐχί) ἡ [ ] ψυχὴ πλεῖόν ἐστιν τῆς τροφῆς
καὶ τὸ σῶμα τοῦ ἐνδύματος

24a) (ἐμβλέψ)ατε (εἰς)
τ[οὺς κόρακας] ὅτι οὐ σπείρουσιν

24b) οὐδὲ θερίζουσιν [ ]
οὐδὲ (συνάγουσιν εἰς) ἀποθήκ(ας)

24c) καὶ ὁ [θε]ὸς τρέφει αὐτ[οὺς]

24d) (οὐχ) /ὑμεῖς\ μᾶλλον /\
διαφέρετε (αὐτ)ῶν

25) τίς δὲ ἐξ ὑμῶν μεριμνῶν δύναται
/προσθεῖναι\ ἐπὶ τὴν ἡλικίαν αὐτοῦ /\
πῆχυν ()

26) (καὶ) /\ περὶ (ἐνδύματος) /τί\ μεριμνᾶτε

27a) Κατα(μάθε)τε τὰ κρίνα () πῶς αὐξάν(ουσιν)

27b) οὐ κοπι(ῶσιν) οὐδὲ νήθ(ουσιν)

27c) λέγω δέ ὑμῖν (ὅτι)

27d) οὐδὲ Σολομὼν ἐν πάσῃ τῇ δόξῃ αὐτοῦ
περιεβάλετο ὡς ἓν τούτων

28a) εἰ δὲ /\ [ἐν] ἀγρ[ῷ] /τὸν χόρτον\
/ὄντα\ σήμερον /\
καὶ αὔριον εἰς κλίβανον βαλλόμενον
ὁ θεὸς οὕτως ἀμφιέ[ννυσιν]

28b) (οὐ) πο(λλ) ῷ μᾶλλον ὑμᾶς ὀλιγόπιστοι

29) μὴ (οὖν) (μεριμνήση)τε (λέγοντες)
τί φάγ(ωμεν) (ἢ) τί πί(ωμεν)
(ἢ) (τί περιβαλώμεθα)

30a) /ταῦτα\ /\ γάρ /\ /πάντα\
τὰ ἔθνη [ ] ἐπιζητοῦσιν

30b) /ὑμῶν\ /\ δὲ ὁ πατὴρ /\ /οἶδεν\
() ὅτι χρῄζετε τούτων ()

31a) /() π[λὴ]ν \
ζητεῖτε /\ τὴν βασιλείαν () αὐτοῦ

31b) καὶ ταῦτα () προστεθήσεται ὑμῖν

BIBLIOGRAPHY

1 KGS 3:2-15

Abou-Assaf, Ali, Pierre Bordreuil, and Alan R. Millard. *La statue de Tell Fekherye et son inscription bilingue assyro-arameenne*. Études Assyriologiques 7. Paris: Éditions Recherche sur les civilisations, 1982.

Albright, William F. "The Phoenician Inscriptions of the Tenth Century BC from Byblos" *JAOS* 67 (1947): 153-160.

Aufrecht, Walter E. "A Bibliography of the Deir ʿAlla Plaster Texts." *Newsletter for Targumic & Cognate Studies*, Supplement no. 2 (1985): 1-7.

Barr, James. *The Semantics of Biblical Language*. New York: Oxford University Press, 1961.

_____. "Theophany and Anthropomorphism in the OT." In *Congress of the International Organization for the Study of the Old Testament, 3rd: 1959; Oxford*. VTSup 7, Leiden: Brill, 1960, 31-38.

Benzinger, Immanuel. *Die Bücher der Könige*. KHAT 9. Freiburg: J. C. B. Mohr, 1899.

_____. *Jahwist und Elohist in den Königsbüchern*. Beiträge zur Wissenschaft vom Alten Testaments, new series, no. 2. Berlin, Stuttgart, Leipzig: W. Kohlhammer, 1921.

Blenkinsopp, Joseph. "Did Saul Make Gibeon His Capital?" *VT* 24 (1974): 1-7.

_____. *Gibeon and Israel: The Role of Gibeon and the Gibeonites in the Political and Religious History of Early Israel*. SOTSMS 2. Cambridge: at the University Press, 1972.

Blum, Erhard. *Die Komposition der Vätergeschichte*. WMANT 57. Neukirchen: Neukirchener Verlag, 1984.

Bottéro, J. "L'Oniromancie en Mésopotamie ancienne." *Ktema* 7 (1982): 5-18.

Brekelmans, C. H. W. "Solomon at Gibeon." In *Von Kanaan bis Kerala: Festschrift für Prof. Mag. Dr. Dr. J. P. M. van der Ploeg O. P. zur Vollendung des siebzigsten Lebensjahres am 4. Juli 1979*. Eds. W. Delsman and others. Neukirschen-Vluyn: Neukirchener Verlag, 1982, 53-59.

Brunner, Hellmut. "Das hörende Herz." *TLZ* 79 (1954): 697-700.

Burney, Charles Fox. *Notes on the Hebrew Text of the Books of Kings*. Oxford: at the Clarendon Press, 1903.

Campbell, Anthony F. *Of Prophets and Kings: A Late Ninth-Century Document (1 Sam 1 - 2 Kings 10)*. CBQMS 17. Washington D. C.: Catholic Biblical Association of America, 1986.

Caquot, André. "Les songes et leur interprétation selon Canaan et Israel." In *Les songes et leur interprétation*. Eds. A.-M. Esnoul and others. Sources Orientales 2. Paris: Éditions du Seuil, 1959, 99-124.

Caquot, André and André Lemaire. "Les textes araméens de Deir ʿAlla." *Syria* 54 (1977): 101-124.

Carlson, Rolf A. *David the Chosen King—A Traditio-Historical Approach to the Second Book of Samuel*. Trans. Eric J. Sharpe and Stanley Rudman. Uppsala: Almqvist & Wiksell, 1964.

Cassuto, Umberto. *The Documentary Hypothesis and the Composition of the Pentateuch: Eight Lectures*. Trans. I. Abrahams. Jerusalem: Magnes, 1963.

Cavalletti, S. "Sogno e profezia nell'Antico Testamento." *RivB* 7 (1959): 356-363.

Clark, W. Malcolm. "A Legal Background of the Yahwist's Use of 'Good and Evil' in Genesis 2-3." *JBL* 88 (1969): 266-278.

Cogan, Mordechai. "Omens and Ideology in the Babylon Inscription of Esarhaddon." In *History, Historiography and Interpretation: Studies in Biblical and Cuneiform Literatures*. Eds. Ḥayyim Tadmor and Moshe Weinfeld. Jerusalem: Magnes, 1984, 76-87.

Cross, Frank Moore. *Canaanite Myth and Hebrew Epic: Essays in the History of the Religion of Israel*. Cambridge: Harvard University Press, 1973.

Crüsemann, Frank. *Der Widerstand gegen das Königtum: Die antiköniglichen Texte des Alten Testamentes und der Kampf um den frühen israelitischen Staat.* WMANT 49. Neukirchen: Neukirchener Verlag, 1978.

De Vries, Simon J. *1 Kings.* WBC 12. Waco, Texas: Word Books, 1985.

De Wette, Wilhelm Martin Leberecht. *Lehrbuch der historisch-kritischen einleitung in die kanonischen und apokryphischen bücher des Alten Testaments.* Revised by Eberhard Schrader. Berlin: G. Reimer, 1869.

Dietrich, Walter. *Prophetie und Geschichte: Eine redaktionsgeschichtliche Untersuchung zum deuteronomistischen Geschichtswerk.* FRLANT 108. Göttingen: Vandenhoeck & Ruprecht, 1972.

Dossin, Georges. "L'inscription de foundation de Iaḫdun-Lim, roi de Mari." *Syria* 32 (1955): 11-16.

Dubarle, André-Marie "Le jugement de Salomon: un coeur a l'écoute." *Revue de sciences philosophiques et théologiques* 63 (1979): 419-427.

Ehrlich, Ernst Ludwig. *Der Traum im Alten Testament.* BZAW 73. Berlin: Alfred Töpelmann, 1953.

Eissfeldt, Otto. "אָדוֹן, אֲדֹנָי" In *Theologisches Wörterbuch zum Alten Testament.* Vol. 1. גלה־אב. Stuttgart: W. Kohlhammer, 1970.

Fensham, F. C. "Legal Aspects of the Dream of Solomon." In *The Fourth World Congress of Jewish Studies.* Vol. 1. Jerusalem: World Union of Jewish Studies, 1967, 67-70.

Fichtner, Joseph. *Das erste Buch von der Königen.* Die Botschaft des Alten Testaments 12/1. Stuttgart: Calwer Verlag Stuttgart, 1964.

Fontaine, Carole. "The Bearing of Wisdom on the Shape of 2 Samuel 11-12 and 1 Kings 3." *JSOT* 34 (1986): 61-77.

Gelb, I. J. "A New Clay-Nail of Ḫamurabi." *JNES* 7 (1948): 267-271.

Gerbrandt, Gerald Eddie. *Kingship According to the Deuteronomistic History.* SBLDS 87. Atlanta: Scholars Press, 1986.

Gerstenberger, Erhard. *Das Bittende Mensch: Bittritual und Klagelied des Einzelnen im Alten Testament.* WMANT 51. Neukirschen-Vluyn: Neukirschener Verlag, 1980.

Gilmer, Harry Wesley. *The If-You Form in Israelite Law.* SBLDS 15. Missoula: Scholars Press, 1975.

Glueck, Nelson. *Ḥesed in the Bible.* Trans. Alfred Gottschalk. Cincinnati: Hebrew Union College Press, 1967.

Gnuse, Robert K. *The Dream Theophany of Samuel: Its Structure in Relation to Ancient Near Eastern Dreams and Its Theological Significance.* Lanham (MD)/New York/London: University Press, 1984.

_____. "Dreams and Their Theological Significance in the Biblical Tradition." *CurTM* 8 (1981): 166-171.

Görg, Manfred. *Gott-König-Reden in Israel und Ägypten*. BWANT, 6th series, no. 5. Stuttgart: W. Kohlhammer, 1975.

Gray, John. *I & II Kings: A Commentary*. 2nd ed. Philadelphia: Westminster, 1963.

Grayson, Albert Kirk. *Assyrian Royal Inscriptions*. 2 vols. RANE 1-2. Wiesbaden: Otto Harrassowitz, 1972, 1976.

_____. "History and Historians of the Ancient Near East: Assyria and Babylonia." *Or* 49 (1980): 140-194.

Güterbock, Hans. "Die historische Tradition bei Babyloniern und Hethitern." *ZA* 42 (1934): 1-91; 44 (1938): 45-149.

_____. "Hittite Historiography: A Survey." In *History, Historiography and Interpretation: Studies in Biblical and Cuneiform Literatures*. Eds. Hayyim Tadmor and Moshe Weinfeld. Jerusalem: Magnes, 1984, 21-35.

Hackett, Jo Ann. *The Balaam Text from Deir Alla*. HSM 31. Chico, CA: Scholars Press, 1984.

Hallo, William. "Assyrian Historiography Revisited." *EI* 14, (1978): *1-*7.

Herrmann, Siegfried. "Die Königsnovelle in Ägypten und Israel." *Wissenschaftliche Zeitschrift der Karl Marx Universität*, Leipzig 3 (1953/54), Gesellschaft und sprachwissenscaftliche Reihe, Heft 1 [Festschrift Albrecht Alt]: 33-44.

Hoffner, Harry A. "Histories and Historians of the Ancient Near East: The Hittites." *Or* 49 (1980): 283-332.

Hoftijzer, Jacob and G. van der Kooij. *Aramaic Texts from Deir Alla*. Documenta et Monumenta Orientis Antiqvi. Leiden: E. J. Brill, 1976.

Hölscher, Gustav. "Das Buch der Könige, seine Quellen und seine Redaktion." In ΕΥΧΑΡΙΣΤΗΡΙΟΝ: *Studien zur Religion und Literatur des Alten und Neuen Testaments*. Ed. Hans Schmidt. Vol. 1. *Zur Religion und Literatur des Alten Testament*. FRLANT 36/1. Göttingen: Vandenhoeck & Ruprecht, 1923, 158-213.

Jepsen, Alfred. *Die Quellen des Königsbuches*. 2nd ed. Halle: Max Niemeyer, 1956.

Johannes, Gottfried. *Unvergleichlichkeitsformulierungen im Alten Testament*. Mainz: Un. Mainz, 1968.

Jones, Gwilym H. *1 & 2 Kings*. Vol. 1. *I Kgs 1-16:34*. NCB Commentary. Grand Rapids: Eerdmans, 1984.

Jongeling, B. "La particule רַק." *OTS* 18 (1973): 97-107.

Joüon, P. *Grammaire de l'Hébreu Biblique.* Rome: Pontifical Institute, 1923.

Kalugila, Leonidas. *The Wise King: Studies in Royal Wisdom as Divine Revelation in the Old Testament and Its Environment.* ConBOT 15. Lund: Gleerup, 1980.

Kapelrud, Arvid S. "Temple Building, a Task for Gods and Kings." *Or* 32 (1963): 56-62.

Kärki, Ilmari. *Die Sumerischen und Akkadischen Königsinschriften Der Altbabylonischen Zeit.* Vol. 1. *Isin, Larsa, Uruk.* StudOr 49. Helsinki: Finnish Oriental Society, 1980.

Kaufmann, Yehezkiel. "פתיחת הספורים על מלכות שלמה" In *Studies in the Bible Presented to Professor M. H. Segal by his Colleagues and Students.* Ed. Jehoshua M. Grintz. Israel Society for Biblical Research 7. Jerusalem: Kiryat Sepher, 1964, 87-93.

Kenik, Helen A. *Design for Kingship: The Deuteronomistic Narrative Technique in 1 Kings 3:4-15.* SBLDS 69. Chico, CA: Scholars Press, 1983.

Kittel, Rudolph. *Die Bücher der Könige.* HAT 1:5. Göttingen: Vandenhoeck & Ruprecht, 1900.

Knierim, Rolf. "Offenbarung im Alten Testament." In *Probleme biblischer Theologie: Gerhard von Rad zum 70. Geburtstag.* Ed. Hans Walter Wolff. Munich: Chr. Kaiser, 1971, 206-235.

_____. "Old Testament Form Criticism Reconsidered." *Int* 27 (1973): 435-468.

Kuenen, Abraham. *Historisch-critisch onderzoek naar het ontstaan en de verzameling van de boeken des Ouden Verbonds.* 3 vols. Amsterdam: S.L. van Looy, 1887-1893.

Kuntz, J. Kenneth. *The Self-Revelation of God.* Philadelphia: Westminster, 1967.

Levine, Baruch. "The Balaam Inscription from Deir Alla: Historical Aspects." In *Biblical Archaeology Today: Proceedings of the International Congress on Biblical Archaeology.* Ed. Janet Amitai. Jerusalem: Israel Exploration Society with the American Schools of Oriental Research, 1985, 326-339.

Lichtenstein, Max Manasse. "The Dream Theophany and the E Document." *JANES* 1 (1969): 45-54.

Lindblom, Johannes. "Theophanies in Holy Places in Hebrew Religion." *HUCA* 32 (1961): 91-106.

Liver, J. "The Book of the Acts of Solomon." *Bib* 48 (1967): 75-101.

Long, Burke. *1 Kings with an Introduction to the Historical Literature*. FOTL 9. Grand Rapids: Eerdmans, 1984.

McCarter, P. Kyle. "The Balaam Texts from Deir ʿAllā: The First Combination." *BASOR* 239 (1980): 49-60.

Machinist, Peter. "Literature as Politics: The Tukulti-Ninurta Epic and the Bible." *CBQ* 38 (1976): 455-474.

Malamat, Abraham. "Longevity: Biblical Concepts and Some Ancient Near Eastern Parallels." *28 Rencontre Assyriologique Internationale in Wien. 6-10. Juli 1981*. AfO Beiheft 19. Horn, Austria: Ferdinand Berger & Söhne Gesellschaft, 1982, 215-224.

Martin-Achard, Robert. "Le songe de Gabaon: I R 3:5. 7-12." *Dimanche ordinaire Assembées du Seigneur* 2/48 (1978): 4-9.

Mayes, Andrew David Hastings. *The Story of Israel between Settlement and Exile: A Redactional Study of the Deuteronomistic History*. London: SCM, 1983.

Mettinger, Tryggve N. *Solomonic State Officials: A Study of the Civil Government Officials of the Israelite Monarchy*. ConBOT 5. Lund: Gleerup, 1971.

Mölle, Herbert. *Das 'Erscheinen Gottes' im Pentateuch: Ein literaturwissenschaftlicher Beitrag zur alttestamentlichen Exegese*. Europäische Hochschulschriften, 23rd Series, no. 18. Bern: Herbert Lang, 1973 and Frankfurt: Peter Lang, 1973.

Montgomery, James. A. *A Critical and Exegetical Commentary on the Books of Kings*. ICC 10. New York: Scribner's, 1951.

Muller, Hans-Peter. "Die aramäische Inschrift von Deir ʿAllā. und die älteren Bileamspruche." *ZAW* 94 (1982): 214-244.

_____. "Die kultische Darstellung der Theophanie." *VT* 14 (1964): 183-191.

_____. "Einige alttestamentliche Probleme zur aramäischen Inschrift von Der ʿAllā." *ZDPV* 94 (1978): 56-67.

Muilenburg, James. "The Speech of Theophany." *Harvard Divinity Bulletin* 28 (1964): 35-47.

Nelson, Richard D. *The Double Redaction of the Deuteronomistic History*. JSOTSup 18. Sheffield: Dept. of Biblical Studies, University of Sheffield, 1981.

Noth, Martin. "Die Bewährung von Salomos 'gottliches Weisheit." In *Wisdom in Israel and in the Ancient Near East: Festschrift H. H. Rowley*.

Eds. Martin Noth and David Winston Thomas, VTSup 3. Leiden: E. J. Brill, 1955, 225-237.

_____. *The Deuteronomistic History.* Trans. Jane Doull, John Barton, and others. JSOTSup 15. Sheffield: University of Sheffield, 1981.

_____. *Könige.* BKAT 9:1. Neukirchen: Neukirchener Verlag, 1968.

_____. *Überlieferungsgeschichte des Pentateuch.* 2nd ed. Stuttgart: W. Kohlhammer, 1960.

_____. *Überlieferungsgeschictliche Studien: Die sammelnden und bearbeitenden Geschichtswerke im Alten Testament.* Tübingen: M. Niemeyer, 1943.

Obermann, Julian. *How Daniel was Blessed with a Son: An Incubation Scene in Ugaritic.* JAOS Supplements 6. New Haven: Yale University Press, 1946.

Oppenheim, A. Leo. *The Interpretation of Dreams in the Ancient Near East.* Transactions of the American Philosophical Society, New Series, no. 46, part 3. Philadelphia: The American Philosophical Society, 1956.

Parlebas, J. "Remarques sur la conception de reves et sur leur interprétation dans la civilization Égyptienne antique." *Ktema* 7 (1982): 19-22.

Puech, Émile. "Respondents." In *Biblical Archaeology Today: Proceedings of the International Congress on Biblical Archaeology.* Ed. Janet Amitai. Jerusalem: Israel Exploration Society with the American Schools of Oriental Research, 1985, 354-365.

Porten, Bezalel. "The Structure and Theme of the Solomon Narrative (I Kgs 3-11)." *HUCA* 38 (1967): 93-128.

Porteous, N. W. "Royal Wisdom." In *Wisdom in Israel and in the Ancient Near East: Festschrift H. H. Rowley.* Eds. Martin Noth and David Winston Thomas, VTSup 3. Leiden: E. J. Brill, 1955, 247-261.

von Rad, Gerhard. "Die deuteronomistische Geschichtstheologie in den Königsbüchern." In *Gesammelte Studien zum Alten Testament.* Vol. 1. Munich: Chr. Kaiser, 1958, 189-204.

Rehm, Martin. *Das erste Buch der Könige: Ein Kommentar.* Würzburg: Echter Verlag, 1979.

_____. *Textkritische Untersuchungen zu den Parallelstellen der Samuel-Königbücher und der Chronik.* ATA 13/3. Munster: Aschendorff, 1937.

Reindl, Joseph. *Das Angesicht Gottes im Sprachgebrauch des Alten Testamentes.* Erfurt Theologische Studien 25. Leipzig: St.-Benno, 1970.

Rendtorff, T. "'Offenbarung' im Alten Testament." *TLZ* 85 (1960): 833-838.

_____. "Die Offenbarungsvorstellungen im Alten Israel." In *Offenbarung als Geschichte*. Ed. Wolfhart Pannenberg. Göttingen: Vandenhoeck & Ruprecht, 1961, 21-41.

Resch, A. *Der Traum im Heilsplan Gottes: Deutung und Bedeutung des Traums im Alten Testament*. Freiburg, Basel, Vienna: Herder, 1964.

Reymond, Philippe. "Le rêve de Salomon (I Rois 3/4-15)." In *Maqqel Shaqedb: La brance d'amandier: W. Vischer*. Ed. S. Amsler. Montpelier: Cuasse Graille Casternau, 1960, 210-215.

Richter, Wolfgang. *Exegese als Literaturwissenschaft: Entwurf einer alttestamentlichen Literaturtheorie und Methodologie*. Göttingen: Vandenhoeck & Ruprecht, 1971.

_____. "Traum und Traumdeutung im AT." *BZ* 7 (1963): 202-215.

Roberts, J. J. M. "Myth *Versus* History: Relating the Comparative Foundations." *CBQ* 38 (1976): 1-13.

Rudolph, W. R. *Der Elohist als Erzähler: Ein Irrweg der Pentatuechkritik?* BZAW 63. Giessen: A. Töpelmann, 1933.

Rummel, Stan. "Narrative Structures in the Ugaritic Texts." In *Ras Shamra Parallels: The Texts from Ugarit and the Hebrew Bible*. Vol. 3. Ed. Stan Rummel. Rome: Pontifical Institute, 1981, 221-334.

Saggs, H. W. F. *The Encounter with the Divine in Mesopotamia and Israel*. London: Athlone, 1978.

Sakenfeld, Katharine Doob. *The Meaning of* חֶסֶד *in the Hebrew Bible: A New Inquiry*. HSM 17. Missoula, MT: Scholars Press, 1978.

Šanda, A. *Die Bücher der Könige*. EHAT 9. Münster: Aschendorffsche Verlagsbuchhandlung, 1911.

Sarowy, A. *Quellenkritische Untersuchungen zur Geschichte König Salmos*. Königsburg: K. Leupold, 1900.

Sauneron, S. "Les songes et leur interprétation dans l'Égypte ancienne." In *Les songes et leur interprétation*. Eds. A.-M. Esnoul and others. Sources Orientales 2. Paris: Éditions du Seuil, 1959, 17-61.

Schmid, Herbert. "Gottesbild, Gottesschau, und Theophanie." *Jud* 24 (1968): 241-254.

Schmidt, Werner H. "Ausprägungen des Bilderverbots? Zur Sichtbarkeit und Vorstellbarkeit Gottes im Alten Testament." In *Das Wort und die Wörter: Festschrift Gerhard Friedriech zum 65. Geburtstag*. Eds.

Horst Robert Balz and Siegfried Schulz. Stuttgart: W. Kohlhammer, 1973, 25-34.

Schnutenhaus, Frank. "Das Kommen und Erscheinen Gottes im AT." *ZAW* 76 (1964): 1-22.

Scott, R. B. Y. "Solomon and the Beginning of Wisdom in Israel." In *Wisdom in Israel and in the Ancient Near East: Festschrift H. H. Rowley.* Eds. Martin Noth and David Winston Thomas. VTSup 3. Leiden: E. J. Brill, 1955, 262-279.

Segal, Moses Hirsch. *The Pentateuch: Its Composition and its Authorship and Other Biblical Studies.* Jerusalem: Magnes, 1967.

Sellin, Ernst. *Introduction to the Old Testament.* Trans. W. Montgomery. London: Hodder and Stoughton Ltd., 1923.

Seow, C. L. "The Syro-Palestinian Context of Solomon's Dream." *HTR* 77 (1984): 141-152.

Shupak, N. "Some Idioms Connected with the Concept of "Heart." In Egypt and the Bible." In *Pharaonic Egypt: The Bible and Christianity.* Ed. Sarah Israelit-Groll. Jerusalem: Magnes, 1985, 202-206.

Skinner, John. *Kings.* The Century Bible. Edinburgh: T. C. & E. C. Jack, 1904.

Smend, Rudolph. "J E in den geschichtlichen Büchern des Alten Testament." *ZAW* 39 (1921): 181-217.

Smend, Rudolph. *Die Entstehung des Alten Testaments.* Theologische Wissenschaft 1. Stuttgart: Kohlhammer, 1978.

_____. "Das Gesetz und die Völker: Ein Beitrag zur deuteronomistischen Redaktionsgeschichte." In *Probleme biblischer Theologie: Gerhard von Rad zum 70. Geburtstag.* Ed. Hans Walter Wolff. Munich: Chr. Kaiser, 1971, 494-509.

Snaith, Norman H. "The First and Second Books of Kings." IB, vol. 3. New York, Nashville: Abingdon, 1954, 3-338.

Sollberger, E. "Šamšu-ilūna's Bilingual Inscriptions C and D." *RA* 63 (1969): 39-44.

Sollberger, E. and J.-R. Kupper. *Inscriptions royales Sumériennes et Akkadiennes.* Littératures anciennes du Proche-orient 3. Paris: Les Éditions du Cerf, 1971.

Stade, Bernhard with Friedrich Schwally. *The Books of Kings: Critical Edition of the Hebrew Text Printed in Colors Exhibiting the Composite Structure of the Books with Notes.* Trans. R. E. Brünnow and Paul

Haupt. The Sacred Books of the Old Testament 9. Leipzig: J. C. Hirichs'sche Buchhandlung, 1904.

Spieckermann, Hermann. *Juda unter Assur in der Sargonidenzeit*. FRLANT 129. Göttingen: Vandenhoeck & Ruprecht, 1982.

Stahl, Rainer. *Aspekte der Geschichte deuteronomistischer Theologie: Zur Traditionsgeschichte der Terminologie und zur Redaktionsgeschichte der Redekompositionen*. Ph.D. diss.: Jena, 1982.

Steuernagel, Carl. *Lehrbuch der Einleitung in das Alte Testament*. Tübingen: J.C.B. Mohr, 1912.

Tadmor, Hayyim. "Autobiographical Apology in the Royal Assyrian Literature." In *History, Historiography and Interpretation: Studies in Biblical and Cuneiform Literatures*. Eds. Hayyim Tadmor and Moshe Weinfeld. Jerusalem: Magnes, 1984, 36-57.

_____. "History and Ideology in the Assyrian Royal Inscriptions." In *Assyrian Royal Inscriptions: New Horizons in Literary, Ideological, and Historical Analysis*. Ed. F. M. Fales. Orientis Antiqvi Collectio 17. Rome: Istituto per l'Oriente, 1981, 13-33.

Thenius, Otto. *Die Bücher der Könige*. KEHAT 9. 2nd ed. Leipzig: Weidmann, 1873.

Trebolle-Barrera, Julio C. *Salomón y Jeroböan: historia de la recensión y redacción de 1 Reyes 2-12, 14*. Bibliotheca Salmanticensis 3. Salamanca: Universidad Pontificia, 1980 and Jerusalem: Inst. Español Biblico y Arqueologico, 1980.

Vaughan, Patrick H. *The Meaning of 'Bamâ' in the Old Testament: A Study of Etymological, Textual, and Archaeological Evidence*. SOTSMS 3. London: Cambridge University Press, 1974.

Vieya, M. "Les songes et leur interprétation chez les Hittites." In *Les songes et leur interprétation*. Ed. A.-M. Esnoul and others. Sources Orientales 2. Paris: Éditions du Seuil, 1959, 89-98.

Veijola, Timo. "Davidverheißung und Staatsvertrag: Beobactungen zum Einfluß altorientalischer Staatsverträge auf die biblische Sprache am Beispiel vom Psalm 89." *ZAW* 95 (1983): 9-29.

_____. *Die ewige Dynastie: David und die Entstehung seiner Dynastie nach der deuteronomistischen Darstellung*. Annalae Academiae Scientiarum Fennicae, Series B., no. 193. Helinski: Suomalainen Tiedeakatemia, 1975

_____. *Das Königtum in der Beurteilung der deuteronomistischen Historiographie*. Annalae Academiae Scientiarum Fennicae, Series B, no. 198. Helinski: Suomalainen Tiedeakatemia, 1977.

Weinfeld, Moshe. *Deuteronomy and the Deuteronomic School*. Oxford: Clarendon, 1972.

Weippert, Helga. "Die Ätiology des Nordreiches und seines Königshauses (1 Reg 11:29-40)." *ZAW* 95 (1983): 344-375.

_____. "Die deuteronomistischen Beurteilungen der Könige von Israel und Judah und das Problem der Redaktion der Königsbücher." *Bib* 53 (1972): 301-339.

Weiser, A. "Zur Frage nach den Beziehungen der Psalmen zum Kult: Die Darstellung der Theophanie in den Psalmen und im Festkult." In *Festschrift Alfred Bertholet zum 80. Geburtstag gewidmet von Kolegen und Freunden*. Ed. W. Baumgartner. Tübingen: J. C. B. Mohr, 1950, 513-531.

Wellhausen, Julius. *Die Komposition des Hexateuchs und der historischen Bücher des Alten Testaments*. 4th ed. Berlin: Walter DeGruyter, 1900.

Williams, Ronald J. "Literature as a medium of political propaganda in Ancient Egypt." In *The Seed of Wisdom: Essays in Honor of T. J. Meek*. Ed. W. S. McCullough. Toronto: University of Toronto Press, 1964, 14-30.

Würthwein, Ernst. *Die Bücher Könige*. 2 vols, ATD 11/1 and 11/2. Göttingen: Vandenhoeck & Ruprecht, 1977, 1984.

Zalevsky, Saul. "חתגלות ה' לשלמה בגעון". *Tarbiz* 42 (1973): 215-258.

2 CHR 1:1-13

Abramsky, Samuel. "שלמה המלך בעיני בעל דברי הימים" *EI* 16 (1982): 3-14.

Ackroyd, Peter R. "History and Theology in the Writings of the Chronicler." *CTM* 38 (1967): 501-515.

_____. *I & II Chronicles, Ezra, and Nehemiah*. Torch Bible Commentaries. London: SCM, 1973.

_____. "The Theology of the Chronicler." *Lexington Theological Quarterly* 8 (1973): 101-116.

Albright, William F. "The Date and Personality of the Chronicler." *JBL* 40 (1921): 104-124.

Baltzer, Klaus. "Das Ende des Staates Juda und die Messias-Frage." In *Studien zur Theologie der alttestamentlichen Überlieferungen*. Eds. Rolf Rendtorff and Klaus Koch. Neukirchen: Neukirchener Verlag, 1961, 33-43.

Barnes, William Emery. *The Books of Chronicles*. Cambridge Bible for Schools and Colleges. Cambridge: at the University Press, 1899.

Barthelémy, Dominique. *Critique textuelle de l'Ancien Testament*. OBO, no 50. Vol. 1. *Josué, Juges, Ruth, Samuel, Rois, Chroniques, Esdras, Néhémie, Esther*. Göttingen: Vandenhoeck & Ruprecht, 1982.

Bea, August. "Neuere Arbeiten zum Problem der biblischen Chronikbücher." *Bib* 22 (1941): 46-58.

Becker, Joachim. "Das historische Bild der messianischen Erwartung im Alten Testament." In *Testimonium Veritati: Philosophische und Theologische studien zu Kirschlichen Fragen der Gegenwart*. Frankfurter Theologische Studien 7. Frankfurt: Josef Knecht, 1971, 125-141.

Benzinger, Immanuel. *Die Bücher der Chronik*, KHAT 20. Tübingen & Leipzig: J. C. B. Mohr, 1901.

Botterweck, G. Johannes. "Zur Eigenart der chronistischen Davidgeschichte." *TQ* 136 (1956): 402-435.

Braun, Roddy L. "Chronicles, Ezra, and Nehemiah: Theology and Literary History." In *Studies in the Historical Books of the Old Testament*. VTSup 30. Leiden: E. J. Brill, 1979, 52-64.

_____. "The Message of Chronicles: Rally Round the Temple." *CTM* 42 (1971): 502-514.

_____. "Solomon the Chosen Temple Builder: The Significance of 1 Chronicles 22, 28, and 29 for the Theology of Chronicles." *JBL* 95 (1976): 581-590.

_____. "Solomonic Apologetic in Chronicles." *JBL* 92 (1973): 503-516.

Brunet, Adrien-M. "La théologie du Chroniste: Théocratie et messianisme." *Sacra pagina: miscellanea biblica Congressus Internationalis Catholici de Re Biblica*. Eds. J. Coppens and others. Vol. 1. Gembloux: Éditions J. Duculot, 1959, 384-397.

Büchers, Hermann. *Die Bücher Chronik oder Paralipomenon*. Herders Bibelkommentar IV/1. Freiburg: Herder, 1952.

Caquot, André. "Peut-on parler de messianisme dans l'oevre du Chroniste?" *RTP* 16 (1966): 110-120.

Cazelles, Henri. *Les livres des Chroniques*. La Sainte Bible. Paris: Les Éditions du Cerf, 1961.

Chang, W. I. "The Tendenz of the Chronicler." Ph.D. diss., Hartford, 1973.

Cross, Frank Moore. "A Reconstruction of the Judean Restoration." *JBL* 94 (1975): 4-18.

Curtis, Eduard Lewis and Albert Alonzo Madsen. *The Books of Chronicles.* ICC 11. Edinburgh: T. & T. Clark, 1910.

De Vries, Simon J. "Moses and David as Cult Founders in Chronicles." *JBL* 107 (1988): 619-639.

Dillard, Raymond B. "The Chronicler's Solomon." *WTJ* 43 (1981): 289-300.

Dumbrell, William J. "The Purpose of the Books of Chronicles." *JEvT* 27 (1984): 257-266.

Elmslie, William Alexander Leslie, ed. *The Books of Chronicles.* Cambridge Bible for Schools and Colleges. Cambridge: at the University Press, 1916.

Fishbane, Michael. *Biblical Interpretation in Ancient Israel.* Oxford: Clarendon, 1985.

Freedman, David Noel. "The Chronicler's Purpose." *CBQ* 23 (1961): 436-442.

Galling, Kurt. *Die Bücher der Chronik, Esra, Nehemia.* ATD 12. Göttingen: Vandenhoeck & Ruprecht, 1954.

Göttsberger, Johann. *Die Bücher der Chronik oder Paralipomenon.* Die Heilige Schrift des Alten Testaments IV/1. Bonn: Peter Hanstein, 1939.

Halpern, Baruch. "Sacred History and Ideology: Chronicles' Thematic Structure—Indications of an Earlier Source." In *The Creation of Sacred Literature.* Ed. Richard E. Friedman. University of California Publications: Near Eastern Studies 22. Berkeley: University of California Press, 1981, 35-54.

Harvey-Jellie, Wallace Raymond. *Chronicles.* NCB. New York: Henry Frowde, 1906.

Im, Tae-Soo. *Das Davidbild in den Chronikbüchern.* Europäische Hochschulschriften XXIII/263. Frankfurt: Peter Lang, 1985.

Japhet, Sarah. אמונות ודעות בספר דברי־הימים ומקומך בעולם המחשבה המקראית. Jerusalem: Bialik Institute, 1977.

_____. "Chronicles, Book of." *EncJud* 5:518-534.

_____. "The Supposed Common Authorship of Chronicles and Ezra-Nehemiah Investigated Anew." *VT* 18 (1968): 330-371.

Kittel, Rudolph. *Die Bücher der Chronik*. HAT, Abt. I, no. 6. Göttingen: Vandenhoeck & Ruprecht, 1902.

McKenzie, Steven L. *The Chronicler's Use of the Deuteronomistic History*. HSM 33. Atlanta: Scholars Press, 1984.

Michaeli, Frank. *Les livres des Chroniques, d'Esdras, et de Nehemie*. Commentaire de l'Ancien Testament 16. Paris: Belachaux et Niestle, 1967.

Mosis, Rudolph. *Untersuchungen zur Theologie des chronistischen Geschichtswerkes*. Freiburger theologische Studien 92. Freiburg: Herder, 1967.

Myers, Jacob. *I Chronicles*. AB. Garden City, New York: Doubleday & Co., 1965.

_____. "The Kerygma of the Chronicler." *Int* 20 (1966): 259-273.

Newsome, James D. "Toward a New Understanding of the Chronicler and his Purposes." *JBL* 94 (1975): 201-217.

Noordtzij, A. "Les intentions du Chroniste." *RB* 49 (1940): 161-168.

North, Robert. "Theology of the Chronicler." *JBL* 82 (1963): 369-381.

Peterca, Vladimer. *L'Immagine di Salomone nella Bibbia Ebraica e Greca*. Rome: Pontificia Universitas Gregoriana, 1981.

Petersen, David L. *Late Israelite Prophecy: Studies in Deutero-Prophetic Literature and in Chronicles*. SBLMS 23. Missoula, MT: Scholars Press, 1977.

Plöger, Otto. *Theocratie und Eschatologie*. 2nd ed. Neukirchen: Neukirchener Verlag, 1962.

Porter, J. R. "Old Testament Historiography." In *Tradition and Interpretation: Essays by Members of the Society for Old Testament Study*. Ed. G. W. Anderson. Oxford: Clarendon, 1979, 125-162.

von Rad, Gerhard. *Das Geschichtsbild des chronistischen Werkes*. BWANT IV/3. Stuttgart: W. Kohlhammer, 1930.

_____. "Die levitische Predigt in den Büchern der Chronik." In *Gesammelte Studien zum Alten Testament*. Vol. 1. Munich: Chr. Kaiser, 1958, 248-261.

Rothstein, Wilhelm. *Kommentar zum ersten Buch der Chronik*. Ed. Johannes Hänel. KAT 18/2. Leipzig: A. Deicherische Verlagsbuchhandlung D. Werner Scholl, 1927.

Rudolph, Wilhelm. *Chronikbücher*. HAT 21. Tübingen: J. C. B. Mohr, 1955.

_____. "Problems of the Books of Chronicles." *VT* 4 (1954): 401-409.

_____. "Zur Theologie des Chronisten." *TLZ* 79 (1954): 285-286.

Saebø, Magne. "Messianism in Chronicles?: Some Remarks to the Old Testament Background of the New Testament Christology." *Horizons in Biblical Theology* 2 (1980): 85-109.

Stinespring, W. F. "Eschatology in Chronicles." *JBL* 80 (1961): 209-219.

Throntveit, Mark A. "Linguistic Analysis and the Question of Authorship in Chronicles, Ezra and Nehemiah." *VT* 32 (1982): 201-216.

Torrey, Charles Cutler. *Ezra Studies.* Chicago: University of Chicago, 1910.

Wilda, G. *Das Königsbild des chronistischen Geschichtswerkes.* Bonn: Rheinische Friedrich-Wilhelms-Universität, 1959.

Willi, Thomas. *Die Chronik als Auslegung: Untersuchungen zur literarischen Gestaltung der historischen Überlieferung Israels.* FRLANT 106. Göttingen: Vandenhoeck & Ruprecht, 1972.

Williamson, H. G. M. "The Accession of Solomon in the Book of Chronicles." *VT* 26 (1976): 351-361.

_____. "Eschatology in Chronicles." *Tyndale Bulletin* 28 (1977): 115-154.

_____. *1 & 2 Chronicles.* NCB Commentary. Grand Rapids: Eerdmans, 1982.

_____. *Israel in the Books of Chronicles.* Cambridge: Cambridge University Press, 1977.

JOSEPHUS

Attridge, Harold. *The Interpretation of Biblical History in the Antiquitates Judaicae of Flavius Josephus.* HDR 7. Missoula, MT: Scholars Press, 1976.

_____. "Josephus and His Works" In *The Literature of the Jewish People in the Period of the Second Temple and the Talmud.* CRINT, section 2. Vol. 2. *Jewish Writings of the Second Temple Period: Apocrypha, Pseudepigrapha, Qumran Sectarian Writings, Philo, Josephus.* Ed. Michael Stone. Assen: Van Gorcum and Philadelphia: Fortress, 1984, 185-232.

Feldman, Louis H. "Josephus as an Apologist to the Greco-Roman World: His Portrait of Solomon." In *Aspects of Religious Propaganda in Judaism and Early Christianity.* Ed. Elizabeth Schussler-Fiorenza. Notre Dame, Ind.: University of Notre Dame Press, 1976, 69-98.

van der Meulen, Harry E. Faber. "Das Salomo-Bild im hellenistisch-jüdischen Schrifttum." Ph.D. diss., Kampen, 1978.

Thackeray , H. St. J. and Ralph Marcus. *Josephus: with an English Translation*. Vol. 5. *Jewish Antiquities, Books V-VIII*. LCL. Cambridge: Harvard University Press, 1958.

Ulrich, Eugene Charles, Jr. *The Qumran Text of Samuel and Josephus*. HSM 19. Missoula, MT: Scholars Press, 1978.

INSTRUCTIONS

Bons, Eberhard. "Zur Gliederung und Kohärenz von Koh 1,12-2,11." *BN* 24 (1984): 80-87.

Brunner, Hellmut. "Die Weisheitsliteratur." In *Handbuch der Orientalistik*. Vol. 1, *Ägyptologie*. Part 2. *Literatur*. Leiden: E. J. Brill, 1952, 90-110.

Bultmann, Rudolph. *Die Geschichte der synoptischen Tradition*. 2nd revised ed. Göttingen: Vandenhoeck & Ruprecht, 1931.

Camp, Claudia V. *Wisdom and the Feminine in the Book of Proverbs*. Bible and Literature Series 11. Decatur, GA: Almond, 1985.

Castillino, George R. "Qohelet and His Wisdom." *CBQ* 30 (1968): 15-28.

Catchpole, D. "The Ravens, the Lilies and the Q hypothesis: A Form-critical Perspective on the Source-critical Problem." *SUNT* 6-7 (1981-1982): 78-83.

Fiorenza, Elizabeth Schüssler. *In Memory of Her: A Feminist Theological Reconstruction of Christian Origins*. New York: Crossroad, 1985.

————. "Wisdom Mythology and the Christological Hymns of the New Testament." In *Aspects of Wisdom in Judaism and Early Christianity*. Ed. Robert L. Wilken. Judaism and Christianity in Antiquity 1. Notre Dame: University of Notre Dame Press, 1975, 17-41.

Fitzmeyer, Joseph. *The Gospel According to Luke, X-XXIV. Introduction, Translation and Notes*. 2 vols., Anchor Bible, nos. 28A and B. Garden City: Doubleday, 1981, 1985

Fohrer, Georg. *Introduction to the Old Testament*. Trans. David Green. Nashville: Abingdon, 1968.

Galling, Kurt. *Der Prediger*. HAT 18. Tübingen: J. C. B. Mohr (Paul Siebeck), 1969.

Gilbert, Maurice. *La critique des dieux dans le livre de la Sagesse*. AnBib 53. Rome: Pontifical Institute, 1973.

_____. "La figure de Salomon en Sg 7-9." In *Études sur le Judaisme Hellénistique.* Eds. R. Kuntzmann and J. Schlosser. LD 119. Paris: Les Éditions du Cerf, 1984, 225-249.

_____. "La structure de la prière de Salomon (Sg 9)." *Bib* 51 (1970): 301-331.

Ginsberg, H. L. "The Structure and Contents of the Book of Koheleth." In *Wisdom in Israel and in the Ancient Near East,* Eds. Martin Noth and D. W. Thomas. VTSup 3. Leiden: E. J. Brill, 1960, 138-149.

von Harnack, Adolf. *Sprüche und Reden Jesu: Die zweite Quelle des Matthäus und Lukas.* Beiträge zur Einleitung in das Neue Testament 2. Leipzig: ET, 1907.

Hengel, Martin. *Judaism and Hellenism.* Trans. John Bowden. 2 vols. Philadelphia: Fortress, 1974.

Hertzberg, Hans Wilhelm. *Der Prediger.* KAT 17/4. Gütersloh: Gütersloyer Verlaghaus Gerd Mohn, 1963.

Jeremias, Joachim. *Die Sprache des Lukasevangeliums: Redaktion und Tradition im Nicht-Markusstoff des dritten Evangeliums.* Göttingen: Vandenhoeck & Ruprecht, 1980.

Kaiser, Otto. *Einleitung in das Alte Testament: Eine Einführung in ihre Ergebnisse und Probleme.* 5th revised ed. Gütersloh: Gütersloher Verlaghaus Gerd Mohn, 1984.

Kayatz, Christa. *Studien zu Proverbien 1-9: Eine form- und motivgeschichtliche Untersuchung unter Einbeziehung Ägyptischen Vergleichsmaterials.* WMANT 22. Neukirchen: Neukirchener Verlag, 1966.

Kloppenborg, John S. *The Formation of Q: Trajectories in Ancient Wisdom Collections.* Studies in Antiquity and Christianity 1. Philadelphia: Fortress, 1987.

_____. "Isis and Sophia in the Book of Wisdom." *HTR* 75 (1982): 57-84.

Klostermann, Erich. *Das Matthäusevangelium.* HNT 4. Tübingen: J. C. B. Mohr, 1927.

Kroeber, Rudi. *Der Prediger.* Schriften und Quellen der Alten Welt 13. Berlin: Akademie, 1963.

Lang, Bernhard. *Die weisheitliche Lehrrede.* Stuttgarter Bibelstudien 54. Stuttgart: KBW, 1972.

_____. *Wisdom and the Book of Proverbs: An Israelite Goddess Redefined.* New York: Pilgrim, 1985.

Larcher, Chrysostrome. *Études le livre de la Sagesse*. Études Bibliques. Paris: J. Gabalda et Cie Éditeurs, 1969.

Lauha, Aarre. *Kohelet*. BKAT 19. Neukirchen: Neukirchener Verlag, 1978.

Loader, James A. *Polar Structures in the Book of Qohelet*. BZAW 152. New York: Walter de Gruyter, 1979.

Lohfink, Norbert. *Kohelet*. Die Neue Echter Bibel. Stuttgart: Echter Verlag, 1980.

Loretz, Oswald. *Qohelet und der alte Orient: Untersuchungen zu Stil und theologischer Thematik des Buches Qohelet*. Freiburg: Herder, 1964.

Mack, Burton. *Logos und Sophia: Untersuchungen zur Weisheitstheologie im hellenistischen Judentum*. SUNT 10. Göttingen: Vandenhoeck & Ruprecht, 1973.

McKane, William. *Proverbs: A New Approach*. Old Testament Library. Philadelphia: Westminster, 1970.

Marshall, I. Howard. *The Gospel of Luke: A Commentary on the Greek Text*. The New International Greek Testament Commentary. Exeter: Paternoster, 1978 and Grand Rapids: Eerdmans, 1978.

Müller, Hans-Peter. "Theonome Skepsis und Lebensfreude." *BZ* (1986): 1-19.

Murphy, Roland E. *Wisdom Literature: Job, Proverbs, Ruth, Canticles, Ecclesiastes, and Esther*. FOTL 13. Grand Rapids, MI: Eerdmans, 1981.

von Rad, Gerhard. *Weisheit in Israel*. Neukirchen: Neukirchener Verlag, 1970.

Reese, James M. *Hellenistic Influence on the Book of Wisdom and Its Consequences*. AnBib 41. Rome: Pontifical Biblical Institute, 1970.

Robinson, James. "Jesus as Sophos and Sophia: Wisdom Tradition and the Gospels." In *Aspects of Wisdom in Judaism and Early Christianity*. Ed. Robert L. Wilken. Judaism and Christianity in Antiquity 1. Notre Dame: University of Notre Dame Press, 1975, 1-16.

Sanders, James. *The Dead Sea Psalms Scroll*. Ithaca, NY: Cornell University Press, 1967.

_____. *The Psalms Scroll of Qumrân Cave 11*. DJD 4. Oxford: Clarendon, 1965.

Schmid, Hans Heinrich. *Wesen und Geschichte der Weisheit: Eine Untersuchung zur alteorientalische und israelistischen Weisheitsliteratur*. BZAW 101. Berlin: Alfred Töpelmann, 1966.

Schürmann, Heinz. *Traditionsgeschichtliche Untersuchungen zu den synoptischen Evangelien*. Düsseldorf: Patmos, 1968.

Schulz, Siegfried. *Q: Spruchquelle der Evangelisten*. Zürich: Theologischer Verlag, 1972.

Skehan, Patrick W. "The Literary Relationship of the Book of Wisdom to Earlier Wisdom Writings." In *Studies in Israelite Poetry and Wisdom*. CBQMS 1. Washington, D. C.: Catholic Biblical Association of America, 1971, 172-236.

Steinhauser, Michael. *Doppelbildworte in den synoptischen Evangelien*. FB 44. Würzburg: Echter Verlag, 1981.

Stern, M. "The Jewish Diaspora." In *The Jewish People in the First Century*. Vol 1. *The Jewish People in the First Century: Historical Geography, Political History, Social, Cultural, and Religious Life and Institutions*. CRINT, section one. Assen: Van Gorcum and Philadelphia: Fortress, 1974, 117-183.

Suggs, M. Jack. *Wisdom, Christology and Law in Matthew's Gospel*. Cambridge, MA: Harvard University Press, 1970.

Weiss, Bernard. *Die Quellen des Lukasevangeliums*. Stuttgart and Berlin: J. G. Cotta, 1907.

Whybray, R. N. *Wisdom in Proverbs: The Concept of Wisdom in Proverbs 1-9*. SBT 45. London: SCM, 1965.

Williams, J. G. *Those Who Ponder Proverbs: Aphoristic Thinking and Biblical Literature*. Sheffield: Almond, 1981.

Winston, David. *The Wisdom of Solomon*. AB 43 (Garden City: Doubleday, 1979).

Wright, Addison. "The Riddle of the Sphinx: the Structure of the Book of Qohelet." *CBQ* 30 (1968): 313-334.

_____. "The Riddle of the Sphinx Revisited: Numerical Patterns in the Book of Qoheleth." *CBQ* 42 (1980): 38-51.

Zeller, Dieter. *Die weisheitlichen Mahnsprüche bei den Synoptikern*. FB 17. Würzburg: Echter Verlag, 1977.

Zimmerli, Walther. "Das Buch Kohelet - Traktat oder Sentenzensammlung?" *VT* 24 (1974): 221-230.

_____. *Prediger*. ATD 16/1. Göttingen: Vandenhoeck & Ruprecht, 1962.

BIBLIOGRAPHY FOR THE INTRODUCTION
AND CONCLUSION

Auerbach, Eric. *Mimesis: The Representation of Reality in Western Literature.* Garden City, NY: Doubleday & Co., 1957.

Bal, Mieke. *Lethal Love: Feminist Literary Readings of Biblical Love Stories.* Indiana Studies in Biblical Literature. Bloomington and Indianapolis: Indiana University Press, 1987.

_____. *Murder and Difference: Gender, Genre, and Scholarship on Sisera's Death.* Trans. M. Gumpert. Indiana Studies in Biblical Literature. Bloomington and Indianapolis: Indiana University Press, 1988.

Bird, Phyllis A. "Images of Women in the Old Testament." In *The Bible and Liberation: Political and Social Hermeneutics.* Ed. Norman K. Gottwald. Orbis: Maryknoll, New York, 1983. Pp. 252-279.

Boff, Clodovis. *Theology and Praxis: Epistomological Foundations.* Maryknoll, NY: Orbis, 1987.

Brown, Raymond. *The Critical Meaning of the Bible.* New York: Paulist, 1981.

Carr, Adrienne and John Carr. *Experiment in Practical Christianity.* 2nd revised ed. Nashville: Discipleship Resources, 1985.

_____. *The Pilgrimage Project: Renewing Our Sense of God's Presence and Purpose.* Nashville: The Upper Room, 1987.

Duling, D. C. "Testament of Solomon." In *The Old Testament Pseudepigrapha.* Ed. James H. Charlesworth. Vol. 1. *Apocalyptic Literature & Testaments.* Garden City: Doubleday, 1983, 935-959.

Färber, R. *König Salomon in der Tradition: Ein historisch-kritischer Beitrag zur Geschichte der Haggada, der Tannaiten und Amoräer.* Vienna: Schlesinger, 1902.

Fierro, Alfredo. *The Militant Gospel: A Critical Introduction to Political Theologies.* Trans. John Drury. Maryknoll, NY: Orbis, 1977.

Fiorenza, Elizabeth Schüssler. "The Will to Choose or to Reject: Continuing Our Critical Work," in *Feminist Interpretation of the Bible,* Letty Russell (Philadelphia: Fortress, 1985), pp. 125-136.

Frei, Hans W. *The Eclipse of Biblical Narrative: A Study in Eighteenth and Nineteenth Century Hermeneutics.* New Haven and London: Yale University Press, 1974.

Gottwald, Norman. *The Hebrew Bible: A Socio-Literary Introduction.* Philadelphia: Fortress, 1985.

Hayes, John and Carl Holladay. *Biblical Exegesis: A Beginner's Handbook.* Revised Edition. Atlanta: John Knox, 1987.

Heyward, Carter. *Our Passion for Justice: Images of Power, Sexuality, and Liberation.* New York: Pilgrim, 1984.

Kaiser, Otto and Werner G. Kümmel. *Exegetical Method: A Student's Handbook.* Trans. E. V. N. Goetschius and M. J. O'Connell. New York: Seabury, 1980.

Kelsey, David. *The Uses of Scripture in Recent Theology.* Philadelphia: Fortress, 1975.

Knierim, Rolf. "Criticism of Literary Features, Form, Tradition, and Redaction." In *The Hebrew Bible and its Modern Interpreters.* Eds. Douglas A. Knight and Gene M. Tucker. Philadelphia: Fortress, 1985 and Chico, CA: Scholars Press, 1985, 123-165.

Krentz, Edgar. *The Historical-Critical Method.* Guides to Biblical Scholarship. Philadelphia: Fortress, 1975.

McKnight, Edgar V. *Post-Modern Use of the Bible: The Emergence of Reader-Oriented Criticism.* Nashville: Abingdon, 1988.

Meyers, Carol. *Discovering Eve: Ancient Israelite Women in Context.* New York: Oxford University Press, 1988.

Mosala, Itumeleng. *Biblical Hermeneutics and Black Theology in South Africa.* Grand Rapids: Eerdmans, 1989.

Plaskow, Judith. "The Coming of Lilith: Toward a Feminist Theology." In *Womanspirit Rising: A Feminist Reader in Religion.* Ed. Carol P. Christ and Judith Plaskow. San Francisco: Harper & Row, 1979. Pp. 198-209

_____. "Jewish Memory from a Feminist Perspective." *Tikkun* 1 (1987): 28-34 (reprinted in *Weaving the Visions: New Patterns in Feminist Spirituality.* Eds. Judith Plaskow and Carol Christ. San Francisco: Harper & Row, 1989. Pp. 39-50)

_____. *Standing Again at Sinai: Judaism from a Feminist Perspective.* New York: Harper & Row, 1990.

Robertson, David. *The Old Testament and the Literary Critic.* Guides to Biblical Scholarship. Philadelphia: Fortress, 1977.

Rowland, Christopher and Mark Corner. *Liberating Exegesis: The Challenge of Liberation Theology to Biblical Studies.* Louisville, KT: Westminster/John Knox, 1989.

Sanders, James A. "Adaptable for Life: The Nature and Function of Canon." In *Magnalia Dei, The Mighty Acts of God: Essays on the Bible and Archeology in Memory of G. Ernest Wright*. Eds. Frank Moore Cross, Werner E. Lemke and Patrick D. Miller. Garden City, NY: Doubleday & Co., 1976, 531-560.

_____. *Canon and Community: A Guide to Canonical Criticism*. Guides to Biblical Scholarship. Philadelphia: Fortress, 1984.

_____. "From Isaiah 61 to Luke 4." In *Christianity, Judaism and Other Greco-Roman Cults: Studies for Morton Smith at Sixty*. SJLA 12. Ed. Jacob Neusner. Part. 1. *New Testament*. Leiden: E. J. Brill, 1975, 75-106.

_____. *From Sacred Story to Sacred Text: Canon as Paradigm*. Philadelphia: Fortress, 1987.

Smith, Jonathan. "Sacred Persistence: Towards A Redescription of Canon." In *Approaches to Ancient Judaism: Theory and Practice*. Ed. William Scott Green. BJS 1. Missoula, MT: Scholars Press, 1978.

Sternberg, Meir. *The Poetics of Biblical Narrative: Ideological Literature and the Drama of Reading*. Indiana Studies in Biblical Literature. Bloomington, IN: Indiana University Press, 1985.

Stuart, Douglas. *Old Testament Exegesis: A Primer for Students and Pastors*. Philadelphia: Westminster, 1980.

Trible, Phyllis. *God and the Rhetoric of Sexuality*. OBT 2. Philadelphia: Fortress, 1978.

_____. *Texts of Terror: Literary-Feminist Readings of Biblical Narratives*. OBT 13. Philadelphia: Fortress, 1984.

Wood, Charles. *The Formation of Christian Understanding: An Essay in Theological Hermeneutics*. Philadelphia: Westminster, 1981.

Zones, Jane Sprague, ed. *Taking the Fruit: Modern Women's Tales of the Bible*. 2nd Edition. San Diego: Woman's Institute for Continuing Education, 1989.

METHOD IN COMPARATIVE STUDY OF EARLY JEWISH INTERPRETATION

Anderson, Bernard W. "Introduction: Martin Noth's Traditio-Historical Approach in the Context of Twentieth-Century Biblical Research." In Martin Noth, *A History of Pentateuchal Traditions*. Trans. Bernard W. Anderson. Chico, CA: Scholars Press, 1981. xiii-xxxii.

Barth, Lewis M. "The Midrashic Enterprise." *Jewish Book Annual* 40 (1982-83): 7-19.

Bernstein, Moshe J. כִּי־קִלְלַת אֱלֹהִים תָּלוּי: A Study in Early Jewish Exegesis." *JQR* 74 (1983): 21-45.

Bloch, Renée. "Midrash." *DBSup.* Vol. 5. cols. 1263-1280.

Bokser, Baruch. "Recent Developments in the Study of Judaism 70-200 C.E." *Second Century* 3 (1983): 1-68.

Callaway, Mary. *Sing, O Barren One: A Study in Comparative Midrash.* SBLDS 91. Atlanta, GA: Scholars Press, 1986.

Childs, Brevard. "Midrash and the Old Testament." in *Understanding the Sacred Text: Essays in honor of Morton S. Enslin on the Hebrew Bible and Christian Beginnings.* Ed. John Reumann. Valley Forge: Judson, 1972. 47-59.

Dinter, Paul, E. "The Remnant of Israel and the Stone of Stumbling in Zion." Ph. D. diss., Union Theological Seminary, 1979.

Evans, Craig A. *To See and Not Perceive: Isaiah 6.9-10 in Early Jewish and Christian Interpretation.* JSOTSup 64. Sheffield: JSOT, 1989.

Fishbane, Michael. *Biblical Interpretation in Ancient Israel.* Oxford: Clarendon, 1985.

Fohrer, Georg. "Tradition und Interpretation im Alten Testament." *ZAW* 73 (1961): 1-30.

Fraade, Steven D. *Enosh and His Generation: Pre-Israelite Hero and History in Postbiblical Interpretation.* SBLMS 30. Chico, CA: Scholars, 1984.

Hilgert, Earle. "The Dual Image of Joseph in Hebrew and Early Jewish Literature." *BR* 30 (1985): 5-21.

Knierim, Rolf. "Criticism of Literary Features, Form, Tradition, and Redaction." In *The Hebrew Bible and its Modern Interpreters.* Eds. Douglas A. Knight and Gene M. Tucker. Philadelphia: Fortress, 1985 and Chico, CA: Scholars Press, 1985, 123-165.

Knight, Douglas A. *Rediscovering the Traditions of Israel: The Development of the Traditio-Historical Research of the Old Testament, with Special Consideration of Scandinavian Contributions.* 2nd revised ed. SBLDS 9. Missoula, MT: Scholars Press, 1975.

_____. Ed. *Tradition and Theology in the Old Testament.* Philadelphia: Fortress, 1977.

Kugel, James L. "On Hidden Hatred and Open Reproach: Early Exegesis of Leviticus 19:17." *HTR* 80 (1987): 43-61.

Le Déaut, Roger. "A propos d'une definition du midrash." *Bib* 50 (1969): 395-413.

_____. *La nuit pascale.* AnBib 22. Rome: Pontifical Institute, 1963.

Miller, Merrill P. "Targum, Midrash and the Use of the Old Testament in the New Testament." *JSJ* 2 (1971): 29-82.

Miller, William. *Mysterious Encounters at Mamre and Jabbok*. BJS 50. Scholars Press: Chico, CA, 1984.

Neusner, Jacob. *Comparative Midrash: The Plan and Program of Genesis and Leviticus Rabbah*. BJS 111. Atlanta, GA: Scholars Press, 1986.

_____. *Midrash in Context: Exegesis in Formative Judaism*. Foundations in Judaism: Method, Teleology, Doctrine, part 1, Method. Philadelphia: Fortress, 1983.

_____. "Scripture and Tradition in Judaism with Special Reference to the Mishnah." In *Approaches to Ancient Judaism*. Ed. William Scott Green. Vol. 2. BJS 9. Chico, CA: Scholars Press, 1980, 173-193.

Page, Sydney H. T. "The Suffering Servant Between the Testaments." *NTS* 31 (1985): 481-497.

Porton, Gary. "Defining Midrash." In *The Study of Ancient Judaism*. Ed. Jacob Neusner. Vol. 1. New York: KTAV, 1981. 55-92.

_____. "Midrash: Palestinian Jews and the Hebrew Bible in the Greco-Roman Period." In *Aufsteig und Niedergang der römischen Welt*. Eds. H. Temporini and Wolfgang Haase. II/19. *Religion (Judentum: Allgemeines; Palästinisches Judentum)*. Vol. 2. Berlin and New York: Walter de Gruyter, 1979, 103-138.

Rowland, Cristopher. "John 1:51, Jewish Apocalyptic, and Targumic Tradition." *NTS* 30 (1984): 498-507.

Sanders, James A. "From Isaiah 61 to Luke 4." In *Christianity, Judaism and Other Greco-Roman Cults: Studies for Morton Smith at Sixty*. SJLA 12. Ed. Jacob Neusner. Part. 1. *New Testament*. Leiden: E. J. Brill, 1975, 75-106.

Sarason, Richard. "Towards a New Agendum for the Study of Rabbinic Midrashic Literature." In *Studies in Aggadah, Targum and Jewish Liturgy in Memory of Joseph Heinemann*. Eds. J. J. Petuchowski and others. Jerusalem: Magnes, 1981, 55-73.

Sweeney, Marvin Alan. *Isaiah 1-4 and the Post-Exilic Understanding of the Isaianic Tradition*. BZAW 171. Berlin: Walter de Gruyter & Co, 1988.

Vermes, Geza. "Bible and Midrash: Early Old Testament Exegesis." In *The Cambridge History of the Bible*. Vol. 1. *From the Beginnings to Jerome*. Eds. Peter R. Ackroyd and Craig F. Evans. Cambridge: Cambridge University Press, 1970, 199-231.

_____. *Scripture and Tradition in Judaism: Haggadic Studies.* 2nd revised ed. SPB 4. Leiden: E. J. Brill, 1973.

Wright, Addison. "The Literary Genre Midrash." *CBQ* 28 (1966): 105-138, 415-457.

_____. *The Literary Genre Midrash.* Staten Island: Alba House, 1967.

York, Anthony D. "The Dating of Targumic Literature." *JSJ* 5 (1974): 114-122.

_____. "The Targum in the Synagogue and in the School." *JSJ* 10 (1979): 74-86.

INDEX OF PASSAGES CITED

Note: Extra note references are provided when the given scripture passage is cited in the text and a note on the same page or in more than one note on the same page. Also, a number of Ancient Near Eastern texts are cited in note 49, page 19. These citations are not indexed below.

BIBLICAL TEXTS

EXTRA-BIBLICAL TEXTS

INDEX OF SCHOLARS CITED

Note: Double entries of note references are provided when the author is cited in more than one note on the same page.